EUROPEAN MUSLIMS AND THE SECULAR STATE

This book is dedicated to the memory of Ottavia Schmidt di Friedberg, colleague and friend, for whom research was an intellectual endeavour, a shared experience and a personal pleasure.

European Muslims and the Secular State

Edited by

JOCELYNE CESARI   SEÁN McLOUGHLIN

CNRS-Paris, France and   *University of Leeds,*
Harvard University, USA   *UK*

The Network of Comparative Research on Islam and Muslims in Europe

ASHGATE

Published by
Ashgate Publishing Limited
Gower House
Croft Road
Aldershot
Hampshire GU11 3HR
England

Ashgate Publishing Company
Suite 420
101 Cherry Street
Burlington, VT 05401-4405
USA

Ashgate website: http://www.ashgate.com

British Library Cataloguing in Publication Data
European Muslims and the secular state
   1. Muslims - Europe - Social conditions - Congresses 2. Islam
  - Europe - Congresses
   I. Cesari, Jocelyn II. McLoughlin, Seán III. Network of
   Comparative Research on Islam and Muslims in Europe
   305.6'97'094

Library of Congress Cataloging-in-Publication Data
European muslims and the secular state / edited by the Network of
   Comparative Research on Islam and Muslims in Europe.
      p. cm.
   Includes bibliographical references and index.
   ISBN 0-7546-4475-8
   1. Muslims--Europe. 2. Islam and politics--Europe. 3. Islam and
social problems--Europe. 4. Islam and state--Europe. I. Network
of Comparative Research on Islam and Muslims in Europe.

   D1056.2.M87E97 2006
   305.6'97'094--dc22

                                  2005021068
ISBN 0 7546 4475 8

Printed and bound in Great Britain by MPG Books Ltd. Bodmin, Cornwall.

Contents

List of Contributors

Valérie Amiraux is Senior Research Fellow in Sociology at the Centre National de la Recherche Scientifique. Her publications include, *Acteurs de l'islam entre Allemagne et Turquie* (Paris: L'Hartmattan, 2001) and, co-edited with Olivier Roy, *Musulmanes, musulmans au Caire, à Téhéran, Istanbul, Paris, Dakar* (Indigène: Marseille, 2004).

Jonathan Birt is undertaking a doctorate in social anthropology at the University of Oxford on Islamic youth movements in Britain. He is also a research fellow at the Islam in Europe Unit, Islamic Foundation, and has published a number of research articles. A collection he is editing, *Challenging Islamophobia*, is currently in preparation.

Alexandre Caeiro is a Doctoral Fellow at the International Institute for the Study of Islam in the Modern World (ISIM), Leiden. His doctorate deals with contemporary Muslim debates on Islamic authority in Western Europe, in particular through the production and consumption of non binding religious advice (*fatwas*) in different settings.

Jocelyne Cesari is Senior Research Fellow at CNRS-Paris and Visiting Professor at Harvard University. Her areas of expertise include the sociology of religion and Islam, and Muslim minorities in Europe and America. Her publications include: *When Islam and Democracy Meet: Muslims in Europe and in the United States* (Palgrave: New York, 2004).

Nadia Fadil is Research Assistant for the Belgian Fund of Scientific Research (FWO-Vlaanderen), which is linked to the Centre for the Sociology of Culture at the University of Leuven. She is currently preparing a PhD on religious individualization, subjectivity and authority among secular and religious second-generation Maghrebi Muslims in Belgium.

Silvio Ferrari teaches Canon law at the University of Milan and Church-State relations at the University of Leuven (Belgium). He has written extensively on the legal status of Islam in Italy and Europe and has edited, together with Anthony Bradney, *Islam and European Legal Systems* (Ashgate: Aldershot, 2000).

Christine Jacobsen is a Doctoral Fellow in International Migration and Ethnic Relations in the Department of Social Anthropology, University of Bergen, Norway. She is preparing a thesis on the role of Islam in the lives of young Muslims in Oslo and has published *Tilhørighetens mange former: Unge muslimer i Norge* (Pax: Oslo, 2002).

Gerdien Jonker is Senior Researcher at the Department of Social and Comparative Anthropology, Viadrina-University Frankfurt (Oder), Germany. Current research focuses on the consequences of 9/11 and after for interaction between Muslim communities and European majority societies. Her publications include, *Eine Wellenlänge zu Gott: Der Verband der Islamischen Kulturzentren in Europa* (Verlag Bielefeld, 2002).

Ana López-Sala is Professor of Sociology at La Laguna University, Tenerife, Spain. Her research interests include citizenship and immigration policies both at the regional level and comparatively across Europe, North America and Spain. Recent publications include *Inmigrantes y Estados* (Anthropos: Barcelona, 2005).

Gema Martín Muñoz is Professor of the Sociology of the Arab and Islamic World at the Autónoma University of Madrid. Her publications include: *El Estado Árabe: Crisis de legitimidad y contestación islamista* (Edicions Bellaterra: Barcelone, 2000), *Islam, Modernism and the West* (I.B. Tauris: London, 1999) and *Percepciones sociales y culturales entre España y Marruecos* (Fundación Repsol: Madrid, 2001).

Seán McLoughlin is Senior Lecturer in Islamic, Religious and South Asian Studies in the Department of Theology and Religious Studies at the University of Leeds, UK. He is the author of several articles on South Asian heritage Muslims in Britain and a forthcoming book, *Representing Muslims: religion, ethnicity and the politics of identity* (London: Pluto Press).

Fabio Perocco teaches in Sociology at the University of Venice, Italy, where he is Director of the Masters in Immigration Studies. His doctoral research examined *Islam in Local Society: the recognition of cultural difference in Tuscany and Venetia*. A recent publication, jointly edited with P. Basso, is *Gli immigrati in Europa: disuguaglianze, razzismo, lotte* (Franco Angeli: Milano, 2003).

Chantal Saint-Blancat is Associate Professor of Sociology at the University of Padova Italy. Her work deals with socio-cultural change amongst minority groups (national, ethno-linguistic, religious) and their social strategies. Recent publications include contributions to: *Cahiers d'Etudes sur la Méditerranée orientale et le monde turco-iranien*, *International Journal of Urban and Regional Research* and *Journal of Ethnic and Migration Studies*.

Thijl Sunier is Senior Lecturer in Cultural Anthropology at the University of Amsterdam, the Netherlands. His doctorate on Turkish youth and Islamic organizations was published as, *Islam in beweging: Turkse jongeren en islamitische organisaties* (Het Spinhuis: Amsterdam, 1996). He is currently writing a book about Islam, religious emancipation and the politics of diversity in France, the Netherlands and Turkey.

Preface

Following workshops in Paris on 24 June 2002 and 3 February 2003, the culmination of the European Commission funded research project on *Islam, Citizenship and the Dynamics of European Integration*, was a final international symposium at La Sorbonne, 30 June to 1 July 2003. Having completed the project, one of the network's commitments to the Commission was a published volume which network organizer and coordinator, Jocelyne Cesari, duly negotiated with Ashgate. Once she had set out the shape of the volume and secured all the contributions, Jocelyne invited me to share the responsibility for reading and editing each individual chapter and, as the only native speaker of English in the network, to produce the final manuscript.

Being a member of the network and editing this book have underlined two simple but important things for me about 'similarity' and 'difference'. Firstly, it is possible to establish a common comparative framework for describing and analysing general processes concerning Islam and Muslims throughout Europe for all the variety that is entailed therein. Indeed, the collective efforts of the contributors in effect 'map' what I consider to be the most important social-scientific dimensions of our interdisciplinary field: the recognition and regulation of Muslims in European nation-states; the consequences of different contexts of migration for Muslims; the institutionalization of Islamic movements, organizations and leaderships; social divisions of class, gender and generation; and the continuing impact of local-global political crises. Secondly, such comparative work firmly puts the familiar 'in context', so that an understanding of particular variations on a theme come much more clearly into view. Certainly this is my experience of reflecting back on Britain from a European perspective.

Finally, I would like to express my own thanks to the contributors for their openness and promptness, patience and tolerance, during the last six months while I was editing their chapters. I hope that I have been able to do their work justice in my attempts to 'translate' their texts from what I affectionately came to refer to as 'Euro-English'. I also owe a special debt to Jocelyne, my co-editor, for her input and advice, drive and encouragement, both on the telephone and via email from Harvard. Finally, thanks to both our families (Jeffrey and Izzy, and Lesley, Thomas and Kate) for their support and understanding, especially in these last weeks as the preparation of the manuscript entered its final, all consuming, stage.

Seán McLoughlin
Leeds, 30 March 2005

Acknowledgements

The present volume owes a debt of gratitude to both institutions and individuals.

We would like to express our thanks to the DG Research of the European Commission in Brussels for funding the collective research project, *Islam, Citizenship and European Integration*, which provides much of the basis for the present volume. Angela Liberatore deserves a special mention for her continuous support and feedback at the different stages of our work.

We are also particularly grateful to the CNRS and especially to the GSRL Institute and its Director, Jean-Paul Willaime, for hosting our meetings in Paris. Thanks too, to Martin Van Bruinessen from ISIM in Leiden, who supported our research and network from the very beginning. In terms of the administration of the network, much of our collective work would not have been possible without the patient efforts and friendly efficiency of Louis Hourmant and Sabrina Pastorelli from GSRL. Their contributions are gladly recognized and warmly appreciated.

We also would like to thank all the scholars, Muslim representatives and experts from the European Commission who participated in our conferences and workshops and who helped us in our collective reflections: Sakina Bargach, Hoceine Benkheira, Didier Bigo, Welmet Boender, Anthony Bradney, Jose Casanova, Lars Dencik, Hakim Elghissassi, Sebastien Fath, Jonathan Friedman, Aristotelis Gavriliadis, Pandeli Glavanis, Elspeth Guild, Dilwar Hussain, Ahmed Jaballah, Moussa Khedimellah, Philip Lewis, Angela Liberatore, Yngve Lithman, Pierre-Jean Luizard, Tung Lai Margue, Patrick Michel, Lydia Nofal, Tariq Ramadan, Olivier Roy, Garbi Schmidt, Tuula Sakaranaho, Martin Van Bruinessen, Sabiha El Zayat, Sami Zemni.

Thanks to all colleagues from the Network of Comparative Research on Islam and Muslims in Europe who made the research possible and, without whom, this book would not exist. We are grateful to Joergen Baek Simonsen, Jonas Otterbeck and Nico Landman who contributed to many of our initial reflections and meetings. Sadly, one other member of the network, who began this project with us, is unable to witness its completion. Ottavia Schmidt di Friedberg, to whom this volume is dedicated, passed away in 2003.

Finally, special thanks to our colleague and friend, Seán McLoughin, for his careful reading and editing of the present volume.

Jocelyne Cesari
On behalf of the Network of Comparative Research on Islam and Muslims in Europe
Cambridge, 30 March 2005

Introduction

Jocelyne Cesari

Islam's presence in Europe is a direct consequence of the paths of immigration established in the early 1960s, leading from former European colonies in Asia, Africa, and the Caribbean. Since the official end of labour migration in 1974, the integration of immigrant populations has become an irreversible fact, particularly as a result of policies on family reunification. These have contributed to the recomposition of 'Muslim' families in Europe and the continent's noticeable increase in family size. In such a context, the assertion of Islamic faith and identity becomes a major issue in terms of the sedentarization of immigrant populations. Throughout Europe, Islam's public visibility is at the root of much questioning, doubt and, often violent, opposition regarding newcomers to the West.

Many researchers in Europe consider that it is Islam's status as a minority religion and culture within a democratic and secularized context which is the decisive element in the transformation of both Muslim practices and their relationship to Islam. Such an approach, however, often amounts to no more than a description of the modalities according to which Muslims adapt to their new social context (see Lewis and Schnapper, 1994; Shadid and Van Kongingsveld, 1995; 2002a; 2002b). This univocal approach takes for granted the political features of the host societies, and fails to look into the transformations of secularism, nationalism and multiculturalism produced within the dominant societies as a result of the establishment of a new religion and new cultures.

In contrast, another, more innovative, approach to these issues seeks to understand the modes of interaction between Muslim groups and the different segments of Western societies. This approach implies a refusal to essentialize either the minority or the dominant culture and leads to an understanding of the social construction of Muslim communities in terms of the dialectical relationship between group resources and their social environment (see Cesari, 2002 and 2004). This is the approach adopted in the research project *Islam, Citizenship and European Integration*, conducted by the Network of Comparative Research on Islam and Muslims in Europe (see Cesari 2003, www.euro-islam.info). This project, which provides much of the basis for the present work, is greatly indebted to a method of research that accords primary importance to a dialectical process in the analysis of interactions between groups and cultures – particularly when the recognition of one group by another dominant group is at stake (see Sakai, 1999), as is the case with Muslims in Western democracies. The contributors to this book have therefore chosen to analyze both the cultural and political principles that structure the organization of religion within Western democracies and the influence of these principles on Muslims' adaptation to secularized societies. In this volume, we present the various interactions between Muslims and secularized spaces in order to apprehend the changes these interactions may imply for both Muslims and Islam itself.

Church-State Relations and its Influence on the Secularization of Islamic Institutions

Throughout Europe, the emergence of Islam has reopened the file – until very recently considered 'case closed' – on the relationship between religion and the state. The very diversity of Euro-Islamic issues is nevertheless a reflection of the specific political and cultural features of individual European countries, rather than a sign of any supposed exceptionality of Islam.

As it is understood by the various European nations, secularism may be characterized according to one of three primary modalities: cooperation between the state and the churches; total separation between the state and religion; or the existence of a state religion. In each case, however, the question of the institutionalization of Islam constitutes a problem which has no equivalent in American society. Unlike the situation in the United States, European 'secularism' means more than the protection of freedom of religion and the autonomy of religious organizations; it is also accompanied by a certain cooperation between church and state. Thus – as Silvio Ferrari's chapter demonstrates – the secularization of Islam is witnessed in the emergence of Islamic institutions adapted to the dominant model of church-state relations in the countries in question.

The influence of dominant political institutions, however, is not limited to church-state relations. It can also be seen in the political responses to the social and economic marginality that currently characterizes the status of many European Muslims. The socio-economic condition of European Muslims is one of great vulnerability. In every country in Europe, the unemployment rate amongst Muslims, immigrants and European-born, is higher than the national average. In the UK, for example, individuals of Bangladeshi and Pakistani heritage are considered to be amongst the most disadvantaged, having a level of unemployment three times higher than that of even other minority communities.

This kind of relegation to the margins has important consequences for the status of Islam in Europe. As Valérie Amiraux demonstrates in her chapter, the association between Islam and poverty has significant political consequences in terms of the equal treatment of Islam *vis-à-vis* other religions. This association also makes it more difficult to identify instances of discrimination specifically on the basis of religion, as racism and economic discrimination are often inextricably bound up with one another. The perception of social differences in terms of religion is very much a factor within the various spaces of Europe, as many of the contributors to this volume (Amiraux, Jacobsen, Jonker, Martín-Muñoz and López-Sala, Saint-Blancat and Perocco) demonstrate.

In looking at the studies contained in this volume, we should also note the intensification, in the majority of the public arenas of Europe, of a hostile and essentializing discourse on Islam. This 'meta-narrative' (Cesari, 2004) is a factor in the construction of Muslim identifications with Islam, particularly amongst the younger generations. In other words, many young Muslims in Europe are answering the pejorative or negative exceptionalism characteristic of mainstream discourse on Islam with an exceptionalism of their own that is at once positive and defensive.

One of the consequences of the events of 11 September 2001 has been the exacerbation of the stigmatization of Muslims, something effected by the linking of Islam, terrorism, and the socioeconomic conditions of the European suburban or inner city ghettos. As Jocelyne Cesari's chapter demonstrates, the '9/11' terrorist attacks have indeed resulted in both an increasingly antagonistic tone in mainstream discourse and stricter policies on immigration and security throughout Europe. A further consequence of the events of 9/11 in the European sphere has been a general questioning of the idea of multiculturalism. Multicultural policy is seen as a contributing factor to economic marginality and to religious segregation, insofar as it reinforces the exceptionality of Muslim immigrants without providing them with a means for real social advancement. While it is still too early to measure the consequences of this political climate on the religious behavior of European Muslims, it is likely that this situation will result in the growth of a reactive and defensive use of Islam (Cesari, 2004).

As the studies contained in the second section of this volume show, the particular institutional and political conditions of European nations have also had the unexpected result of influencing both the emergence of prominent Muslim figures, and the strategies they adopt. Gerdien Jonker's chapter demonstrates how the strategies of leading Muslims have been shaped by the 'structures of opportunity' offered by the society in which they live. In Germany, for example, the sole possible point of entry to public space for Muslims as 'Muslims' before 9/11, was the space of inter-religious dialogue. Similarly, Thijl Sunier indicates how the norms and values of Dutch society have strongly influenced the debate on Islam and Islam's assimilation into the public sphere – whether it is a question of 'pillarization', of multiculturalism, or of tolerance towards homosexuality. His study illustrates the evolution of the representational dynamic of Muslim populations: while Muslim communities once identified themselves primarily on the basis of ethnicity, they are identifying themselves with increasing frequency in terms of religion. In the past three years, the debate has become focused around the status of *imams* and their ability to promote the 'core values' of Dutch society in their communities.

As Chantal Saint-Blancat and Fabio Perroco correctly emphasize in their chapter, it is the local level, more than the level of governmental policy or Islamic organizations, which is a crucial space for the redefinition of Islamic leadership. This is particularly so because of the emergence of a new generation of leaders, who act as 'mediators' between Muslim communities and dominant institutions (local authorities, the media, the Church). In France, as Alexandre Caeiro demonstrates, the process of Islam's institutionalization begun by the Minister of the Interior has restructured the balance of power amongst the different influential figures. A tense relationship continues to exist between those bureaucratic leaders recognized by the French government and the preference of lay Muslims for those leaders associated with transnational movements such as the Muslim Brothers and/or in touch with the daily reality of local Muslim communities.

Seán McLoughlin's study confirms the growing influence in the British public sphere of reformist leaders who trace their Islamic heritage to the ideas of movements including the Muslim Brothers but, more especially in the UK, the Jama'at-i Islami of the Indian-subcontinent. Indeed, it would seem that Europe has become a new centre for the expansion of reformist movements such as the Muslim Brothers or the Jama'at-i Islami. Their positions on democracy and European culture should be clearly distinguished from those of the Wahhabis or post-Salafis. The former promote an inclusive attitude, arguing in favor of Islam's compatibility and engagement with the ideals and norms of democracy, whereas the latter take up a defensive position, refusing any form of adaptation to the European environment. To label all of these groups 'fundamentalist' only makes for confusion, and reinforces both an essentializing discourse and the construction of so-called Muslim exceptionalism.

The Influence of Secularism on Religious Practice

Secularism is more than the functional separation of politics and religion: it also, and especially, signifies the decline of religion's influence in society. Particularly in the European public sphere, the term has an ideological character, and has become, through various modes of political and cultural representation, one of the cornerstones of European identity. It is in this way that Islam's establishment in Europe may be seen as a potential threat to secularism as the cultural norm – a fact attested to, for example, by the heated nature of France's debate on the 'Islamic headscarf', or *hijab*. The justifications given for this fear of Islam invoke *ad nauseum* the commonplace that 'in Islam, there is no separation between the political and the religious'.

Certainly, none of the post-colonial states of the Muslim world have rejected the use of Islam as a means of creating a national community. In Muslim countries Islam is always either the state religion or under state control, even in nominally 'secular' nations such as Turkey or Iraq. As a result, the state becomes the custodian of the legitimate interpretation of tradition. The result is the de-vitalization of Islamic thought, not only on the question of political power, but on any topic of cultural or social import. That is to say, it is not that 'the Muslim mind' is somehow lacking in critical faculties but, rather, that this critical faculty has been stifled by authoritarian political control.

The establishment of Muslim communities in Europe and the United States therefore provides a release from the 'iron grip' of authoritarian Muslim states on Islamic tradition. In concrete terms, this 'liberation' can take a variety of forms. What is common to all, however, is the increasing individualization of Islamic practice – which should, nonetheless, not be taken to mean that Islam becomes a private matter.

The phenomenon of individualization has a variety of facets, of which the most important is perhaps the centrality of the notion of individual responsibility in religious choice. This individualization is accompanied by a growing distrust amongst believers of religious mediation – whether this mediation is on the part of a cleric, a religious leader, or a religious institution. This is something demonstrated by Gema Martín-Muñoz and Ana López-Sala in their chapter on religious practice amongst immigrant Muslim women in Spain. The suspicion of institutionalized or bureaucratized authority has precedents in the history of Islam: in Sufi practice, for example. However, the distrust of religious authority assumes a new tone in a secularized context, as Gerdien Jonker shows in her analysis of Sufi movements in Germany.

The principle mode of individualization among European Muslim populations takes the form of an attempt to reconcile the maximum amount of personal freedom with a belief in a more or less well-defined form of transcendence, which can then be adjusted to the constraints of the dominant societies. An adjustment to the boundaries between public and private space proper to the various European cultures can be seen in the ever more frequent relocation of religious practice to private spaces (praying in one's home, for example, rather than praying at the workplace). These various readjustments are accompanied by an increased emphasis on Islamic values, in contrast to orthopraxis. Religious practice proper is often limited to the observance of key rites of passage: circumcision, marriage, and burial.

It would be a mistake, nevertheless, to confuse the individualization of religious faith with an automatic decline in religious practice. As Nadia Fadil, Christine Jacobsen and Gema Martín-Muñoz and Ana López-Sala demonstrate, the relationship between individualization and faith is more complex than it might initially appear. In fact, for some Muslims, especially amongst the younger generations, faith is seen as something indistinguishable from the observance of Islamic laws. Here, religion is indeed defined as orthopraxis: in other words, as the literal observance of religious prescriptions, as well as the demand to embody them in one's daily life. Identification with Islam thus offers the individual a way to structure everyday reality, and provides a framework that s/he can use to organize and give sense to his/her life.

For the young women in Belgium interviewed by Nadia Fadil, such orthopraxis can actually mean emancipation from cultural, ethnic, and patriarchal constraints. Affirming one's 'Muslimness' becomes a way of affirming one's individuality, and of distancing oneself from the male discourse on women in Islam. Religious affirmation can also take on a more social connotation. Gerdien Jonker notes that, in Germany, 'lay' Sufi practice tends to emphasize ideas of spirituality and transcendence less, and the cohesion of the religious community and the religion-based activities that reinforce it (mutual aid societies, social activities, and so on) more. Christine Jacobsen similarly describes the Muslim Youth of Norway's investment in civic, social and educational activities.

This trend of constituting one's individuality through the affirmation of one's 'Muslimness' is naturally extremely diverse in terms of religious involvement, ranging from strict orthopraxis to more ethnically-oriented forms of religious participation. It is necessary, however, to make a distinction between those forms of religious affirmation which encourage openness and dialogue with the 'host' society (see Jacobsen, Fadil, Martín-Muñoz and López-Sala) and those which reject the secularized or non-Muslim environment. The practitioners of the latter are often disciples of transnational movements promoting a variety of Islamic 'fundamentalisms', such as the Deobandis, Tablighis or Wahhabis described by Jonathan Birt.

What these transnational movements have in common is the endorsement of a return to the Qur'an and the imitation of the life and *sunna* (custom) of the Prophet, especially during his spiritual and communal leadership in Medina. These movements' attitudes towards sacred texts and traditions finds its expression in an essentialization and a de-historicization of the religious message, as well as a rejection of values or cultural elements with a provenance outside the Qur'an. This is true of innovations issuing from Muslim societies, but especially those originating in the countries of the West. However, at least in the British context, as shown in Birt's chapter, Deobandis are beginning to engage with the non-Muslim public sector (universities, prisons, the army), something still anathema to Wahhabis. The question remains, however, of the political loyalties of the leaders and followers of such religious movements, especially when a very conservative interpretation of Islam is combined with socio-economic marginality. This combination of factors can easily have political consequences, which may in turn lead to radical political activity in the name of Islam.

Islam in Europe: One of the Various Dimensions of Global Islam

As a result of the significance of transnational networks in the education and activities of Muslim communities, any analysis which limits itself to their processes of adaptation within national societies risks presenting only a partial image of the cultural and religious reality of these communities. Islam's adaptation to the democratic context is, rather, a multidimensional process, involving forms of identification both national and transnational.

Furthermore, this evolution is even more complicated in that, since the end of the twentieth century, global Islam has experienced a profound and oftentimes chaotic metamorphosis, marked especially by the crisis of authoritarian regimes in the Muslim world and the rise of a theology of intolerance and a discourse of hate. The Muslim communities of Europe are, thus, just so many echo chambers of this crisis. Their position at the centre of Western civilization crystallizes the debates and upheavals of the entire Muslim world, including the crisis of religious authority, the question of democracy, relationships with 'the Other', the status of women and the appeal of 'fundamentalisms'.

The real challenge for the coming decades is in the continuing evolution of the tension between the two extremes of Islam – one, reformist and open to influence, the other, radical and closed in on itself – which continue to polarize the Muslim communities of the West. The evolution of this tension will be determined both by Muslims themselves, and by the various policies of Western governments on the integration and institutionalization of Islam.

References

Cesari, J. (ed.) (2002), *Cahiers d'études sur la Méditerranée orientale et le monde turco-iranien*, 33, 'Musulmans d'Europe', special edition, Paris.

Cesari, J. (ed.) (2003), 'European Muslims and the Secular State in a Comparative Perspective', Research Report, *Islam, Citizenship and European Integration*, European Commission, DG Research, Brussels, September.

Cesari, J. (2004), *When Islam and Democracy Meet: Muslims in Europe and in the United States*, New York, Palgrave.

Lewis, B. and Schnapper, D. (eds) (1994), *Muslims in Europe*, London: Pinter.

Sakai, N. (1999), 'Modernity and its Critique: The Problem of Universalism and Particularism', in Harootunian, H. and Myoshi, M. (eds), *Postmodernism and Japan*, Durham, NC: Duke University Press, pp. 93-122.

Shadid, W.A.R. and Van Koningsveld, P.S. (eds) (1995), *Religious Freedom and the Position of Islam in Western Europe*, The Netherlands: Kampen.

Shadid, W.A.R. and Van Koningsveld, P.S. (eds) (2002a), *Intercultural Relations and Religious Authorities: Muslims in the European Union*, Leuven, Sterling, Arlington: Peeters.

Shadid, W.A.R. and Van Koningsveld, P.S. (eds) (2002b), *Religious Freedom and the Neutrality of the State: The Position of Islam in the European Union*, Leuven, Dudley, Mass: Peeters.

Section I
Secularity in Europe and the Institutionalization of Islam: Legal Regulation and Political Recognition

Chapter 1

The Secularity of the State and the Shaping of Muslim Representative Organizations in Western Europe

Silvio Ferrari

Introduction

The establishing of Muslim representative organizations is a fundamental step towards the development of an Islamic community in Europe that is able to establish a fruitful relationship of cooperation with the political and social institutions of nation-states. The multiplicity of cultural traditions and historical experiences that constitute Europe itself are very much reflected in the variety of attempts that have been made to achieve such an objective. However, even the most convinced supporters of the need to respect national diversity also feel the need to identify, more precisely, the contexts within which an institutionalized European Islam can find its place. The notion of the secularity of the state is at the centre of this consideration. This chapter begins with the identification of some of the secular state's fundamental features, continues with a description of the initiatives taken in some European countries to provide a more precise legal status to Muslim communities, and concludes with some observations aimed at defining the limits within which public administrations can accompany this process.

The Secularity of the State: Legal Profiles

The 'secularity of the state' is an expression which today enjoys great popularity in Europe and few are the states that would hesitate to define themselves as secular. At the same time, this expression does not have a univocal meaning and it is therefore necessary to explain its contents more precisely. The main features of European political and legal secularity are two (Ferrari, 2003: 124):

1. Individual religious freedom, which means the irrelevance of one's religious convictions with regard to the enjoyment of political and civil rights (or in other words the civil and political equality of citizens and the prohibition of discrimination).

2.   The distinction between state and church. On the one hand, there is the autonomy of religious organizations and the absence of state intervention in their doctrines and internal organization. On the other, there is the independence of the state from every form of religious legitimization of its own power, as the state is ultimately founded only on the will of its citizens.

Individual religious freedom is guaranteed as much by international conventions signed by the European countries[1] as by their own constitutional laws.[2] Naturally this does not mean that no religious discrimination exists: in some countries – for example Denmark, Great Britain and Norway – the most important state authorities have to profess a certain religion (Davis, 2000). But these provisions, although they possess considerable symbolic value, concern an extremely limited number of people. In general, it is possible to state that, as much in Western Europe as in Eastern Europe, among Roman Catholics as among Protestants and the Orthodox Churches, the apostate, the atheist and the follower of a minority religion suffer no diminution of their civil and political rights, which are due to all citizens, on account of their religion or conscience.

The independence and autonomy of religious organizations also has a solid basis in the Constitutional Charters of the European countries and in the concordats and agreements that many have stipulated with some religious denominations (Warnink, 2001; Robbers, 2001). Countries certainly do exist – see, in particular, the states of Northern Europe, where there is an established or state church – where the bishops are appointed by the head of state and the ministers of religion are considered public employees. However, in these countries the autonomy of religious denominations is also increasingly considered a necessary consequence of the principle of collective religious freedom and therefore a limit exists before which the authority of the state has to stop. Throughout the twentieth century, the history of the Church of England, or of the Church of Norway, clearly displayed a tendency to recognize ever more fully, not only the doctrinal autonomy, but also the organizational autonomy, of religious denominations even in those countries that have kept the closest ties between state and church (Rhodes, 1991: 317ff; Thorson Plesner, 2000: 317-26).

Within the limits now outlined it is possible to maintain that 'the secular state' constitutes a model of organization of relations between religion and politics that is widely shared in European countries, beyond the legal superstructures still hinging on the existence of concordats, state churches or dominant religions. Within this picture the presence of Muslim communities constitutes a dual challenge: on the one hand, for the Muslims themselves who have to find a means of integration in a reality (the secular state) that is culturally alien to many of them, and on the other, for the Europeans who have to understand how far the secularity of the state can go in integrating this reality.

The Organization of Muslim Communities: The Terms of the Question

The fundamental principle underlying the secularity of the state – that is, the distinction between religion and politics – is affected in both its aspects by the establishment of representative institutions amongst the Muslim communities of Europe. On legal ground, this distinction has historically been translated into the enucleation of two different institutions, the state and the church, which have been placed in charge of disciplining the temporal and spiritual profiles of human life. As these two profiles intersect on several points, it is considered opportune to regulate them through dialogue and cooperation between the two distinct authorities that govern them. The distinction between these two institutions, each of which are endowed with their own sphere of autonomy, and their cooperation for the development of the human person and of the social community, are two fundamental coordinates of the system of relations between states and religions in Europe today. This is independent of the various legal regimes into which this system of relations is divided at the national level: 'concordatarian' Italy and 'separatist' France, and (however surprising this statement may appear to be) the countries where a state church exists, are all characterized, albeit in different forms and emphases, by a system founded on these two benchmarks.[3]

This is the cultural and legal background that lies behind the request which many states have addressed to the Muslim communities resident in their territories, namely, to provide a representative organization at the national level which is capable of functioning as an interlocutor of the state. Such an organization is necessary to ensure the possibility of effective cooperation on the subject of the teaching of religion in schools, spiritual assistance, the financing of religious activities and institutions and so on. This request has sometimes been formulated in an excessively inflexible way, with the state insisting on the need for unitary representation, something not always required of other religious communities (for instance, the Christians, who have separate representative institutions). The experience of some countries, such as Sweden,[4] shows that the legal recognition of several Muslim communities does not impede effective cooperation with the state. At other times, the demand to create a single representative institution at the national level has masked delaying tactics by public administrations that were not ready for a productive engagement with Muslims (Hussain, 2003: 246). However, besides this lack of flexibility and willingness on the part of the state, the formation of Muslim representative institutions has run into other and more important difficulties. On the one hand, in many countries Muslim immigration is a recent phenomenon which is numerically considerable and still very much in progress. There has not been a sufficiently long period of sedimentation that might allow suitable representative institutions to grow up within the Muslim communities. On the other hand, these communities have shown the tendency to diversify along a multiplicity of lines (nationality, ethnicity, theology, ideology, and so on) all of which has impeded the establishment of a representative body of 'the Muslim community' as such. Finally, the need for structured representation at the national level is alien to the Islamic tradition and it thus seems unusual to many Muslims who come from countries where the relationships between state and religion are not organized according to such a model.[5]

For these reasons it would be advisable not to underestimate the time required to institutionalize Islam in Europe. Nevertheless, in recent years the need to have bodies able to speak in the name of all Muslims resident in a state has become more pressing. Indeed, many governments consider that, in order to prevent the Muslim communities from drifting towards 'fundamentalism', it is necessary to consolidate their legal status at the national level and to put it on a similar plane to the status enjoyed by other religious denominations. This involves greater cooperation between the state and the Islamic communities, something that would be considerably facilitated by the prior identification of a sufficiently representative interlocutor.

The Organization of Muslim Communities: Attempts to Find a Solution

The experiments conducted in various European countries have employed different approaches and they depend not only on history and the social situation but also on the legal system of each state.[6] In Austria, the Muslim community was recognized by a law of 1912, when half a million Muslims still lived within the borders of the Austro-Hungarian Empire (Heine, 2002: 28-29). On this basis the Islamic Religious Community of Austria was created in 1979.[7] In Poland a similar path was followed and the Muslim community has been recognized since 1936 (Rynkowski, 2004). It is probably no accident that in these countries, where Islam obtained legal recognition some decades or so ago, the problem of Muslim representative institutions causes fewer difficulties than elsewhere.

In Spain this same question was tackled in the context of the overall reorganization of the relations between the state and religious denominations following the transition from the Franco regime to a democratic one (see Martín-Muñoz and López-Sala, this volume). The *Comisión Islamica de España* was created in concomitance with the federations that grouped together the organizations of Jews and Evangelicals, giving them the status of official interlocutors of the public administration and thus allowing the stipulation of *acuerdos* (agreement) with the state. Although the 'forced' aspects of this process rapidly emerged and severely slowed down the application of the agreement stipulated between the Spanish State and the *Comisión Islamica*, this body appears to be endowed with relative stability and it is reasonable to think that, with the passing of time, it may work with increasing effectiveness (Ciaurriz, 2004: 23-64; Mantecón, 2004: 214-18).

In contrast to the countries hitherto considered, in Great Britain no formally recognized representative organization of the Islamic communities exists at the national level. Various associations are active, with a more or less considerable number of adherents, none of which, however, has historically been able to carry out a representative function similar, for example, to that of the *British Board of Deputies* for Jewish communities (Khaliq, 2004: 228-30). However, as McLoughlin (this volume) shows, this situation has begun to change in recent years, although not yet decisively, with the emergence of the Muslim Council of Britain (MCB) which the New Labour government has accorded a semi-official status as privileged Muslim interlocutor of the state. This historical absence of a formally recognized representative Muslim body in Great Britain, which is important from the political point of view, has however a relatively reduced impact in legal terms. The system of relations between state and religions in Great Britain does not in fact provide any form of recognition or registration of religious communities. Nor does it require the constitution of a national representative body as spokesperson of the religious interests of a particular community or interlocutor of the public administration (Lyall and McClean, 1995: 148-49; Doe, 1994: 304-06). The major obstacle to effective cooperation between the state and the Muslim communities has not in the past derived from their (albeit real) organizational deficit, but instead from the historical preference shown by the British legal system for the protection of ethnic and racial minorities compared to religious ones. This 'ethnic-racial axis' has excluded Muslims (like some other religious groups but not Jews or Sikhs) from the system of protection based on the 1976 *Race Relations Act* and from a good deal of initiatives aimed at promoting the integration of minority groups.[8]

In Italy, also, no organization exists that can represent Muslim communities at the national level, but this absence has a far greater impact than in Great Britain. Indeed, the Italian legal system sustains a system of agreements with different religious groups from which Muslims remain excluded: negotiations for the conclusion of an agreement between the state and Muslim communities have never taken off. In this situation it is impossible to tackle some central issues, such as the teaching of Islam in state schools or the financing of Muslim communities through legal mechanisms already operating for the other most important denominations (Aluffi Beck-Peccoz, 2004: 181-98). The typically Italian vitality of initiatives at the local level, whose aim is to respond to such needs as prayer facilities in the workplace, absences for Ramadan, the provision of separate space for Muslims in cemeteries, compensate in part for this deficiency (see Saint-Blancat and Perocco, this volume). However, in the absence of a coherent legal picture at the national level, the risk of contradictory and short-lived initiatives increases.

Similar problems have arisen in another country, Germany, where the support of the state is graduated according to the recognition of a particular legal status for different religious communities.[9] The absence of a stable and authoritative representative organization has impeded the Muslim communities from being recognized – both at the national level and at that of the *Länder* (individual federal states) – as corporations of public law.[10] This has prevented them from being able to accede to the financial system which hinges on the 'ecclesiastical tax'[11] and so to benefit from the advantages enjoyed by the most important religious groups. Muslims are therefore placed in a position of inferiority compared to other religious groups (among which the Jews; see Jonker, 2002: 41 and Chapter 8, this volume). Nevertheless, the possibility of organizing themselves as registered associations has allowed Muslims to make use of other rights, including that of teaching Islam in state schools.[12]

The greatest difficulties have arisen in other countries, however, where the attempts to build Muslim representative organizations emerged late in the day (when tensions between Muslims and the autochthonous population were high) and when attempts were conducted in isolation, outside a project of the overall re-arrangement of the relations between the state and religions. This is the case in France and Belgium, both of which deserve a more detailed consideration now.

In France the process of the constitution of a Muslim representative body on the national scale began at the end of the 1980s. Previously this role had been assumed by the Great Mosque of Paris but this was closely connected to the Algerian community and government. Therefore it was not well suited to expressing the wishes of the other Muslim constituencies that, from the 1980s onwards, had acquired importance in French Islam (Terrel, 2004: 69). To overcome this difficulty Pierre Joxe, at that time the Minister of the Interior, set up the first consultative body in 1989. Other consultative bodies followed, although the course was not always a linear one, until the 2003 elections which brought into being the *Conseil français du culte musulman* (see Caeiro, this volume).[13]

This process was marked by the constant interest and activity of those at the helm of the Ministry of the Interior. These were the people who initiated the first consultations, who participated in meetings to define the procedure of election to the *Conseil*, who drew up the criteria to ensure broad representation of all Muslim perspectives, and who provided the organizational support for these elections.[14] In the course of these encounters the French administration was careful to avoid taking decisions on behalf of the different Muslim constituencies. The statement that it has, 'pleinement joué son rôle de médiateur et de facilitateur en veillant à ne pas exercer de tutelle' (Sevaistre, 2004: 41) is therefore justified. However, it is likewise undeniable that the administration interpreted its competencies in a 'Bonapartist' fashion,[15] which is little consonant with the French tradition of *laïcité* and separation (Basdevant Gaudemet, 2004: 68).[16]

A fundamental stage in the journey of the establishment of Muslim representative organizations in France was the signing, in January 2000, of the *Principes et fondements juridiques régissant les rapports entre les pouvoirs public et le culte musulman en France*.[17] This document was drawn up by the Minister of the Interior, Jean-Pierre Chevènement, and it summarizes the fundamental principles of the system of relations between state and religious denominations in France. In the introduction the document states that the Muslim groups and associations which participate in the process of consultation:

> confirment solennellement leur attachement aux principes fondamentaux de la République française et notamment [...] à la liberté de pensée et à la liberté de religion, à l'art. 1 de la Constitution affirmant le caractère laïque de la République et le respect par celle-ci de toutes les croyances et enfin aux dispositions de la loi du 9 décembre 1905 concernant la séparation des Eglises et de l'Etat.[18]

This document may be criticized on two levels. The first remark regards its contents, which sometimes appear to be excessively specific. To require adherence to the principle of separation between state and church may be justified. However, to demand the acceptance of the provisions by which it was defined in the law of 1905 appears unreasonable, above all when a considerable part of French public opinion considers that it should be changed. The second criticism hinges on the fact that a similar declaration of adherence to the *laicité* of the state and to the principles of religious freedom and equality was not required of the representatives of other religious groups. In this case there is an evident disparity in treatment, which Chevènement has justified in the name of the exceptional nature of the situation,[19] and by the 'difficulty' that parts of the Muslim world encounter in keeping religion and politics separate.[20]

In Belgium the process of the creation of Muslim representative bodies was conceived in similar terms but had a far less linear development. Although Islam had been recognized since 1974,[21] it was only in the 1990s that the procedures for creating a Muslim representative institution on a national basis were set in motion. Hitherto, the functions of a similar body had for some years been carried out by the (Saudi inspired) Islamic and Cultural Centre of Belgium (Hallet, 2004: 43-48). After numerous moments of tension, both among the various Muslim constituencies within the body charged with preparing the elections and between this and the Belgian administration (Hallet, 2004: 44-45), the elections finally took place in 1998. These in turn led to the creation of a constituent assembly which then appointed an executive committee which was finally recognized by a royal decree of 25 May 1999 as the Belgian government's official interlocutor both at the federal level and at the level of individual federal bodies.[22]

Also in this case, the Belgian administration played an active part in the process of the formation of the Muslim representative institution, creating a special commission to check on the conduct of the elections, validating the results and sustaining all the costs of the election procedure (Hallet, 2004: 45-46; Foblets and Overbeeke, 2004: 14, 19-20). However, the interventions of the administration, which gave rise to the greatest controversy, came after the elections. In 1999 over half of the members designated to take part in the executive committee were rejected by the Ministry of Justice as they were considered to be of an excessively radical orientation on the basis of a confidential assessment conducted by the security services (Hallet, 2004: 47; Foblets and Overbeeke, 2004: 14-15). In 2004 the constituent assembly was dissolved before its natural term of office had expired, and new elections were called. These satisfied the demands of some Islamic organizations but went against the wishes of the Muslim representatives elected to the constituent assembly.[23]

These state interventions were justified by the fear of extremist infiltration and by the conflicts between groups of Turkish and Moroccan origin. However, it is difficult to maintain that they respect the principle of autonomy of the religious group, which is implicit in the distinction between politics and religion that is a qualifying feature of European identity. That the state should dissolve a regularly constituted religious body, or that it should preclude, on the basis of an assessment entirely lacking in transparency, the presentation of candidatures to the steering committee of that body, is scarcely compatible with either the jurisprudence based on Article 9 of the European Convention on Human Rights.[24] Nor is it compatible with the laws contained in the Constitutional Charters of many countries (including Belgium), not only on the subject of autonomy (Warnink, 2001; Robbers, 2001)[25] but also on that of equality among religious groups (Foblets and Overbeeke, 2004: 21).

Conclusion: Rights of Freedom, Autonomy of Religious Groups and Cooperation between the State and Religions

The foregoing brief examination of the organizational models framing the presence of Islam in Europe poses a question: how can European states properly comprehend the institutionalization of Islam and channel this process, without too much trauma, towards a system of relations between states and religions, that is characteristic of the European tradition? The key to the question may be found, in my opinion, in the correct distinction between the fundamental principles underlying the relations between states and religions: freedom, cooperation and autonomy.

Rights of freedom, both individual and collective, are guaranteed by international law and by the constitutional laws of European countries in terms that cannot be conditioned by the adoption of a specific legal organization by a particular religious community. The *cooperation* of the state with the various religious groups can instead be subordinated to the respecting of certain requirements, such as the acceptance of the democratic and secular rules of the state. However, these requisites only concern the spheres of political and civil society. They cannot affect the *autonomy* of religious groups, for example, by requiring that the latter should organize themselves in democratic ways or that, within their own communities, they should respect equality between men and women in the same way that this value is respected in civil society.

These three profiles of the relations between states and religions need to be taken into account and developed together. On the one hand a platform of rights and freedoms should be recognized and consolidated which are the Muslim's due, just as they are for every other religious group. Into this first category falls, for example, the right of associations of believers to obtain legal status, to have their own places of worship, to celebrate religious ceremonies, to prepare and choose freely the religious staff to whom they wish to entrust the leadership of the community, to teach their own doctrine, to receive the economic support of their own followers and so on. These rights are due to religious communities – and therefore also to Muslim communities – without other restrictions apart from those provided by the laws of general application.

On the other hand, the state's cooperation with religious groups need not necessarily be indiscriminate. The public powers' 'incompetency' in matters of religion does not exclude the capacity to appreciate the external repercussions of a religious doctrine, in other words, that behaviour which corresponds to the precepts of a religion may also have a direct and significant impact on civil coexistence. Moreover, when such behaviour is legitimate and therefore protected by the freedom referred to above, from the state's point of view it may present a different degree of merit. It is in fact possible that religious behaviour contributes to the development of those values – the dignity of the human being, democratic coexistence, the freedom of conscience, equality and so on – that are at the foundation of the political system and of social peace. On the subject of the public financing of a religion, of the civil recognition of religious acts, of the teaching of a religion in state schools – all of which are activities that involve state intervention – the public administration can graduate its support within certain limits and maintaining certain proportions.

Nevertheless, the conditions to which the state subordinates its cooperation with a religious community should be maintained within the defined horizon of civil society and the organization of its policies. These conditions cannot affect the internal autonomy of a religious group by expecting the latter to be structured according to the principles and values on which coexistence in civil society is modelled. Also the Christian Churches, with which cooperation with the state is closest, present different structures that are more or less respectful of the principles of democracy, of the *rule of law* and of the rights of their followers. The same autonomy and the same organizational pluralism must be recognized in respect of Muslim associations and institutions. An authentically secular state stops at the threshold of the internal organization of religions, vigilant only that in the latter's internal relations, respect of that hard core of fundamental rights, which may not be neglected even in religious communities, is guaranteed.

The request for institutionalization directed at European Muslims does not concern the rights of freedom but instead those of cooperation. When this aspect is involved the public administration may legitimately request that Muslim communities provide themselves with a structure in the absence of which it is impossible to conduct effective interaction with the state. However, the public administration should not go so far as to define the features that this structure should possess 'on the inside'. The interest of the state is to have a Muslim counterpart that is willing to operate within civil society in the respect of the principles of secularity and democracy. This counterpart also needs to possess the requirements of stability, representativeness and authority that are indispensable for establishing a relationship of cooperation with the public powers. However, these requirements can be guaranteed by different means according to the different national situations: there is no single recipe for Europe, but rather as many models as there are historical, social and cultural realities that make up the Old Continent. In some cases it will be preferable to have a single institution that represents all the Muslim communities at the national level, as in France. In others, it will be a federation of several organizations expressing the various theological, ethnic and political currents that comprise Islam, as in Spain. In others still, it will be a multiplicity of independent institutions recognized by the state as being on an equal plane, as in Sweden.

An examination of the experiences of the various parts of Europe shows that even the paths by which the institutionalization of Islam has been achieved can be very different. In some countries it was simply a question of giving legal recognition to a reality that already existed in fact (the case in Austria). In others the choice was to follow the more difficult path of democratic elections, as in France and Belgium. The controversy that followed these attempts, and the uncertain results that have been achieved, underline that it may not be possible to transpose instruments that have produced good results in the political field into the sphere of religions. In any case, before venturing down this road, it is necessary to bear in mind that the outcome of the elections may be different from the one hoped for by the governments and political parties that encouraged them. Getting cold feet half way through, as happened in Belgium, weakens faith in the democratic approach and throws a shadow over precisely that principle of the secularity of the state that it is indispensable to safeguard.

References

Aluffi Beck Peccoz, R. (2004), 'Islam in the European Union: Italy', in Potz, R. and Wieshaider, W. (eds), *Islam and the European Union*, Leuven: Peeters.

Alwall, J. (1998), *Muslim Rights and Plights: The Religious Liberty Situation of a Minority in Sweden*, Lund: Lund University Press.

Basdevant Gaudemet, B. (2004), 'Islam in France', in Aluffi Beck Peccoz, R. and Zincone, G., *The Legal Treatment of Islamic Minorities in Europe*, Leuven: Peeters.

Cesari, J. (2002), 'Islam in France: the Shaping of a Religious Minority', in Yazbeck Haddad, Y., *Muslims in the West: From Sojourners to Citizens*, Oxford: Oxford University Press.

Ciáurriz, M.J. (2004), 'La situación jurídica de las comunidades islámicas en España', in Motilla, A. (ed.), *Los musulmanes en España: Libertad religiosa e identidad cultural*, Madrid: Trotta.

Davis, D. (2000), *Religious Liberty in Northern Europe in the Twenty-first Century*, Waco: Baylor University.

Doe, N. (1994), 'The legal position of religious minorities in the United Kingdom', in European Consortium for Church-State Research, *The Legal Status of Religious Minorities in the Countries of the European Union*, Thessaloniki-Milano: Sakkoulas-Giuffrè.

Ferrari, S., Durham, C. and Sewell, E. (2003), *Law and Religion in Post-Communist Europe*, Leuven: Peeters.

Foblets, M.C. and Overbeeke, A. (2004), 'Islam in Belgium: The Search for a Legal Status of a New Religious Minority', in Potz, R. and Wieshaider, W. (eds), *Islam and the European Union*, Leuven: Peeters.

Frégosi, F. (2004), 'Quelle organisation de l'islam dans la République: institutionnalisation et/ou instrumentalisation?', in Yves Charles Zarka (dir.), *L'Islam en France*, Paris: PUF.

Hallet, J. (2004), 'The Status of Muslim Minorities in Belgium', in Aluffi Beck Peccoz, R. and Zincone, G., *The Legal Treatment of Islamic Minorities in Europe*, Leuven: Peeters.

Heine, S. (2002), 'Islam in Austria: Between Integration Politics and Persisting Prejudices', in Shadid, W.A.R. and van Koningsveld, P.S. (eds), *Intercultural Relations and Religious Authorities: Muslims in the European Union*, Leuven: Peeters.

Hussain, D. (2003), 'The Holy Grail of Muslims in Western Europe: Representation and their Relationship with the State', in Esposito, J. and Burgat, F. (eds), *Modernizing Islam: Religion in the Public Sphere in Europe and the Middle East*, London: Hurst & Company.

Islam en Europe: Législation relative aux Communautés Musulmanes (2001), Bruxelles: Comece.

Jonker, G. (2002), 'Muslim Emancipation? Germany's Struggle over Religious Pluralism', in Shadid. W.A.R. and Van Koningsveld, P.S. (eds), *Religious Freedom and the Neutrality of the State: the Position of Islam in the European Union*, Leuven: Peeters.

Khaliq, U. (2004), 'Islam and the European Union: Report on the United Kingdom', in Potz, R. and Wieshaider, W. (eds), *Islam and the European Union*, Leuven: Peeters.

Lyall, F. and McClean, D. (1995), 'The Constitutional Status of Churches in Great Britain', in European Consortium for Church-State Research, *The Constitutional Status of Churches in the European Union Countries*, Paris-Milano: Litec-Giuffrè.

Mantecón, J. (2004), 'Islam in Spain', in Aluffi Beck Peccoz, R. and Zincone, G., *The Legal Treatment of Islamic Minorities in Europe*, Leuven: Peeters.

Minnerath, R. (2001), 'Church autonomy in Europe', in Robbers, G. (ed.), *Church Autonomy*, Frankfurt: Lang.

Muckel, S. (2004), 'Islam in Germany', in Potz, R. and Wieshaider, W. (eds), *Islam and the European Union*, Leuven: Peeters.

Otterbeck, J. (2004), 'The Legal Status of Islamic Minorities in Sweden', in Aluffi Beck Peccoz, R. and Zincone, G., *The Legal Treatment of Islamic Minorities in Europe*, Leuven: Peeters.

Rhodes, E.R. (1991), *Law and Modernization in the Church of England*, Notre Dame and London: The University of Notre Dame Press.

Roald, A.S. (2002), 'From "People's Home" to "Multiculturalism"': Muslims in Sweden', in Yazbeck Haddad, Y. (2002), *Muslims in the West: From Sojourners to Citizens*, Oxford: Oxford University Press.

Robbers, G. (2001), *Church Autonomy*, Frankfurt: Lang.

Robbers, G. (ed.) (2005), *State and Church in the European Union*, Baden-Baden: Nomos.

Rohe, M. (2004), 'The Legal Treatment of Muslims in Germany', in Aluffi Beck Peccoz, R. and Zincone, G., *The Legal Treatment of Islamic Minorities in Europe*, Leuven: Peeters.

Rynkowski, M. (2005), 'Poland', in Puza, R. (ed.), *Religion and Law in Dialogue* (proceedings of the meeting of the European Consortium for Church and State Research, Tübingen, 18-21 November 2004).

Sander, Å. and Larsson, G. (2002), 'The Mobilisation of Islam in Sweden 1990-2000: From Green to Blue and Yellow Islam?', in Shadid. W.A.R. and Van Koningsveld, P.S. (eds), *Religious Freedom and the Neutrality of the State: The Position of Islam in the European Union*, Leuven: Peeters.

Schmied, M. and Wieshaider, W. (2004), 'Islam and the European Union: The Austrian Way', in Potz, R. and Wieshaider, W. (eds), *Islam and the European Union*, Leuven: Peeters.

Sevaistre, V. (2004), 'L'islam dans la République: le CFCM', in *La documentation française*, 298, 33-48.

Terrel, H. (2004), 'L'État et la création du Conseil français du culte musulman (CFCM)', in Yves Charles Zarka (dir.), *L'Islam en France*, Paris: PUF.

Thorson Plesner, I. (2000), 'State and Religion in Norway', in *European Journal for Church and State Research*, 8.

Torfs, R. (2001), 'Autonomy of Churches in Belgium. Status Quaestionis and Current Debate', in Warnink, H., *Legal Position of Churches and Church Autonomy*, Leuven: Peeters.

Torfs, R. (2005), 'State and Church in Belgium', in Robbers, G. (ed.), *State and Church in the European Union*, Baden-Baden: Nomos.

Troll, C.W. (2003), 'Christian-Muslim Relations in Germany: A Critical Survey', in *Islamochristiana*, 29, 165-83.

Vogt, K. (2002), 'Integration through Islam? Muslims in Norway', in Yazbeck Haddad, Y., *Muslims in the West: From Sojourners to Citizens*, Oxford: Oxford University Press.

Warnink, H. (2001), 'Legal Position of Churches and Church Autonomy', Leuven: Peeters.

Notes

1 Most Western and Eastern European countries have signed the European Convention for the Protection of Human Rights and Fundamental Freedoms (1950) and the International Covenant on Civil and Political Rights (1966). Article 18 of the Covenant and Article 9 of the Convention guarantee the respect of freedom of thought, conscience and religion and the recognition of the right to manifest, individually or together with others, in public or in private, one's religion or conviction. In addition the Member States of the European Union have recently (2004) signed a Constitution that contains a ruling of similar content (art. II-10).

2 All European countries' constitutions contain at least one provision that protects freedom of religion in ways which, explicitly or through interpretation by the different

Constitutional Courts, replicate those outlined by the articles mentioned in the previous footnote. See Robbers (2005) and, for the countries that are not members of the European Union, Ferrari, Durham and Sewell (2003).

3 The same principles of distinction and cooperation also underlie the relationship between the European Union and religious groups, as defined by Article 52 of the Constitutional Treaty signed in Rome on 29 October 2004.

4 In Sweden, the state has recognized three Muslim organizations: they operate within an 'Islamic Council for Cooperation' that works as an interlocutor for the state body in charge of relations with religious communities and which contributes financially towards supporting their activities (Otterbeck, 2004: 238-41; Sander and Larsson, 2002: 108-11; Roald, 2002: 108-09; Alwall, 1998: 184-87). In Norway, there is also a countrywide umbrella organization (the Islamic Council of Norway) that operates as the state counterpart (Vogt, 2002, 95-96).

5 This has been a difficulty, not only for Muslims. European Jewish communities during the eighteenth and nineteenth centuries went through the same processes of institutionalization.

6 For an overall picture, see Hussain (2003: 215-250).

7 See Schmied and Wieshaider (2004: 202-04). The most important legal provisions regarding the Muslim community in Austria are published in Islam (2001: 72-99).

8 However, things are changing quickly. The Anti-Terrorism, Crime and Security Act of 2001 extended the provisions concerning incitement to racial hatred to cover religious hatred and a bill that makes 'incitement to religious hatred' an autonomous offence has been recently proposed: see Special Issue: Religious hate and free speech in UK, February 2, 2005, at http://www.hrwf.net.

9 For an up-to-date picture of Muslim organizations and their position in the German legal system, see Troll (2003: 29, 165-83); also Rohe (2004: 86-88).

10 On the conditions required to obtain this recognition, and on the difficulty that they pose in relation to Muslim organizations, see Muckel (2004: 47-49).

11 On this system, see Robbers (2005).

12 This has begun to be provided experimentally: see Rohe (2004: 95-97). For a description of the more strictly legal aspects of the question, see Muckel (2004: 71-75).

13 This process is described in detail by Sevaistre (2004: 33-48). New Conseil elections scheduled for 26 April 2005 were postponed and a new date (19 June 2005) has been proposed.

14 For other examples of the involvement of the French administration in the formation of Muslim representative institutions, see Terrel (2004: 82, 87, 90).

15 It is symptomatic that Bonaparte's work has been repeatedly evoked during the organization of Islam in France: again, see Terrel (2004: 71-74).

16 For the criticisms, beginning with this remark, that were made by Muslims, see Frégosi (2004: 101-05).

17 The document may be found at: www.pourinfo.ouvaton.org/immigration/dossierchenement/chevenement.htm [accessed on 25 November 2004]. It was preceded, in 1994, by the Charte du culte musulman en France (published in Islam, 2001: 160-72), signed by the members of the Conseil consultatif des Musulmans de France, guided by the Paris Mosque. Many Muslim representatives considered the request to sign this declaration a demonstration of suspicion and lack of trust: see Cesari (2002: 40).

18 In the introduction, it also contains the statement that 'toute discrimination fondée sur le sexe, la religion, l'appartenance ethnique, les mœurs, l'état de santé ou le handicap est contraire à ce principe et pénalement répréhensible'. A reference, originally contained in the document, to the freedom to change one's religion was omitted in the final version.

19 According to Chevènement, 'la situation que nous connaissons aujourd'hui a d'inédit, tant pour les pouvoirs publics que pour les musulmans'. Indeed, it is a question of applying a legal system defined in 1905 to a new religious group and that 'appelle la manifestation d'un consentement mutuel: les Pouvoirs Publics doivent accueillir l'exercice d'un culte qui s'est progressivement implanté en France depuis le début du siècle et plus particulièrement depuis une quarantaine d'années; l'islam de France doit s'organiser en tant que culte minoritaire dans un pays laïque'. These passages are contained in a speech of 28 January 2000 available at: www.pourinfo.ouvaton.org/immigration/dossierchenement/chevenement.htm, [accessed 25 November 2004].

20 Islam, Chevènement (ibid.) states, 'à la différence du christianisme, n'a connu ni la Renaissance ni la Réforme. Certes, l'Islam distingue le domaine religieux et le domaine mondain. Mais il ne manque pas de musulmans pour faire observer que cette distinction appelle une coordination et, par conséquent, une implication permanente du religieux dans le mondain'. However, co-ordination between the temporal and spiritual is not only a Muslim characteristic: it is often advanced by representatives of other religions, including Roman Catholics.

21 In Belgium a system of legal recognition of religions is in force: six communities have been recognized so far (Roman Catholic, Protestant, Jewish, Anglican, Muslim, Greek and Russian Orthodox). See Torfs (2005).

22 Besides Hallet's work, see Foblets and Overbeeke (2004: 3-23). The main legal texts regarding this issue are published in Islam (2001: 100-133).

23 See 'Law imposing elections on the Muslim community voted' (22 July 2004) at www.hrwf.net/html/belgium_2004.html#_Toc86135577 [accessed 25 November 2004]. The law was approved on 16 July 2004 with elections set for 20 March 2005. According to an agreement concluded before the elections of 1998, the constituent assembly should remain in office until 2009 and a third of its components were to have been renewed in 2004; in this same year the mandate of the executive committee expired. See also 'Minister of Justice justifies the state's intervention in the internal affairs of the Muslim community' (12 July 2004) and 'Ongoing tension between the state and the representative bodies of the Muslim community' (24 May 2004), ibidem. On the same web-site other writings provide a more detailed picture of this complex question. See also: www.suffrage-universel.be.

24 In a series of recent decisions the European Court of Human Rights has placed precise limits on the power of the public administration to interfere with the internal organization of a religious community: see the decisions in the cases of Hasan and Chaush v. Bulgaria of 26 October 2000 (where, at paragraph 78, it is stated that; 'State action favouring one leader of a divided religious community or undertaken with the purpose of forcing the community to come together under a single leadership against its own wishes would likewise constitute an interference with freedom of religion'). See also the decision in the case of the Metropolitan Church of Bessarabia v. Moldova, 13 July 2001 (in particular paragraph 117). Texts available at: www.olir.it/ricerca/index.php?Form_Document=1182 and Document=1579 [accessed 6 December 2004]. On the contrast between the orientation expressed in these sentences and the activity of the Belgian government regarding the Muslim Executive, see Foblets and Overbeeke (2004: 16-18).

25 The Belgian Constitution contains a provision (Article 21) that forbids the state to interfere with the appointment of ministers of any religion: see Torfs (2001: 83).

Chapter 2

Discrimination and Claims for Equal Rights Amongst Muslims in Europe

Valérie Amiraux

Introduction

Few would question the existence of negative perceptions and representations of Muslims in Europe, although these feelings are expressed and translated very differently from country to country (Allen and Nielsen, 2002). Indeed, studies of the post 9/11 context have shown that anti-Muslim feeling and hostility – sometimes called 'Islamophobia' – is growing all over Europe.[1] Media coverage of the attacks on the USA has been incriminated in the increasing distrust and suspicion experienced by Muslim populations. However, this negative perception of Islam in European public opinion has also opened up new opportunities for Muslims to express their own requirements and interests. Individually and collectively, experiences of discrimination and unequal treatment have been publicly denounced by Muslims and, in a few cases, even taken to the courts. This chapter is an attempt to elaborate on such matters and especially a double dynamic of 'juridicization'[2] and 'judicialization'[3] which appears to be emerging. This dialectic designates a general tendency to work towards the resolution of issues that are a source of political conflict through the legal system. My argument, regarding a growing recourse to legal argumentation, concerns both state policies as well as the initiatives of Muslim citizens.[4]

In an age of globalization domestic politics and decision-making is increasingly constrained by international legal provisions. No European state can, for instance, ignore the existence of international conventions protecting human rights or behave as if these have no importance. Nation-states can no longer do as they will on a national level, being embedded in larger frameworks that highlight moral and ethical values ('common goods') apparently shared and protected by an 'international community'. At the same time, citizens also appear to rely more systematically than before upon legal provisions to resolve situations or conflicts, acting in the name of a collective or as private individuals. In this respect, my focus will be the way in which 'judicial' treatment may help a cause (for example, equality between Muslims and non-Muslims) to gain political relevance and visibility.

This chapter begins, firstly, by examining the legal conditions framing and determining the social and political life of Muslims in France, Germany, Great Britain and Italy. In terms of a European perspective, I enquire: where do the national specificities lie? Secondly, the chapter considers the way in which individual claims for equality made by Muslim citizens, in particular their use of anti-discrimination legislation, affects the perception of Islam as a public issue.[5] Beyond a 'resource mobilization' interpretation, what do such moves indicate in terms of the political commitment of Muslims in public arenas? What is the political impact of this 'juridicization' of the discussion over Islam at national and European levels? Far from being the simple by-product of national migration waves, the presence of Muslims is shaped by the larger framework of European integration. So, what sorts of social dynamics are created by an implementation of 'equality' that relies on courts and trials as the main sites for its construction? What does the 'discrimination repertoire' bring to discussions about Islam in the West?

The Legal Regulation of Religion in Europe and the Fact of Religious Discrimination

Reviewing the settlement processes of Muslims in the European Union (EU), scholars have sought to elaborate a comprehensive and comparative perspective within which it is possible to identify institutional models of relations between Muslims and non-Muslims. A major focus of interest has been existing relations between particular churches and states and the way that this frames the interactions of Muslims in the contexts in which they now reside. Of course, the 'bewildering variety' (Davie, 2000: 15) of church-state relations in Europe is central. The usual classification distinguishes between: a) 'concordat type' regimes (that is, the state recognizes denominations or has signed agreements with representative religious hierarchies as in Italy or Germany); b) systems with official state churches (such as the established Church of England); and c) systems of strict separation between churches and the state (for instance, France).[6] These different systems of regulation can influence, constrain and even empower Muslims as they participate in the respective national political cultures, although other factors cannot be discounted.

Trying to delimit the apparent uniqueness of the different national 'models' is difficult. Religious freedom, tolerance, the neutrality of the state, and the autonomy of religious hierarchies vis-à-vis the state (the latter being 'incompetent' as far as religious matters are concerned) are all European 'common goods'. Moreover, such principles also follow international standards of law. For instance, when it comes to individual rights, all EU member-states constitutionally protect, both individually and collectively, their citizens' freedom of conscience and religion.[7] European states are 'neutral' vis-à-vis religious denominations and prohibit discrimination on the basis of an individual's belief.[8] Indeed, this neutrality 'guarantees' the equal treatment of denominations in European liberal democratic contexts.[9] Parallel to this protection against all forms of individual or collective discrimination on grounds of religion, freedom to practice one's faith is also guaranteed. However, this general frame of protection does not preclude minority denominations from sometimes experiencing highly differentiated, and thus unequal, treatment. Over the last decade especially Islam and Muslims have gradually become a systematic illustration of this fact.

From a juridical point of view, the stable presence of Islam in European political spaces raises questions about the current compromises and balances inherited from a religious history that was sometimes extremely violent. The central question for European states now incorporating Muslim minorities has most often been presented as a juridical one: in a pluralistic and democratic setting, what place and status should Muslims be allowed as the institutionalization of Islam gathers apace? How should equality between faiths and the neutrality of the state be enacted in the case of Islam and Muslims? Even if this 'does not pose legally unsolvable problems or, on close examination, particularly new ones' (Ferrari, 2004: 4), the legal provisions that already exist to address the Muslim presence often need more effective application. Indeed, and this is my main point here, the legal regulation of different religious denominations may also create all sorts of indirect discrimination: administrative and procedural obstacles to the opening of places of worship; strict conditions for the teaching of Islam in public schools;[10] difficulties recognizing Islam on the basis of the 'there-is-no-unique-partner' argument.

In France, for example, the 'neutrality' of the state and the separation and privatization of religion, does structure a certain 'equality' between faith communities. Nevertheless, it also produces indirect discrimination towards certain minority religious communities. Some French MPs interviewed recently confessed their ignorance of the room for manoeuvre actually allowed by the 1905 Law of Separation. Facing demands for new Muslim places of worship, they resorted to arguments about the neutrality of the state in order to construct a convenient legal barrier protecting them from making interventions in discussions about the allocation of a piece of land or the granting of planning permission. Their situation in many ways resembles that of teachers and head-teachers of schools requesting the government's help in defining a coherent and pragmatic position on managing the presence of Muslim students wearing veils in French public schools.

The major change in the position of religion in European public space came as the result of a significant historical shift, which, again, assumed a somewhat different shape from country to country. From the sixteenth to the eighteenth century European history saw the more or less peaceful coexistence of states organized along confessional lines, whether this was formally institutionalized or not. Membership of the political community was often dependent on membership of the dominant religious denomination. Therefore, one major evolution in the emergence of contemporary Europe was the shift from such confessional regimes of citizenship to ultra liberal ones where no such test exists. Religious pluralism and the individualization of religious belonging are directly related to this change. Individuals may now choose to believe or not to believe, exercising a fundamental right protected by constitutional national provisions, European texts and international treaties.[11] This fundamental change induces another one: *the integration into national political culture of the idea that religious pluralism should be, if not actively supported, at least tolerated and protected.*

In the management of growing religious pluralism, a distinction seems to be appearing between countries with a dominant Catholic culture (Italy, France) and countries with either a clear Protestant majority (Great Britain) or bi-confessional population (Germany). Here, the degree of intimacy of each national context with *de facto* religious diversity remains a key variable which helps to explain why the latter contexts are more sensitive, or at least indifferent, to Muslims' practices and needs,[12] and why the former, on the contrary, would seem to produce explosive controversies such as wearing the veil, the right to open a mosque, or the presence of religious symbols in public buildings. Furthermore, it may be necessary to distinguish between Muslim claims in countries that follow in the footsteps of other denominations (for example, the recognition of Sikhs' right to wear turbans in Great Britain or Jewish slaughter rites in Germany), and countries in which Muslims had have to 'do it for themselves' in environments intolerant to religion such as France.

In Italy, the legitimacy of certain symbols (for example, cribs at Christmas[13] and the crucifix in public primary schools – see Saint-Blancat and Perocco, this volume) is regularly discussed,[14] and more and more so in connection with the question of religious pluralism and the direct competition between faiths. So, what place should be given to 'Otherness' without alienating the 'Self'? The problem is a highly sensitive one in Europe not only because it raises the issue of pluralism inside a specific nation-state, but also because it highlights, crucially, the religious vitality of the respective religious communities, Christian and non-Christian (Davie, 2002). Moreover, as this chapter demonstrates, some existing national provision for religious freedom and the public administration of worship can produce indirect discrimination as an unintended consequence. The British law of blasphemy, for example, which applies only to Christianity, undoubtedly has some discriminatory implications for other denominations as illustrated by the Rushdie Affair.[15]

Nationality, Citizenship and International Crises

Analysing the public regulation mechanisms of religious denominations is thus insufficient in terms of mapping the variety of situations faced by Muslims in Europe. Beyond their position as 'believers', Muslims are also generally 'citizens' of their place of residence and, moreover, 'economic' agents. Here the picture becomes complex as each country offers diverse access to nationality and citizenship. If Muslims are recent minorities in the four countries referred to at the outset of this chapter, they trace their heritage to different countries,[16] sometimes echoing a colonial past as in the French or British cases, sometimes symbolizing a dynamic economic period of recruiting unskilled workers as in Germany, or reflecting the change of status from 'home-country' to 'host-country' as in Italy.

At first glance, the difficulties faced by Muslim populations in Europe are not different from one country to another. Most countries receiving migrant workers in the 1960s had to come to terms with the same practical issues, relating to the different stages of migration and settlement, the educational needs of children, and the move away from policy concerning 'migration' to (in some cases) a policy of 'integration'. For migrants themselves, the price to pay is more or less expensive, depending on whether you lived as a Turk in Solingen during 1989, as a fourth generation member of a family of Algerian migrants in Lille, as a Pakistani taxi driver in Bradford or as a Moroccan waiter in Milan. Nevertheless, the current situation is one of radical convergence between contexts that have previously always been compared and contrasted.

Independent of the policies implemented in public sectors such as education or housing, of church-state relations, of the origin of the original migrants, and of the degree of secularization, European societies are now converging in constructing Islam as domestic threat to cohesive citizenship. For instance, notwithstanding the reform of the nationality law (applied 1 January 2000) which made it somewhat easier for 'foreign workers' to become 'citizens', public attacks are becoming a daily experience for Muslims in Germany. From 1961 until the end of the 1990s, the public perception of Islam was mostly considered a foreign policy and diplomatic issue. However, immediately after 9/11, the automatic equation between migrants from Muslim backgrounds and a sense of 'threat' to the federal territory gained a new force (see Jonker, Chapter 8, this volume). One of those involved in the 9/11 attacks, M. Attah, had been living and studying in Germany.

Islam and Muslims have certainly gained a new kind of public visibility in Europe during the last two decades (Amman and Göle, 2004). This visibility is not exclusively based on the growing fear of Islamism and terrorism at the international level, or on new political demands for recognition which have been made by Muslims, especially of a younger generation, since the mid-1980s. Part of this 'new' visibility, and in particular the media focus on Muslims, can be related to the impact of international crises on European contexts. International events have an important effect on local perceptions of Muslims by their fellow citizens (Cesari, 2004). These are incorporated into public policy-making, in particular when selecting 'good Muslims' and denouncing 'bad ones' (Bonnefoy, 2003, comparing Britain and France). However, part of this emerging visibility is also tied to the construction of Islam as a public 'problem' in most European contexts, a construction which draws on different narratives stemming from national security policy (especially in the aftermath of 9/11), [17] controversial representations of Muslims as enemies (Cesari, 2001), the institutionalization of Islam in general and more specific controversies (Amiraux, 2004a).

The public character of Islam is therefore multiple: 'As phenomena are open to various modes of conceptualizing them as problems, so too their public character is open to various means of conceiving their resolution' (Gusfield, 1981: 5). The 'public-ization' of Islam in most European countries has thus created a set of narratives that work as a constraint on Muslim citizens. It either forces them to justify their personal choices and ways of life, or invites them to react personally to anything related to Islam, from the Israeli-Palestinian conflict, to the public stoning of women in Iran, to the necessity of wearing the veil as Muslim woman.

Serving the Cause of Equality

Having established some of the context of my argument, I now want to return to my main focus. If Islam requires the same equal treatment from pluralistic European democracies as other confessions, the implementation of this principle of equality of religions seems to be increasingly elaborated in the courts and local jurisdictions. In particular, it relies upon the fight against all forms of discrimination. This general shift has occurred for various reasons and reflects multiple interests. On the one hand, local and regional Muslim associations or federations have organized in an effort to secure the institutional status that could eventually lead to equal treatment by public authorities at a national level. On the other hand, individuals and collectives have sued in defence of their rights as believers but also as victims of racial injustice and discrimination. In both cases respect for, and tolerance of, 'Otherness' lies at the heart of the relevant discourse. There are different 'registers' however.

The first register, 'mobilization', clearly refers to the 'public recognition' of Islam as a denomination, its claims for equal treatment and a willingness to translate this into the creation of a representative body,[18] with all the associated symbolic and practical outcomes. The discussion here routinely focuses on the realm of religious practice and its public regulation. It has given birth to some very eclectic institutions, each doing their best to cope with the local requirements of their country of residence. For instance, Islamic institutions are often expected to provide public agencies with a hierarchy and it is assumed that they should be able to represent all Muslims.

In respect of the second register, the focus is on two different repertoires, the respect for religious minorities' 'freedom of conscience' and the 'fight against discrimination'. Both types of experience of exclusion are apparent in empirical studies of Islam and Muslims in Europe. This second register also illustrates the way that experiences of injustice and discrimination have affected motives and investments in the judicial and political arenas as a means of resolving potential conflicts between Muslims and non-Muslims in some EU member-states.

Religious identity and the meaning of being a Muslim has changed amongst believers settled in Europe. The entire literature, whichever country is in question, emphasizes the diversity and heterogeneity of Muslim populations, not only in terms of origins and ethnic background, but also in terms of definitions of being a Muslim and the practices and relationships to the community of belief that follow from this (see the chapters in Section III, this volume). The grammar of religious belonging has become more and more complex, depending on the type of identification that the individual wants to prioritise: a strict obedience to rites, the adoption of a 'life ethic', the defence and eventual promotion of a cultural patrimony. Indeed, religious practice alone is no longer a sufficient indicator of the religious 'belonging' of individuals that may choose to be identified as 'Muslims' in certain circumstances but not in others. Of course, certain visible signs become clear markers of 'religious' difference: clothes, names, faces, veils and beards. After 9/11, the study of the resultant rise of Islamophobia identified the profile of the 'ideal victim': 'The headscarf seems to have become the primary visual identifier as a target for hatred, with Muslim women being routinely abused and attacked' (EUMC Newsletter, Issue 13, June 2002: 1).

Again, the relative sensitivity of different European contexts, and the justification for policy makers to take a position against the wearing of the veil in public schools, is totally different in Germany and France. During the 2003-4 episode in France, secularism, gender equality and the precarious situation of women in certain urban settings were the main arguments motivating the law that eventually banned ostentatious religious symbols from public schools (European Parliament, 2004: 50). By contrast, the stigmatization of the Islamic veil in Germany was essentially because it was perceived as a 'political' rather than a 'religious' symbol (see Jonker, this volume). In a way, the French legal answer appears to be less discriminatory of Muslims than the German interpretation, which saw fit to ban the headscarf amongst civil servants working in the field of education. The January 2004 declaration by the German President, Johannes Rau, that all religious symbols, including the crucifix, should be banned from public schools was an attempt to re-balance this discussion.

Common usage of the term 'discrimination' is rather loose, seeking to unify multilevel experiences that encompass various degrees of intensity, from passivity to hostility, intolerance to racial hatred and violence. Here a distinction should be drawn between reference to 'discrimination' as a means to denounce a situation of unequal treatment of one or more parts of a population, and the mobilization of that constituency in the context of legal action and lawsuits. In this respect, a second distinction between 'direct' and 'indirect' discrimination is crucial to refine the use of the concept in legal terms. With the notion of 'indirect' discrimination, it is no longer necessary to establish the passive (*de jure*) intention motivating discrimination. Rather, judges are invited to assess the concrete effects (*de facto*) of texts and norms on the life of individuals, even when explicit intention does not appear as such in the legal data. Judgements should refer to situations produced by the application of 'neutral criteria' to a specific population which, because of its belonging to a certain group, remains the victim of unequal treatment.

As is the case for women and other vulnerable groups, Muslims are mostly victims of indirect discrimination. The application of the 1905 law and the understanding of the principle of *laïcité* in France, in particular in relation to the opening of places of worship, or the blasphemy law in England, are both good illustrations of this. In France, the text of the law in itself does not contain explicit provisions against non-Catholic denominations, but it was designed as a tool to prevent the Catholic Church from intervening in politics. The principle of *laïcité* and, especially, the neutrality of the state, is most often understood by local public authorities who too often rely on a literal interpretation of the concept of 'separation' that is at the core of the 1905 legislation. Similarly, not being recognized as an 'ethnic' group, Britain's Muslims have historically been denied direct access to important legal rights and public goods.

Religion as a criterion of discrimination has not yet been properly researched and applied to the situation of Muslims in the European Union.[19] When it has been researched, for instance by sociologists, the reference to discrimination is a rather loose one ('discrimination' = 'unequal treatment'), being variously set in the context of: assessing public policies; advocating the replacement of 'integration' discourse with an (anti-racist) 'fight against discrimination' discourse; or simply examining 'representation' amongst groups such as 'Muslims'. Public discussions of Islam were also, until recently, rather confined to debates over the definition of norms and rules of behaviour in a context where Muslims are a minority. Can Muslims be incorporated as citizens? Is Islam compatible with European political values?

In such a context, the emergence of the word 'discrimination' in relation to the situation of Muslims in Europe refers to the way that public agencies imagine Islam: an 'Otherness' that automatically inspires fear and suspicion. Discrimination must therefore be understood in terms of the tensions between 'host-societies', their national history and tradition of citizenship on the one hand, and the specific requests by Muslims on the other. The extensive use of the word 'Islamophobia' – no longer limited to the United Kingdom as it was before 2001 – has developed in France, where some Muslims and non-Muslims use it as a legitimate word to describe forms of racism which articulate with religious identity (Geisser, 2003). Considering the blurred border separating racism from discrimination, Islamophobia has been defined as:

> a two-stranded form of racism – rooted in both the 'different' physical appearance of Muslims and also an intolerance of their religious and cultural beliefs, and should be considered as a modern epidemic of an age-old prejudice towards, and fear of, Islam. (Sheridan, 2002: 87)

What, then, can be the 'cause' of 'Muslims' in Europe? What can be the common denominator that helps to organize a collective identification 'of Muslims as Muslims'? If the notion of religious discrimination is new to academic discussions, it is also new to the political vocabulary of Muslim organizations. In England and Wales, religious discrimination is a widespread problem, more prevalent than racial abuse according to some authors (Sheridan, 2002). Used now as a catchword to encompass diverse forms of hatred or distrust vis-à-vis Muslims, the notion of religious discrimination is not without problems or difficulties in terms of its definition, the question of 'intention' (is it really about the religious belonging of the victim?) and the lack of data (OSI, 2002: 227, 260).

Since 9/11, the analysis of a growing anti-Muslim and anti-Islamic feeling has been more extensively studied. This is also part of a broader climate of the 'ethnicization' of Islam – resulting from the conflation of culture and religion (Roy, 2003: 68-69) – and also, to some extent, part of the competition (at least in the media) between victims of racism. In most of the cases where the religious belonging of the victim of discrimination could be at stake, it remains implicit. There is generally no evidence of the centrality of the religious variables, even if religion 'appeared to trigger both implicit racism and general discrimination to a greater extent than did race or ethnicity, both before and post-September 11' (Sheridan, 2002: 90).

A Community of Suffering? Injustice and the Muslim Common Good

Another important and often ignored dimension of the religious discrimination debate is reflected in the fact that experiences of injustice seem to operate as 'common goods' between Muslim populations otherwise defined by an intrinsic heterogeneity. 'Islam' is inscribed in a form of daily experience that works 'as a horizontal social imaginary bonding many different Muslim actors, in different contexts, who act together simultaneously' (Göle, 2003: 814). For the Muslims who choose their religion as a motive for associative commitment, racism and other injustices are often experienced not personally but 'by proxy'. This strong identification with the feelings of victims (relatives or friends but sometimes anonymous individuals) generates a sense of shared experience of vulnerability and exclusion that is perhaps the most striking aspect of the renewal of the idea of the *umma* in a non-Muslim context.[20] Indeed, as a member of the community of believers, even if you have never suffered from intolerance, racism or discrimination as a 'Muslim', you may strongly empathize with the victims and therefore adopt discourses and practices of activism, even militancy, that re-connect you with the 'real victims'.[21] The community ceases simply to be a spiritual imaginary and becomes a shared 'community of suffering' with its own icons and martyrs.[22]

To analyse claims structured around repertoires centred on emotions and affects, Göle uses the concept of 'stigma' as used by Goffman. It is an attribute that profoundly discredits the individual, but which is also the subject of public perception 'to the extent that it articulates the private corporeal realm to the public domain of perception, social interaction, and communication' (Göle, 2003: 809). Far from the usual association of stigma with the process of exclusion, she mobilizes the notion of stigma to 'understand the ways in which social difference and public exclusion are carried out by bodily signs and practices' (Göle, 2003: 810). In terms of the technique of systematizing the use of legal resources (texts, laws, case law) to attract the attention of a larger public and create a voice in the public space, the identification with one case, one figure that symbolizes a singular experience, appears as central in this 'juridicization' process. It helps to organize the narrative, to formulate concrete expectations, to seduce different publics. Public opinion relates more easily to individual cases, charged with an emotional capacity to gather people together. Certain cases gain more attention and become 'affairs' while others do not. In 1989 and 2003, for example, the controversies over the veil in France produced a quasi 'iconology' of the victims of unfair treatment or injustice: 'Cases can be part of an effort to elevate an issue to the political agenda, occupying time in Parliament and the newspapers' (Sterett, 1998: 310).

Commitment to the fight against discrimination has aided in the more systematic use of legal tools in the cause of Muslim equality with other citizens. As in the case of anti-racist NGOs, most of the Muslims committed in associations dealing with Islamophobia are familiar with the law, most of them holding degrees in that discipline. At the intersection of law and politics, professional skills serve moral ends. Law firms are being created by Muslims and lawyers are engaging in Muslim associations after they obtain their degree, as was the case of one of the young women working for the recently created *Collectif Contre l'Islamophobie en France* (2004). As law plays a more central role in political regulation and intervenes more systematically in the juridical reformulation of social problems, the mobilization of legal resources to serve the cause of the equality of Muslims is becoming more systematic. In some cases Muslim lawyers act as 'gate-keepers' defining the 'entrance' and 'exit' to particular topics and actors, even controlling the production of media and academic discourse on such matters. In Germany, for example, some members of the Islamische Gemeinshaft Milli Görüş (IGMG) have, since 9/11, systematized the lawsuits against journalists, writers and scholars that were said to be publishing unverified allegations against Muslims and therefore negatively affecting the public image of the movement. Tribunals and courts become some of the main sites for translating the specific claims and needs of Muslims into politics. This both domesticates Islam as a public issue at a national level and contributes to the Europeanization of the cause of equality for Muslims.

The ability to elaborate a cause such as 'equality' between Muslim and non-Muslim citizens and to promote justice through a defence of rights engaging other types of publics is a new and recent outcome of the equality discourse emerging in Europe. The defence of Muslims' rights to live as 'Muslims' is a cause that can even attract the support of other groups, moving beyond a simple 'community' politics. The emergence of an organized denunciation of Islamophobia and religious discrimination is also opening up a new perspective centred on a more systematic use of judicial tools to gain recognition of rights and specific claims. This process is made possible thanks to the intervention of Muslims, who are not only activists but also professionals working for their fellows' rights. The 'professionalization' of activism is neither a new thing, nor peculiar to Muslims however. Putting one's professional competence in the service of empowering a peculiar (and often vulnerable) group is, for some, at the heart of a moral commitment to the practice of 'lawyering' as a form of advocacy: '(...) their real goal is to contribute to the kind of transformative politics that will redistribute political power and material benefits in a more egalitarian fashion' (Sarat and Scheingold, 1998: 7).

Conclusion

Muslims are not a group of citizens that can easily be understood in terms of the more general banners associated with the study of collective action and other social groups such as gays, women or immigrants. The claim for specific rights based upon collective, ritual and other aspects of their religious life also reduces Muslims' ability to be considered as legitimate actors in the civil rights debate in more or less secularized societies. Muslims are, in a way, 'obliged' to associate with other groups in order to gain legitimacy, credibility and visibility (Bouzar, 2004). However, sustaining and defending a vision of the 'good society' where equality occupies a central position is entirely commensurate with the 'ethic' of Muslims' commitment to associative activity in European countries (Roy, 2003). Moreover, their public claims for equality can also attract non-Muslim fellow citizens who would not 'naturally' feel attracted to their 'motives':

> The particular features of a group's culture, which are identified as significant by members and outsiders, and precisely where the boundary is drawn with other groups, especially the majority community, often depend upon the context or situation in which an issue arises. (Poulter, 1998: 7)

Increasing racism, Islamophobia and discrimination indicates the multiple difficulties Muslims are experiencing on a daily basis in many European societies.

Still, the number of people experiencing discrimination that file lawsuits remains low when compared with the increasing and generalized use of the term 'discrimination' in common parlance. Understanding the challenges posed by the settlement of Muslims in the EU requires two processes to be distinguished. The first one is rather institutional and refers to the public regulation of worship. What should individual European states do as far as religious practices and the representation of Islamic communities is concerned? A second process, parallel to the previous one, invites us to focus on the specific tensions that are emerging between Muslims and the rest of society. How do the former produce differences? How do they accept or deny their identification as Muslims? How does the latter deal with this? This second dynamic cannot be treated separately from the first but both should not be considered as equivalents. If the terms 'Islam' and 'Muslims' sometimes overlap, they do not always refer to the same population, nor to the same challenges.

References

Allen, C. and Nielsen, J. (2002), *Summary Report on Islamophobia in the European Union after 11 September 2001*, Vienna: European Union Monitoring Centre on Racism and Xenophobia.

Amiraux, V. (2004a), 'Expertises, savoir et politique. La constitution de l'islam comme problème public en France et en Allemagne', in Bénédicte Zimmermann (ed.), *Les sciences sociales à l'épreuve de l'action*, Paris: EHESS, 209-245.

Amiraux, V. (2004b), 'Peut-on parler de "discrimination religieuse"? Réflexions à partir de la situation des musulmans en France', *Confluences Méditerranée*, April: 50-61.

Amman, L. and Göle, N. (eds) (2004), *Islam in Sicht: Der Auftritt von Muslimen im öffentlichen Raum*, Bielefeld: Transcript.

Bhargava, R. (ed.) (1988), *Secularism and its Critics*, Delhi and Oxford: Oxford University Press.

Bonnefoy, L. (2003), 'Public institutions and Islam: A new stigmatization?', *ISIM Newsletter*, December (13), 22.

Bouzar, D. (2004), *'Monsieur Islam' n'existe pas: Pour une désislamisation des débats*, Paris: Hachette (Littératures).

Bradney, A. and Ferrari, S. (eds) (2000), *Islam and European Legal Systems*, Aldershot: Ashgate.

Cesari, J. (2004), *L'islam à l'épreuve de l'occident*, Paris: La découverte.

Davie, G. (2000), *Religion in Modern Europe: A Memory Mutates*, Oxford: Oxford University Press.

Davie, G. (2002), *Europe: The Exceptional Case*, London: Darton, Longman and Todd.

Debray, R. (2002), *L'enseignement du fait religieux dans l'école laïque*, http://www.education.gouv.fr/rapport/debray/debray.pdf [accessed, 27 December 2004].

European Commission against Racism and Intolerance (ECRI) (2000), *General Policy Recommendation n°5: Combating Intolerance and Discrimination against Muslims*, Strasbourg: 27 April.

European Parliament (2004), *Report on the Situation as Regards Fundamental Rights in the European Union*, A5–0207/2004.

Ferrari, S. (2004), 'Islam in Europe: An Introduction to Legal Problems and Perspectives', in Aluffi, R. and Zincone, G. (eds), *The Legal Treatment of Islamic Minorities in Europe*, Leuven: Peeters, 1-9.

Göle, N. (2003), 'The Voluntary Adoption of Islamic Stigma Symbols', *Social Research*, 70 (3), 809-828.

Madeley, J.T.S. (2003), 'European Liberal Democracy and the Principle of State Religious Neutrality', *West European Politics*, 26 (1): 1-22.

Manço, U. (2004), *Reconnaissance et discrimination. Présence de l'islam en Europea occidentale et en Amérique du Nord*, Paris: L'Harmattan.

Marongiu-Perria, O. (2004), 'Politique publique et islam depuis la loi de 1905', *Hommes et migrations*, 03/04 (1248), 89-97.

McLoughlin, S. (1996), 'In the name of the *umma*: globalisation, race relations and Muslim identity politics in Bradford', in Shadid, W.A.R. and van Koningsveld, P.S. (eds), *Political Participation and Identities of Muslims in Non-Muslim States*, Kampen, the Netherlands: Kok Pharos, 206-228.

Poulter, S. (1998), *Ethnicity, Law and Human Rights: The English Experience*, Oxford: Clarendon Press.

Roy, O. (2003), *L'islam mondialisé*, Paris: Seuil (la couleur des idées).

Sarat, A. and Scheingold, S. (eds) (1998), *Cause Lawyering. Political Commitments and Professional Responsibilities*, Oxford: Oxford University Press.

Scheingold, S. (1998), 'The struggle to politicise legal practice: a case study of left activist lawyering in Seattle', in Sarat, A. and Scheingold, S. (eds), *Cause Lawyering: Political Commitments and Professional Responsibilities*, Oxford: Oxford University Press, 118-148.

Sheridan, L. (2002), 'Religious discrimination: The new racism', in Muslim Council of Britain (ed.), *The Quest for Sanity: Reflections on September 11 and the Aftermath*, London: Muslim Council of Britain, 86-93.

Sterett, S. (1998), 'Caring about individual cases: Immigration lawyering in Britain', in Sarat, A. and Scheingold, S. (eds), *Cause Lawyering: Political Commitments and Professional Responsibilities*, Oxford: Oxford University Press, 293-316.

Stone Sweet, A. (2002), 'Constitutional Politics in France and Germany', in Shapiro, M. and Stone Sweet, A., *On Law, Politics, and Judicialization*, Oxford: Oxford University Press, 184-208.

Werbner, P. (2002), *Imagined Diasporas among Manchester Muslims*, Oxford: James Currey.

Notes

1 See, for example, ECRI (2000) and EUMC (2001).
2 'Juridicization' refers to the use, by individuals, of juridical tools and arenas (courts) to seek satisfaction of their needs, answers to their complaints and, eventually, reparation for damages.
3 Stone (2002: 187-188) argues that, 'The 'judicialization of politics' refers to the general process by which legal discourse – norms of behaviour and language – penetrate and are absorbed by political discourse', implementing a 'spectre of court intervention'.
4 This is particularly well illustrated by the law of 15 March 2004 banning the wearing of certain religious symbols from French public schools. One could also quote the decision by some of the 15 German Länder (individual states) to ban the wearing of the veil by teachers working in public schools, following the decision, taken by the Constitutional Court in October 2003, not to outlaw the veil at a federal level.

5   Discrimination is intended unequal treatment of individuals based on the illegal reference to their real or supposed belonging to a 'race' or ethnic group. Direct discrimination is based on an intention to treat two persons differently because of their racial or ethnic grouping, this motivation being illegal.

6   See Ferrari (this volume); Bradney and Ferrari (2000); Shadid and van Koningsveld (2002); and Cesari (2004: 100-117).

7   Legal provisions protecting individuals and collectives in terms of 'freedom of conscience', 'of religion' and 'of worship' include: in France, the 1905 law, 1901 law, 1907 law, 1958 Constitution (Article 2 and Preamble of the 1946 Constitution); in Italy, Articles 3, 8 and 9 of the Constitution; in Germany, Articles 4, 3-3, 33-3, 116-2, and 140 are the central references to constitutional provisions; in Great Britain, the Bills of Rights defines the main principles related to religion. The Human Rights Act (1998) includes a section (13) dedicated to religious freedom. The right to change one's religion, the right not to believe in any religion, the right not to practice (even being a believer) are part of religious freedom and therefore constitutionally protected. In some cases, the recognition of these rights may have created difficulties during the negotiations between state representatives and Muslim leaders, in particular, regarding the question of apostasy.

8   Each national administration uses its own labels in this respect. For example, 'culte' in France (literally 'worship', designating the institutional and mostly collective aspect of religious life). Elsewhere, 'religion', 'faith', 'community of the faithful', 'denomination'.

9   A liberal state does not impose any constraints in terms of defining what a 'good life' may be (Madeley, 2003).

10 Even if the way Islam is taught in French public schools has been improving since 1996 (Debray, 2002).

11 Even if the way Islam is taught in French public schools has been improving since 1996 (Debray, 2002).

12 To quote but a few examples: dietary requirements; the possibility to pray in public buildings; the recognition of holidays; the presence of chaplains in public services; the right to slaughter animals according to specific religious rules; Muslim plots in cemeteries.

13 In December 2004, certain episodes led to the explosion of a polemic on the preparation of cribs in public schools. In particular, the discussion revealed competing positions between representatives of the Catholic Church and non-Catholic citizens.

14 In December 2004, concerning the constitutionality of the presence of the crucifix in public primary schools, the Italian Constitutional Court explained that the authority to decide to install such religious symbols or not lay with head-teachers and not any law. However, as pointed out by Margiotta Broglio, the Constitutional Court has replaced the crucifix in its own building with paintings of la Madonna. See www.olir.it/areetematiche/75/documents/Chizzoniti_Corte_e_crocifisso.pdf, [accessed 27 December 2004].

15 Without reviewing the law of blasphemy, the British government is currently drafting a new law that should protect all religions.

16 Most Muslims in France trace their heritage to North Africa, in Great Britain the Indian sub-continent and in Germany most are Turks. In Italy, Moroccans are the largest group of Muslims, just ahead of Albanians.

17 As far as the French context is concerned, some surveys have stressed the relative quietness that dominated public opinion immediately after the 9/11 attacks. This does not mean that racism and xenophobia was not an issue or that the public perception of Islam, both as a faith and as culture, is a positive or tolerant one.

18 None of the four European countries discussed have been able to escape the logic of the need to create a representative Muslim body to act as a 'partner' for the public authorities. See Caeiro, Jonker, McLoughlin, and Saint-Blancat and Perocco, this volume.

19 With the exception of the British case (Poulter, 2002), few works deal with the question of religious discrimination in other European countries. See Manço (2004) and Marongiu-Perria (2004) for the French case. For an attempt to blend a juridical approach and a sociological reading of the experience of injustice and discrimination, see Amiraux (2004b).

20 See McLoughlin (1996) for an account of the impact of the Bosnian war on British Muslims.

21 The words of a convert to Islam interviewed by the author and Samir Amghar, Paris, 19 November 2004.

22 For example, profaned places (attacks against mosques or tombs) or persons (in Corsica, the personification of racist violence against religious authorities, *imams*). N.B. Werbner (2002) also discusses the idea of a 'community of suffering'.

Chapter 3

Islam, Secularism and Multiculturalism After 9/11: A Transatlantic Comparison

Jocelyne Cesari

Introduction

One common element of mainstream discourse on Islam in the post-9/11 world has been the constant correlation between Islam as a religion and Islam as a factor in political violence. One of the effects of this correlation can be seen in the acts of aggression against Muslims in both the United States and Europe. This continued conflation of international politics with issues of Muslim immigration demonstrates the persistence of an essentializing of both Islam and its practitioners. Developed over several centuries of confrontation between the Muslim and European worlds (Daniel, 1960; Said, 1978; Cesari, 1997), such an attitude is far from dead, it seems. Indeed, it is striking how the idea of Islam as an international 'risk factor', current since the 1980s, is bolstered by centuries-old representations of Islam that would be familiar in the eighteenth century or even earlier. The same fixed ideas of Islam as an inherently violent and fanatical religion are continually re-invoked and readjusted to fit changes in international and domestic situations.

In Europe, this perception of the international or political manifestation of Islam was a significant factor in shaping the condition of Muslim minorities long before the events of 9/11. In the United States, on the other hand, a political distinction was generally maintained between Islam in the Muslim world and Muslim immigrants living in the West – a distinction, however, which is no longer necessarily true (Cesari, 2001: 97-116).

The convergence of European and American political discourse is noteworthy for the automatic correlation between the war on terrorism, internal security measures, and immigration policy – always, it seems, with a focus on individuals of a Muslim background. Such a correlation increasingly invalidates the distinction between international and domestic policy, and has consequences not only for the status of Muslim minorities, but also for more general issues of secularism and multiculturalism in the democratic nations concerned.

Anti-terrorism, Security, Immigration: Ties that Bind

For some European nations, the linking of Muslim immigration to international political crises is nothing new. In France, for example, while immigrants were building prayer-rooms in low-income housing projects during the 1980s, certain commentators, including members of the academic community, looked to international events, such as the Islamic Revolution in Iran or the Islamist movements in Egypt and Algeria, to explain this phenomenon. The re-emergence of Islam in France, therefore, was considered to be a result of foreign manipulation, and thus a potential source of political unrest. Such applications of the international political situation to internal French issues – perpetually reinvigorated by the latest foreign crisis – have also led to a tendency to analyze any expression of Islam from a political perspective. The habit, in France, of automatically considering any form of Islamic expression to be influenced by the ongoing political crisis in Algeria, for example, ultimately obscured the real nature of the new social and cultural dynamics of diasporic Muslim communities.

Since 9/11, the perception of Islam as an internal as well as an external threat has been at the forefront of both European and American political discourse. One of its practical manifestations has been special legislation relating to the fight against terrorism. Common to all the new laws is an expansion of the definition of the term 'terrorism', now enlarged to cover any association with terrorist organizations or activities. The United State's 1952 Immigration and Naturalization Act (INA), for example, includes in the definition of terrorism such acts as: hijacking, kidnapping, assassination, and use of biological or chemical agents, explosives, or firearms with intent to harm persons or property. The INA defines 'terrorist activity' as any individual or organization committing an act 'which the actor knows, or reasonably should know, affords material support to any individual, organization or government in conducting a terrorist activity at any time'. The USA Patriot Act (2001) struck the qualification 'should know', from this statement. Thus the law now implicitly presumes knowledge on the part of the accused; it is for the accused to prove his lack of knowledge (i.e., that his actions 'materially supported' terrorist activity) (Lebowitz and Podheiser, 2002: 3). The European Union (EU) Common Positions and Framework Decision on Combating Terrorism (December 2001) has similarly expanded the definition of terrorism (2001/930, OJ 2001 L 344/90). The term no longer refers exclusively to the use of violence for political ends, but encompasses any act that constitutes a threat to a country or international organization. The new definition also specifies that terrorism can be either the passive or active support of terrorist acts or organizations (Fekete, 2004: 6).

In general, these and other such anti-terrorism measures provide for the granting of increased judicial powers to police and other security forces, the authorization of arbitrary imprisonment, and the toughening of immigration and refugee laws. The USA Patriot Acts, passed on 26 October 2001, only six weeks after the 9/11 attacks, authorized the government to incarcerate and detain non-US citizens on the basis of mere suspicion, as long as the government had reasonable cause to believe that an individual posed a threat to national security.

Security, of course, was a political concern well before 9/11, sometimes related to a broader international agenda, as in the United States' anti-terrorist law of 1996,[1] and sometimes dealing more with domestic concerns, as in France and Germany. Nevertheless, one of the principal responses to 9/11 in the West has been a collective tightening of existing security policy, to such an extent that there is now an almost total identification of domestic security and the international war against terrorism. One example of this is the French law, passed on 15 November 2001, on 'day-to-day security'. In the course of the deliberations on this law, the French National Assembly introduced a whole series of categories to serve in the fight against terrorism, merging domestic security, juvenile delinquency, and terrorism – a combination that has also intensified the marginalization of poor youth in the suburbs. Two provisions of this law in particular – one concerning noise in the communal areas of apartment buildings, the other stipulating a maximum penalty of six months in prison for 'serial' subway turnstile-jumpers – appear to have no relation to terrorism at all, nor to high-level delinquency, and will most likely have little impact on either.

In Germany, two laws were voted into effect regarding this issue: the first on 9 September 2001 (First Anti-Terrorism Package) and the second on 1 January 2002. The laws gave increased funding and investigative powers to German security forces, provided for armed security agents on German air carriers, and revised a law that granted privileges to religious organizations as public law corporations. The Act's abolishing of 'religious privilege' was written into law on 8 December 2001. This abolition had previously been a subject of contention, but its passage was expedited by the events of 9/11 (Brower, 2003: 404). An immediate effect of this abolition was the outlawing of Metin Kaplan's 'Caliphal State' organization (Christian, 2003: 1-58).

Patterning itself on the American model, Great Britain passed a sweeping Anti-Terrorism, Crime and Security bill on 14 December 2001. At the same time, the country's declaration of a state of emergency elicited widespread debate on the restriction of civil liberties, primarily in response to the vastly expanded powers given to police for information-gathering and surveillance of citizens. The act provides for a variety of anti-terrorism measures, most notably the freezing of financial assets and policies having to do with immigration and asylum. The Act's definition of what constitutes an international terrorist is based on a definition set out in the previous Terrorism Act of 2000 but is expanded to include any individual that the state deems a threat to national security. In Italy, a law of 18 October 2001 expanded a 1965 anti-Mafia law, giving increased powers to the police in a manner similar to other anti-terrorism laws.

The primary result of these new measures in the 'international fight against terrorism', however, is a targeting of all individuals defined as – or assumed to be – 'Muslim'. In the United States, this takes the form of increased surveillance of immigrants and visitors coming from Muslim countries, racial profiling, and Department of Justice interviews and investigations of Muslims already present in the country. Nearly 1200 resident aliens of Muslim origin were arrested in the United States after 9/11, largely on the basis of their ethnicity or country of origin. Even if these practices have since tapered off somewhat, they continue to spark debate on the tension between the necessity to respect human rights and the concern for national security. The US Citizenship and Immigration Services, or CIS (formerly the Bureau of Immigration and Nationalization Services), has the power to hold and/or deport any resident alien or visitor who overstays his or her visa. Immigration control procedures have been significantly tightened by requiring immigrants to register at immigration offices and to notify the government of any change of residence during their stay.

In December 2002 more than 200 Iranians were held for several days in California before being turned over to the CIS for registration. Under the terms of the Patriot Act the government may hold people in detention on unspecified charges for indeterminate lengths of time. It also has the power to conduct investigations in ways that potentially violate Fourth Amendment protections against illegal search and seizure. In November 2001 Attorney General John Ashcroft announced that the government would conduct investigations of nearly 5000 Muslim foreigners living on American soil. By the end of 2002 more than 3000 additional investigations had been announced. According to official sources, only around twenty people from the first group of 'interviewees' were eventually arrested and accused and these for reasons other than terrorist activities. Most Muslims perceive such investigation, leading to so few arrests, as discriminatory or biased against Islam.

In Germany, a new registration and screening procedure was instituted after 9/11. The procedure targets Muslim men, aged 18 to 41, who either are, or were, students. The procedure is administered by the individual states (Länder). However, in state administrative courts, both Hessen's and Berlin's data screening (Rasterfahndung) laws failed to meet the criteria for legality (rechtmässigkeit). The courts explained their rulings by arguing that the fear of another '9/11-style attack' did not provide sufficient justification for initiating the practice of racial profiling. Nonetheless, around 8 million individuals have been affected by the procedure (Achelpohler and Niehaus, 2004: 504).

Immigration policies have been similarly tightened, with increased surveillance of people from Muslim countries and tougher conditions for entry. Since November 2001, the American government has enforced a twenty-day waiting period for all men between 18 and 45 arriving from Muslim countries. The new procedures for receiving foreigners into the country, in force since 5 June 2002, consist of the following provisions: the taking of photographs and digital fingerprints at passport control; regular surveillance of any foreigner in the country for a stay of less than 30 days; and greater authority on the part of the CIS to deport foreigners whose visas have expired. These measures apply to visitors from any country designated by the United States as a supporter of terrorism, particularly Iran, Iraq, Sudan, Libya, and Syria. Certain cases in which these measures have actually been applied to American citizens have been the subject of criticism. As of January 2003, 54,242 individuals had been registered, almost all from the Middle East or the Indian subcontinent (Tumlin, 2004: 1173). One-quarter of those who register face deportation as a result of technical immigration violations, such as failure to maintain an adequate number of college-credits on a student visa. The 2003 creation of the Department of Homeland Security, which combines 22 agencies and 180,000 workers from the fields of immigration and intelligence as well as counterterrorism and foreign policy, has further reinforced the link between immigration and global terrorism.

Similarly, in Europe, Germany, the UK, France, Italy and Spain have all adopted new immigration and asylum regulations. A distinction can be made between laws concerning the entry of foreigners included within anti-terrorism legislation – as in Germany and Great Britain – and new, separate, anti-immigration laws, such as those enacted in France, Italy, and Spain. An example of the former, Germany's Prevention Act, included changes to the Alien Acts, which were subsequently included in the law on immigration adopted by the Bundestag on 22 March 2002. This law gives the government the power to bar entry to any foreigner deemed to be a danger to German democracy and security (Brower, 2003: 409). On 1 January 2005, Germany began enforcement of its Immigration Act, which contains such security measures as expedited deportation procedures in cases of suspected terrorist threat. Possible causes for deportation now include incitement to racial hatred.

Similarly, the UK's Anti-Terrorism, Crime and Security Act of 2001 states that any person fitting the definition of a terrorist will be forbidden entry into the country. The aim of both the UK and German laws is to limit the entry of potential terrorists by regulating or barring their access to the nation. The domestic security legislation voted into law by the French National Assembly on 23 January 2003 also contains provisions on immigration. The law specifies that police may deport any non-European Union citizen 'who has committed acts justifying a criminal trial' or whose behavior 'threatens public order'. Earlier versions of this law gave police the power to deport foreigners for participating in political demonstrations.

The newly adopted immigration laws in Italy (3 June 2002) and France (26 November 2003) share the following provisions: increased penalties for illegal immigration, more temporary detention centres and limits on family reunification. France's law further introduces digital fingerprint files for those seeking French visas and close surveillance of mixed-nationality marriages. Since the Madrid attacks of 11 March 2004, Spain's policies on immigration and foreigners have also been made to do 'double-duty' in the war against terrorism. Thus several individuals who have been suspected of terrorist activity have been deported from Spain under laws governing the movement of foreigners (*El País*, 30-31 May 2004). The same logic applies in laws governing political asylum and refugee status. In France, a December 2003 amendment of asylum law included a list of 'safe countries' in terms of their respect for international human rights (10 December 2003, Law No. 20031176). The government is thus able to refuse right of entry to anyone hailing from any of the countries on the list. The political consequence of these measures is the tightening of immigration policy and the association of illegal immigrants with terrorism.

Europe's political concern with issues of immigration arises from the perceived link between international terrorism and Muslim immigrants. One current statistic maintains that 1 to 2 per cent of all European Muslims (between 250,000 to 500,000 people) have been suspected of involvement in terrorist activities (Savage, 2004: 25-50). This statistic is due less to the fear that Europe might serve as a strategic base for terrorist operations, than the idea that Muslims residing or born in Europe tend to be drawn to radical organizations or groups. Of the 660 plus detainees at Guantanamo Bay, representing over 42 countries, more than 20 claim European citizenship, while only two are American nationals. Since 9/11, the nations of the EU have arrested more than 20 times the number of terrorist suspects as the United States (Kempe, 2003).

The designation 'foreign enemy', technically applicable only to those outside a country's borders, is beginning to be applied to certain targeted domestic groups such as students or religious leaders. The fight against terrorism thus has significant consequences for Muslims living in western countries. Not only 'foreign enemies', but also Muslim citizens and residents are considered possible threats, and any activity relating to Islam is potentially suspect and subject to police surveillance. The primary reason for this generalized suspicion is the quasi-impossibility of differentiating between Islam as a religion and Islam as a political tool. Since the enactment of the USA Patriot Act, Muslim charitable organizations in the United States have also been the frequent target of police investigations. On 4 December 2001, the government designated The Holy Foundation for Relief and Development (HLF) as a terrorist organization and froze its assets, alleging that the foundation had ties to Hamas, a 'terrorist' organization according to US diplomatic regulations. The Global Relief Foundation (GRF) and the Benevolence International Foundation (BIF) were also penalized financially. More than 50,000 people were affected by the shutting-down of these three organizations. Indeed, it has become increasingly difficult to practice *zakat* – the Islamic duty of charitable giving – without being subject to the FBI's scrutiny, even to the point of interrogation. The assets of a fourth US-based charity – the Islamic American Relief Agency, in Columbia, Missouri – were frozen in mid-October 2004, just at the beginning of Ramadan. The following week (19 October), a request from several Muslim groups for the US government to provide a list of 'approved' organizations for charitable giving was denied. US officials claimed that such a request was not feasible, since new information could come to light at any time (*Christian Science Monitor*, 17 November 2004).

On 20 March 2002 FBI agents searched several Muslim offices and houses in Virginia and Georgia, looking for evidence of terrorist support. Even academic institutions like the International Institute of Islamic Thought (IIIT) and the University of Islamic and Social Sciences have been among the FBI's targets. These investigations were part of the Green Task Initiative, the objective of which is to dismantle the financial resources of terrorist groups. During the first four months of the Green Task Initiative's operation, more than 10.3 million dollars in assets were seized.

Mosques are a particularly sensitive locus, largely due to the support they receive from foreign countries in the form of monetary donations or religious personnel. The Islamic Center of Boston, for example, came under fire several times from the local media because one of its founding members, Sheikh Yusuf al-Qaradawi – an Egyptian-born follower of the Muslim Brothers and world-renowned *mufti* – had appeared on the Al Jazeera network (*Boston Herald Tribune*, 28 and 29 October 2003). Any form of support given to a country or group listed as 'terrorist' can be considered passive support for terrorism, even if the money is designated for humanitarian ends and not strictly to any political group. At the same time, increased police powers have allowed officers to conduct raids on mosques and Islamic associations throughout Europe. In January 2003, the main Islamic organizations of Germany launched a protest after simultaneous police raids were conducted in Stuttgart, Mannheim, and Freiburg, with more than 617 Muslims being arrested and detained for several hours (Fekete, 2004: 11). Such actions tend to exacerbate the feelings of foreignness and alienation already endemic among European Muslims. They widen the gap between Muslims and the rest of the population, and reinforce a reactionary and defensive stance on the part of western Muslims, not only towards the non-Muslim environment, but also towards their own Islamic tradition (Cesari, 2004: 91-109).

For American Muslims with immigrant backgrounds, the situation is something altogether new. Some have spoken out against their ghettoization, comparing their situation – in the words of the Muslim Public Affairs Council (MPAC) President, Salam Maryatti – to confinement in a 'virtual camp'. [2] Particularly amongst immigrants of middle and upper class origin, the once common view of America as an environment relatively favorable to Islam is gone. Not only do Muslims now feel vulnerable in the United States, they also experience a feeling of being watched and the constant threat of arrest (Cesari, 2004: 41).

Multiculturalism and Secularism

The idea of a 'war' between the West and the Islamic world necessarily affects how Islam is perceived in western contexts. Discussion of Islam's public status has become markedly less tolerant since 9/11. In Europe, discussions around the issue are accompanied by the often aggressive re-evaluation of multiculturalism as a social policy and practice. In the United States, meanwhile, it influences the balance between recognizing religion and the protection of civil liberties.

First, however, we should note the increasing virulence of current anti-Islamic rhetoric: in other words, the growing prevalence of what in Europe is called 'Islamophobia'. In France of the 1990s, anti-Islamic statements were almost exclusively the prerogative of the far right. Today, however, intellectuals, journalists, writers and artists unashamedly express their aversion to Islam. In an interview in the September 2001 issue of the magazine *Lire*, writer Michel Houellebecq stated, 'Islam is definitely the most f***** up of all the religions'. Oriana Fallaci's *Rage and Pride*, which sold more than a million copies in Italy and France, is a collection of slurs aimed at Islam and Muslims that resulted in the author being indicted for incitement to racial hatred in October 2003. That same year (on 24 October), the founder of the newspaper *Le Point* publicly declared himself an 'Islamophobe', calling Islam an 'inanity of various archaisms' (LCI, 24 October 2003). In the United States, examples of anti-Muslim invective continue to multiply, even if the term 'Islamophobia' is less widespread than in Europe. On 23 April 2004, a Boston radio announcer voiced his opinion that all Muslims should be killed. Since 9/11, evangelical leaders have produced myriad pronouncements and publications attacking the idea of any possibility of coexistence with Islam or with Muslims. This same antipathy can even be found at the highest levels of government, for example, in statements by the Attorney General and high-ranking military personnel (Cesari, 2004: 40-41).

Since 9/11, the crucial division is no longer between a foreign politicized and radical Islam and individual Muslims; now, the main distinction is between 'good' and 'bad' Muslims: in other words, between those Muslims who accept the norms and political values of western societies and those who reject them (Mamdani, 2004). The evaluation of such acceptance or rejection is often based, not on facts, but on what politicians and intellectuals presume to know about Islam. In some cases, the mere fact of being religiously observant may be sufficient to put one in the category of being a 'bad' Muslim, as religious observance is associated, increasingly, with radicalism. The 'good Muslim/bad Muslim' dichotomy is at the heart of all future negotiations for Islam's representation in Europe and its status in the public sphere. It is also the underlying motif of debates such as the *hijab* question and the legal status of *imams*.

The question of Islam's public self-representation is one peculiar to the European cultural situation, and rests on an attempt to model the public status of Islam according to the preexisting relationships between church and state (see Ferrari, this volume). Even before 9/11, negotiations and agreements were already underway in Belgium and Spain. In France, the events of 9/11 led to the establishment of, and elections for, the French Council on Islam (Conseil Français du Culte Musulman), whose primary mission was to be a barricade against the 'bad' 'fundamentalist' Muslims who posed a threat to national and international security (see Caeiro, this volume).

Meanwhile, resistance to the increased visibility of Islamic symbols is on the rise due to a logic that automatically associates the practice of Islam with 'fundamentalism' and thus a potential transition to terrorist activity or the support of terrorist activity. France's headscarf controversy exemplifies this kind of semantic slippage. Certainly, the March 2004 law prohibiting the wearing of all religious symbols in public schools has its basis in a conception of secularism significantly more rigid than that of other European countries and definitely more so than that of the United States. Nevertheless, the arguments offered in the course of this controversy were largely political or cultural in nature. *Hijab* was perceived as a symptom of 'communautarisme'. In French political and intellectual circles, such a term refers to the ethnic and political 'self-isolation' of Muslim 'immigrants', an isolation exacerbated by Muslims' vulnerable socio-economic status and the violence in the economically depressed suburbs. Women, according to this argument, are the first victims of the failure to integrate into society, a failure which has, as one of its results, an extremist and militant form of religious practice. Bernard Stasi, the president of the Presidential Commission on Secularism (Laïcité), describes the commission (which was instrumental in getting the law banning religious symbols passed) in the following terms:

The concept of *laïcité* is something this commission has insisted upon throughout the course of its work. Many of us are shocked to see the rise in certain acts and forms of agitation that seek to undermine this concept, particularly in the public sphere. We are not exaggerating when we say that it is the duty of all those who hold positions of responsibility in this country to keep their eyes open. The reasons for the deterioration of the situation are well known. The difficulties of integration experienced by new immigrants to France during the past few decades, the dismal living conditions of many of our cities' suburbs, unemployment, the feeling experienced by many of our country's residents that they are subject to discrimination or even exclusion from the national community – all these causes contribute to the fact that many people have turned a willing ear to those who advocate the destruction of our Republic's values. (Stasi, address to the President of the French State on the day of the release of the report of the commission, 11 December 2003)

Today, Islam has come to embody a representation of women that some find distasteful or loathsome. As a consequence, a debate has emerged in Europe regarding the Muslim headscarf, or *hijab*. The wearing of *hijab* is usually perceived by non-Muslims as an attack on female dignity but this is reliant upon a *reconstruction* of what is known (or what one thinks one knows) about Islam. In July 1998, for example, the Minister of Baden-Württemberg upheld a Stuttgart school's decision to not hire a Muslim woman as a teacher because she chose to wear a veil. The minister declared that in Islam *hijab* was a political symbol of female submission, and not an actual religious requirement (US Department of State, 1998; Germany Country Report on Human Rights Practices, 1998). Since then, the polemical stakes have only increased. In a 2003 decision, the Federal Court of Germany ruled that decisions regarding *hijab* were the responsibility of the individual states, based on the principle that education policy fell under state jurisdiction. In the wake of this ruling, seven German states declared – at an October 2003 meeting of 16 regional ministers for culture, education and religious affairs in the city of Darmstadt – that they were backing legislation to ban teachers from wearing the headscarf.[3] In late March of 2004, the regional government of Berlin outlawed the wearing of all religious symbols by civil servants. On 1 April 2004, the southern state of Baden-Württemberg became the first German state to ban teachers from wearing *hijab*. The state assembly, dominated by a coalition of opposition Christian Democratic Union and liberal Free Democrats, approved the law almost unanimously (*BBC News Online*, 1 April 2004). Another five of 16 states, including Bavaria and Lower Saxony, are in the process of passing similar bans.

Similarly, the debate on the legal and social status of *imams* has intensified since 9/11 (see also Birt, this volume). Linked, again, with the issue of terrorism, the religious conservatism of many *imams* is commonly seen as presaging political disturbance. For example, the Algerian *imam* of Vénissieux, who had spoken out in favor of polygamy and the stoning of adulterous women, was deported from France on 21 April 2004 by the Ministry of the Interior. The administrative court of Lyon eventually stayed the deportation on the grounds that the case had no basis in fact but was rather based on 'general statements resting on subjective opinions' (Landrin, 2004). Despite the stay, however, the *imam*'s deportation was confirmed.

Religious training for *imams* has thus become a political matter since 9/11, not only in France, but throughout Europe. In May 2001, a Moroccan *imam*, speaking on Dutch television, stated that homosexuality was a disease and a danger for the Netherlands (see Sunier, this volume). The statements caused a public uproar, creating debate on freedom of religious expression and the need for *imams* to respect the values of Dutch society. The controversy – only heightened by the events of 9/11 – hastened the January 2002 adoption of a law requiring all foreign-born *imams* entering the territory to be trained in Dutch language and culture. (For those already residing in the Netherlands, the training is optional.) The first Dutch language and culture class, consisting of around thirty *imams* from Morocco and Turkey, graduated in January 2003 (Bœnder, 2003).

The debate on Islam's public legitimacy often takes the form of a reassessment of multicultural policies. Since 9/11, a strong desire for cultural homogeneity can be felt throughout Europe, even in countries long considered hospitable to the ideals of multiculturalism, such as the countries of Scandinavia and Great Britain (see McLoughlin, this volume). The recent shift in the Netherlands is also a striking example of this phenomenon, in which the emergence of an extremist right-wing political party reflects the general cooling of public opinion towards non-Europeans and a growing skepticism of cultural and religious diversity. On 6 March 2002, the Leeftbaar Rotterdam Viable party obtained 36 per cent of the Dutch vote in the first round of municipal elections. The party's leader, Pim Fortuyn, a sociology professor and open homosexual, was the first person in the history of Dutch politics to have publicly expressed anti-Islamic sentiments. Fortuyn's remarks warning that the presence of Muslims was a danger to Dutch society earned him expulsion from the national party, Leeftbaar Nederland, shortly before the 2002 elections. Nevertheless, the author of *Against the Islamization of Our Culture* remained as the party's candidate at the local level and eventually he founded his own party, Lijst Fortuyn, in order to compete in municipal elections. Fortuyn was assassinated on 6 May 2002. Despite his death, his party came second in the 15 May 2002 parliamentary elections, just behind the Christian Democrats, with 26 seats (out of 150) in the Chamber of Deputies and 17 per cent of the popular vote. (In the January 2003 elections, however, this number fell to only 6 per cent of the vote.) Similarly, the 2 November 2004 assassination of film-maker Theo van Gogh – by a Muslim male angered by van Gogh's critical portrayal of Islam in his film on Muslim women – led to a wave of violence against Muslims and Muslim places of worship. Since then, debate has raged on whether Islam can be compatible with the basic values and cultural and political principles of Dutch society. This has been accompanied by severe criticism of the multiculturalism of the 1980s:

> A cross parliamentary report published in January 2004 concluded that the attempt to create a multiethnic society had been a dismal failure, huge ethnic ghettos and subcultures were tearing the country apart and the risk of polarization could only be countered by Muslims effectively becoming Dutch. (Fekete, 2004: 20)

The idea of cultural integration as a 'contract' has come increasingly to the fore in current discussions on Islam's legitimacy in European societies, with each country interpreting this idea in terms of its own existing legal structures. In the Netherlands, the UK, France and several other countries, under the new immigration laws described above, official passage into society is dependant upon the successful completion of a test, not only of language ability, but also of cultural knowledge. There is a punitive dimension to these policies: those who fail the tests are forced to leave the country (Austria), have fines imposed on them or suffer cuts in their social assistance payments (the Netherlands), or find their residency rights removed or limited (France).

Islam's presence in western societies, therefore, prompts a re-evaluation of the principle of cultural equality, and a redefinition of the very concepts of tolerance and pluralism. None of the various multicultural policies currently active in Europe truly allow the concepts of equality and pluralism to be rethought in terms of the incorporation of a minority's values. In addition, there is a great deal of misunderstanding and false perceptions regarding the rights and privileges accorded to ethnic groups. A cursory glance at the situation in Europe and in the United States reveals that, far from the often fantasized perception of privileging specific communities or ethnic groups, the policies put in place are, for the most part, aimed at preventing and fighting against unequal treatment and discrimination based on race or ethnicity. Such policies can be found even in an officially assimilationist country like France. Multiculturalist policy also takes the form of what Audrey Kobayashi calls 'red boot' multiculturalism: i.e., the financing of various cultural events such as a festival of Berber music, a rap concert, or an exhibition of African art (1993: 205-31).

What is currently understood as multiculturalism, then, is a partial assimilation to the dominant public culture, together with the preservation of individual cultures in the private sphere (not only the family, but also the neighborhood and the world of volunteer organizations). Islam's integration into European societies leaves this model open to question, sparking debate on what constitutes 'public culture'. The debate stems particularly from the claim made by certain Muslims for the recognition of Islamic norms, a claim perceived by some as a threat to western political principles. In other words, the religious demands of Muslims – especially those relating to *hijab* and the separation of the sexes – are seen as an attack on secularism and human rights. In such conditions, one might wonder whether agreement on cultural and social principles is still possible.

Conclusion: Religion and Fundamental Liberties

In the United States, the question of Islam is less one of religious and cultural differences and more of the right to the free exercise of religion. One result of this emphasis is the racialization of Islam: i.e. the subjection of Islam to a form of religious discrimination more or less identical to the categories of ethnicity. In other words, while Muslim immigrants and Muslims of overseas ancestry have experienced increasing restrictions on their freedom, this has not been the case with Muslims of African-American heritage. A distinction based on ethnicity, therefore, is evidently being used, a distinction that also deepens the racial divide within the Muslim community itself.

The new powers exercised by the government in the fight against terrorism have challenged the erstwhile separation between church and state, allowing an unprecedented level of government intrusion into the religious life and practices of a particular group. With the possible exception of certain human rights organizations and intellectual figures, the situation does not appear to have had much of an impact on American popular opinion. One study conducted by Cornell University (December 2004), for example, revealed that 44 per cent of Americans surveyed were not opposed to the restricting of certain basic civil liberties in the case of Muslims (*Associated Press*, 17 December 2004).

Europe's example would appear to indicate that these conditions, even if they are perceived or described as exceptional, are likely to have permanent consequences for the balance of religious powers and for religion's status in American civil society. Indeed, governmental powers, once acquired, are rarely ever again put into question; as Danièle Lochak has observed, in politics, the exception tends to become the rule. Thus the 1939 law which subjected foreign organizations to preliminary approval and close scrutiny by the Ministry of the Interior was repealed only in 1981 (Lochak, 2003: 2812).

In conclusion, the government's increased powers for the monitoring of both citizens and religious or political associations in the name of the 'War on Terror' appears as a given in both Europe and the United States. 9/11 appears to have effectively legitimized a more coercive form of government control: one that was always discussed and debated, but never completely accepted before this date.

References

Achelpohler, W. and Niehaus, H. (2004), 'Data screening as a means of Preventing Islamist Terrorist Attacks on Germany', *German Law Journal*, 5 (5), 495-513.

Bœnder, W. (2003), 'Teaching Dutch Ways to Foreign Imams, Between Government Policy and Muslim Initiative', paper presented at the Sorbonne 'European Muslims and the Secular State Conference', Paris, 30 June–1 July, www.euro-Islam-info.

Brower, E. (2003), 'Immigration, Asylum and Terrorism: A Changing Dynamic. Legal and Practical Development in the EU in Response to the Terrorist Attack of 11.09', *European Journal of Migration and Law*, 4, 399-424.

Cesari, J. (1997), *Faut-il avoir peur de l'islam?*, Paris: Presses de Science Po.

Cesari, J. (2001), 'Islam de l'extérieur, musulmans de l'intérieur: deux visions après le 11 septembre 2001', *Cultures et Conflits*, 44, Winter, 97-116.

Cesari, J. (2004), *When Islam and Democracy Meet: Muslims in Europe and in the United States*, New York: Palgrave.

Daniel, N. (1960), *Islam and the West: The Making of an Image*, Edinburgh: Edinburgh University Press.

Fekete, L. (2004), 'Anti-Muslim Racism and the European Security State, Race and Class', *Race and Class*, 46 (1), 3-29.

Kempe, F.S. (2003), 'Europe's Middle East Side Story', *Wall Street Journal*, 29 July.

Kobayashi, A. (1993), 'Multiculturalism: Representing a Canadian Institution', in Duncan, J. and Ley, D. (eds), *Place/Cultures/Representation*, London: Routledge, 205-31.

Landrin, S. (2004), 'La justice suspend l'expulsion de l'imam de Vénissieux', *Le Monde*, 24 April.

Lebowits, L.M. and Podheiser, I.L. (2002), 'Summary of the changes in immigration policies and practices after the terrorist attack of September 11, 2001: The USA Patriot Act and other measures', *University of Pittsburgh Law Review*, Summer, 1-13.

Lochak, D. (2003), *Gazette du Palais*, September–October, 2811-2812.

Mamdani, M. (2004), *Good Muslim, Bad Muslim: America, the Cold War and the Roots of Terror*, New York: Pantheon Books.

Said, E. (1978), *Orientalism*, New York: Pantheon Books.

Savage, T.M. (2004), 'Europe and Islam: Crescent Waxing, Cultures Clashing', *The Washington Quarterly*, 27 (3), 25-50.

Stasi, B. (2003), speech of 11 December, www.elysee.fr.

Tumlin, K.C. (2004), 'Suspects First: How Terrorism is Reshaping Immigration Policy', *California Law Review*, 92, July, 1173-1203.

Walter, C., Silja, V., Volker, R. and Schorkopf, F. (eds) (2004), *Terrorism as a Challenge for National and International Law: Security versus Liberty?*, Berlin: Heidelberg, Springer 2003: 1-58.

Notes

1 The 1996 law lists organizations and groups considered to be 'terrorist'. Particularly for anyone wishing to become a US citizen or permanent resident, any form of association with, or support for, a listed group can lead to arrest and the secret handling of evidence. 'Secret Evidence' is a part of pre-existing legislation (Illegal Immigration Reform Law) designed to curb illegal immigration. According to the procedure, the government can create ad hoc tribunals for illegal immigrants, in which certain elements in the government's case may be kept from defense attorneys for reasons of national security. Muslim immigrants have been special targets of this procedure and many Muslim organizations have mobilized against it. Ironically, during his first campaign for the presidency, George W. Bush had promised to put an end to the practice.

2 Comment made at the 'Islam in America' conference, held at Harvard University, 8-9 March 2003. Recorded by the author on 9 March 2003.

3 See www.islamonline.net/English/News/2003-10/11/article08.shtml.

Section II
The State, Civil Society and Muslim Leaderships: Contested Representations of Islam in Europe

Chapter 4

The State, New Muslim Leaderships and Islam as a Resource for Public Engagement in Britain

Seán McLoughlin

Introduction

In this chapter I start from the premise that scholarly accounts of Muslims in Western Europe ought to reflect more deliberately on the relationship between all three of the structure of particular states, the cultural capital of social actors and the 'resources' of the Islamic tradition. Where Islam is a resource for the articulation of quite different strategies of adaptation to minority status, I want to explore two short case studies of the ways in which mainly middle-class Muslim activists, with a good deal invested personally and professionally in the 'mainstream', are prioritizing 'engagement' over 'isolation' or 'resistance' (Lewis, 2002: 219) in the context of contemporary Britain.

My account begins with an overview of the ways in which the structure of the British State, in terms of legislation, policymaking and the existence of an established church, has provided the framework within which a distinctively 'Muslim' identity politics has evolved in recent decades. In particular, my account examines the current New Labour government's emphasis on 'civic renewal' and the related emergence of what I call the 'faith relations industry'. Thereafter, in my first case study, I trace a shift in the main focus of Muslim leaders' engagement with the state, from 'old' ethnically-oriented grassroots networks in the 1980s, to a new, more 'professionalized' national focus for representation in the 1990s, culminating in the inauguration of the Muslim Council of Britain (MCB) in 1997.[1]

While many Muslims have found 'non-Islamic' routes to pursue participation, not least through the established political parties, it has most often been 'reformist Islamist' activists with historical links to movements such as Jama'at-i Islami (JI, the Islamic Party, formed India, 1941) that have sought to engage the public sphere in Britain on an avowedly 'Islamic' basis.[2] Since the 1970s and 1980s 'reformists' in Britain have pioneered (selective) access to the resources of the Islamic tradition in English as part of the project of rethinking what it means to be a European Muslim. In a second case study focusing on the engagement of the Islamic Foundation (IF), then, I consider what it might mean for the JI tradition to become transformed, not only as the movement has 'travelled' (Mandaville, 2001) from a

Muslim majority to a non-Muslim state context, but also as the cultural capital of a British-born generation has begun to impact organically on the intellectual activism of this institution.[3]

From 'Race' to 'Faith' Relations: State, Multiculturalism and Established Church

As members of the Commonwealth, South Asian heritage Muslims became *de facto* 'citizens' as soon as they settled in Britain during the 1950s and 1960s. However, immigration legislation since 1962 has progressively reproduced narrower conceptions of 'citizenship' (Husband, 1994). Indeed, recalling the administration of colonial affairs, state management of non-European immigrants in Britain has been organized in terms of the pragmatic recognition of essentialized 'cultural communities' rather than individual civil rights (Baumann, 1999). Anti-discrimination legislation of 1966 and 1976 established the racial and ethnic basis of this paradigm and witnessed the emergence of a so-called 'race relations industry' to oversee minority affairs. As members of 'ethnic' groups, Jews and Sikhs were afforded protection by the law, but not Muslims, given the multiethnic and transnational nature of Islam.

'Race' relations in Britain have also been administered in terms of state policymaking under the rubric of 'multiculturalism' (compare Sunier, this volume). As Parekh (2000: 42) suggests in the report of the Commission on the Future of Multi-Ethnic Britain, the main political debate in this respect has been between 'nationalists' and 'liberals', both of whom emphasize the importance of social cohesion over plurality. Since the 1960s, 'nationalists' have advocated an 'assimilationism' which maintains that 'minorities' should conform to British 'norms'. In contrast, 'liberals' have posited a public space which claims to be ideologically 'neutral' but is still avowedly secular and prioritizes 'equality' at the expense of 'difference'. However, with minorities refusing assimilation and advancing religion as a major basis for public recognition, Parekh (2000: 48) concludes that if Britain is to become a more inclusive and harmonious society, it must expose itself to a conversation between liberalism and greater pluralism. Indeed, in a postcolonial age of 'transnational citizenship', he has asked the radical question, could Britain recognize itself as, a 'multicultural post-nation' (2000: 39)?

Perhaps not surprisingly, Parekh's report was not well received by 'nationalists' or 'liberals'.[4] Moreover, the possibility of any progressive debate about the future of multi-ethnic Britain was quickly overtaken by local and global 'crises' when, in the summer of 2001, there were disorders involving Pakistani Muslim heritage youth in the 'northern towns' of Bradford, Burnley and Oldham, events quickly followed by the attacks of 9/11. By the end of the year the New Labour government had articulated a concern for 'community cohesion' in a series of its own reports.[5] Without reference to Parekh (2000), Home Office Minister, Denham, proposed the need for a debate about 'shared values' and 'common citizenship' in order to 'minimise the risk of further disorder' (2002: 1-2). Denham also maintained that the aim of the new policy of 'community cohesion' would not be to revisit assimilationism (2002: 21) but rather to promote a commitment to 'civic identity' (2002: 11-12) and 'civic renewal' (2002: 18). Here, it is possible to detect the influence of the 'communitarian' political philosophy that achieved prominence in the USA under the Clinton presidency.[6] Indeed, ironically echoing the New Right backlash against local authorities' 'multicultural' policies in the 1980s (Husband, 1994), here was a UK-based communitarian critique of the 'old' Labour culture of 'rights', now said to have neglected citizens' 'responsibilities' and so reinforced ethnic 'segregation'.

In such a context, any remaining taboos against publicly challenging aspects of minority 'culture' understood to inhibit 'cohesion' have finally been broken. In February 2002, for example, a Home Office White Paper, 'Secure Borders, Safe Haven' proposed a new citizenship ceremony for Britain, an oath of allegiance, language tests (especially for ministers of religion including *imams*) and a debate on the desirability of the custom of transcontinental marriage (which Anne Cryer, Member of Parliament for Keighley, near Bradford, has described as 'importing poverty', *The Guardian*, 12 July 2001).[7] Together with a raft of new anti- and counter-terrorism measures, which in the main targeted Islamic groups (see Birt, this volume), Muslim communities, in particular, are currently subject to unprecedented levels of intervention and regulation by the British State.[8] In the face of new local-global crises, there has been a deepening of the 'moral panic' about those allegedly 'in' but not 'of' the West, with transnationalism seen unambiguously as a threat and the real dilemmas of diasporas at the grassroots generally overlooked.

Of course, Britain is unusual amongst liberal democracies in that religion has an 'established' position in the structure of the state (Modood, 1997). One outcome of Anglican privilege has been that no system of formally recognizing 'other faiths' exists. Nevertheless, Muslims have benefited from the presence of a Church of England which not only legitimates space for religion in public life but has also been hospitable to sharing that space with others (Lewis, 2002; compare Jonker, Chapter 8, this volume). For some Muslims this has meant that they can support 'establishment' both as a symbolic recognition of God's sovereignty and a more tangible critique of secularism's presumed 'neutrality' (Modood, 1997). Lacking the capacities and infrastructure of the Church of England, interfaith activity has also provided Muslims with opportunities for making alliances and learning how best to negotiate with the state as was the case during the successful campaign for a 'religion' question at the 2001 Census.[9]

Even beyond the specialized sphere of interfaith relations, there has been a new openness to religion in British politics over the last decade or so. In 1992, the Department of Environment, in collaboration with the Church of England and with the help of the Interfaith Network for the UK (founded 1987), formed the Inner Cities Religious Council (ICRC).[10] With a view to tapping into religious communities' resources – people, networks, organizations, buildings – as a part of urban regeneration, the ICRC provided the first government forum for multifaith representation and consultation on a national level (McLoughlin, 2002). However, religion remained a somewhat ambiguous presence in politics during the early to mid-1990s. Rather than government it was independent public policy bodies such as the Runnymede Trust (1997) which took the lead in commissioning research and producing reports on such matters as 'Islamophobia'.

Since 1997, when New Labour came to power, government has engaged 'faith' more publicly and controversially. 'Communitarianism' regards religious communities as a particular source of social capital, especially in deprived areas where other forms of social infrastructure may be absent (Putnam, 2001). Indeed, in New Labour's first year of office, the Department of Environment, Transport and the Regions issued advice to all local authorities on 'involving faith communities' in neighbourhood renewal.[11] More recently, in October 2003, 'the religious issues section of the Home Office Race Equality Unit was reconstituted to form the new Faith Communities Unit', suggesting that 'faith' is becoming as important as 'race' in the state's management of minority ethnic affairs.[12] Legitimated by the 2001 Census, which produced the politically 'useful' statistic of 76.8 per cent religious affiliation in Britain, such developments reflect the emergence of a new 'faith relations industry'.[13] This exists to: i) engage the many (socially excluded) 'newcomers' to Britain (especially 'Muslims') whose principal mode of communal identification and organization has been 'faith' based; ii) facilitate government consultation with the main faith groups on policy-making and service delivery; and iii) promote 'community cohesion' through interfaith activity. Nevertheless, there are still many elements of 'hard' secularism in government and Britain's public culture per se, something reflected in the continuing opposition to recent attempts at legislation on 'incitement to religious hatred' (*The Guardian*, 6 December 2004).[14]

'Old' and 'New' Muslim Leaderships: The Emergence of the Muslim Council of Britain

The British State has stopped short of officially recognizing existing, or creating newly elected, 'Muslim' representative institutions as in some other European countries (see Ferrari and Caeiro this volume). Nevertheless, at the local level in the 1980s, and on the national level since the late 1990s, government has periodically leant unelected Muslim bodies and their leadership public legitimacy, mainly through consultation but sometimes by channelling resources in their direction.

Not unlike the leaders of the Pakistan movement, Muslim 'community' leaders in Britain have usually been 'lay' rather than religious specialists.[15] Their 'authority' has drawn upon a 'cultural capital' (Bourdieu and Passeron, 1977) that overlaps with, but is distinctive from, the traditional leadership associated with the *'ulama* (religious scholars) and *shaykhs* (Sufi masters). Amongst the first generation of economic migrants, the men who emerged as the chairmen of grassroots mosque committees in the 1960s, 1970s and 1980s, and subsequently acted as the interlocutors of local government, often shared certain characteristics. These characteristics at once reflected their South Asian cultural heritage and yet set them apart from other first generation migrants, the majority of whom were illiterate and of rural peasant farming origin: membership of a powerful and well-established regional and/or patri-lineal kinship (*biradari*) group; a reputation as a well connected and effective political operator – a 'strong man'; some limited education, including basic competence in English; and, finally, experience of engagement with members of 'wider society', perhaps through a public service occupation (for example, transport) or, more usually, a small business (for example, owning a shop or restaurant).

This sort of cultural capital allowed a first generation of grassroots Muslim leaders to build up mosque institutions which sustained the life-worlds, and maintained the localized hegemony, of dislocated male migrants in particular (McLoughlin, in press). For this segment of the Muslim population, the resources of the Islamic tradition were selectively employed to maintain ethnic boundaries, legitimate the authority of South Asian cultural 'norms' and reinforce conservative adaptation strategies. Moreover, within the 'doing deals culture' (Ouseley, 2001: 10) operated by some local councils as they sought to recognize large Muslim populations, the public engagement of mosques and their leaders has routinely been limited to competition for scarce resources, securing 'rights' and participating as required in photo-calls to 'celebrate the community' (McLoughlin, in press). In this context 'Islam' becomes reified as part of the dominant discourse of what Baumann (1999) calls 'difference multiculturalism' and 'engagement' is limited to a rhetorical transaction between community leaders and the state.

More than any event, the Rushdie Affair of 1988-89 illuminated the strengths and weaknesses of a Muslim community leadership grounded in grassroots networks and associations. If the early 1980s witnessed the local state consult representatives of Islam on questions of public recognition, by the end of the decade the numbers of 'Muslim' councillors was also beginning to rise (Lewis, 1994). However, there was not a single Muslim Member of Parliament and no national body with the authority to represent Muslims to an increasingly centralized government.[16] Having been informed of the offending passages in *The Satanic Verses* by co-religionists in India (Ahsan and Kidwai, 1993), an alliance of mainly 'reformist Islamist' and 'neo-traditionalist' heritage elites recognized both the realities and the opportunities of this situation. Feeling that they possessed the professional, scholarly and social skills necessary to do business with government ministers, senior civil servants, publishers and the media, the UK Action Committee on Islamic Affairs (UKACIA) was formed in London. However, despite the letter-writing, petitions, telephone-calls and meetings, the UKACIA's peaceful lobbying failed to make an impact on the Conservative government of the day. Indeed, this 'new' leadership was eventually outmanoeuvred by the 'old' grassroots' leadership associated with Bradford Council for Mosques (BCM) which had mobilized working class Muslims during the *halal* meat and Honeyford affairs earlier in the decade (McLoughlin, 2002). Strategies of 'accommodation' having failed, BCM resorted to protest and publicly burned Rushdie's book, something the UKACIA's middle-class leadership neither sanctioned nor approved of.

Into the 1990s, the UKACIA took its campaigning to the legal system, arguing in the High Court that Britain's blasphemy laws, still protecting only the Church of England, should be reformed and extended to defend Islam. While this project, too, was unsuccessful, the organization doggedly persisted with engaged representational strategies on the national level, seeking recognition especially in terms of legislation on 'religious' (as well as racial and ethnic) discrimination (UKACIA, 1993). Indeed, all Muslim activists were disappointed by their slow rate of progress during this period. However, himself frustrated at the continuing divisions between Islamic organizations, Conservative Home Secretary, Michael Howard, advised Muslim activists to speak with one voice should they wish to exercise more influence over government (*Q-News*, 25 March 1994).

Within a couple of months this intervention had prompted the UKACIA to form a National Interim Committee on Muslim Affairs. Having consulted over 1000 organizations on the need for a new national umbrella body (*The Muslim News*, 31 May 2002), and studied the constitutions of similar organizations such as the Board of Deputies of British Jews, the committee finally inaugurated the Muslim Council of Britain (MCB) in 1997. Regarding its constituency as 'British citizens with an Islamic heritage', the stated aims and objectives of the MCB included 'a more enlightened appreciation of Islam and Muslims in the wider society' and 'better community relations and work[ing] for the good of society as a whole'.[17]

Today the MCB is run by a skeleton staff who, for the most part, work on a voluntary basis. Both general secretaries to date, Iqbal Sacranie (1998-2000, 2002-04) and Yousef Bhailok (2000-02), have been able to assume the role only because they are prosperous middle-aged businessmen. Indeed, a cursory glance at the biography of each begins to reveal the particular cultural capital of the MCB's most senior leadership. Sacranie and Bhailok are of 'African-Asian' ('twice-migrant') and 'Gujerati Indian' origin respectively, both relatively small but significant 'ethnic' segments of the British-Muslim population exhibiting a more upwardly mobile trajectory than the larger 'Pakistani' or 'Bangladeshi' constituencies. At the same time, both have experience not only of grassroots mosque institutions but also organizations with national profiles in sectors such as charity and education (*The Common Good*, 1(2): 2). Notably, Sacranie was also Joint-Convenor of the UKACIA.[18]

While Sacranie and Bhailok have associations with the 'neo-traditionalist' Deobandi tradition, many other MCB activists appear to be associated with 'reformist Islamist', and especially JI-related, organizations such as UK Islamic Mission, the Islamic Foundation, Young Muslims UK and the Islamic Society of Britain. Based on an analysis of the membership of the MCB's Central Working Committee available at www.mcb.org.uk in January 2003, I estimate that one-third to one-half of members' affiliations could be described as 'reformist Islamist' heritage. Moreover, the contents of the organization's occasional newsletter, *The Common Good*, reveal that it is the activities of such organizations that have the highest profile. However, while Muslim magazine, *Q-News*, has labelled the MCB as 'lassi Islamists' (March-April 2002: 22-3) – a *halal* version of New Labour's 'champagne socialists' – such a representation is somewhat misleading. JI-related organizations may be home to a significant body of activists who have the requisite aptitude and energy for the MCB's political work. However, the organization also depends on its fair share of British-born, university-educated, young Muslim professionals in their thirties, a *new* rising middle-class first politicized by events such as the Rushdie Affair, the Gulf War and Bosnia, and who may or may not be (or have been) affiliated to JI-related or other organizations.[19] So it is then that the

MCB is best viewed as providing a non-sectarian space for the advance of a Muslim politics of recognition.[20]

Perhaps fortuitously, the MCB's consolidation of a 'new', professionalized and media-friendly Muslim representative body coincided with the election of New Labour. As we have seen, the party has been committed to an important role for faith in the more general project of civic renewal. However, as the elections of 1992 and 1997 had shown, it was also no longer in a position to take the votes of Muslims for granted (Nielsen, 2001). In any case, having received a positive response to its initial enquiries, the MCB soon found itself invited to regular meetings and receptions at the Home Office and Foreign and Commonwealth Office, even representing the latter as a part of delegations to Muslim countries (McLoughlin, 2003). Various government departments, agencies and civil society organizations, all now required to engage multifaith (as well as multiracial and multiethnic) 'partners' as part of the 'stakeholder society', also started to consult the MCB which provided user-friendly access to the necessary Muslim 'voices'.

By May 2004 the MCB had 395 affiliates at local, regional and national levels.[21] Seeing itself as the 'first port of call' for government,[22] it can certainly point to an increasing recognition of 'Muslims' on the national level since its inauguration.[23] However, it also seems clear that the changing place of faith in the policymaking of the British government has been equally, if not more important, in shaping these new developments. Moreover, the MCB is just one amongst many lobbies at Whitehall and has been unable to significantly influence 'higher' arenas of debate such as foreign policy (Radcliffe, 2004). 'Loyalty' was always going to be part of New Labour's attempt to incorporate a 'moderate' Muslim leadership. So, while the MCB was able to support military intervention in Kosovo during 1999 (*The Muslim News*, 28 May 1999), and issued a statement of condemnation within hours of 9/11, its 'failure' to support the war in Afghanistan in late 2001,[24] resulted in the government publicly questioning the very 'authority' it had taken a key role in ascribing. Birt (2005), for example, argues that while attempts to 'groom' the MCB ultimately failed, this provoked 'coded' public messages from New Labour 'spin doctors' expressing 'disappointment' at the failure of the 'moderates' to marginalize an 'extremist' fringe.

For the MCB, such experiences highlighted the problems of state patronage. Indeed, all minority leaderships must strike a balance between strategies of accommodation and protest (Werbner, 1991). So it was then that the organization was to belatedly take a more public role in supporting the Stop the War Coalition. One of its own affiliates, the 'reformist Islamist' Ikhwan al-Muslimun (the Muslim Brothers) related, Muslim Association of Britain (MAB), had taken a lead in the alliance alongside the Socialist Workers' Party, the Campaign for Nuclear Disarmament and others.[25] Nevertheless, despite 'meagre resources' and the somewhat 'intangible outcomes' of its work,[26] against the context of huge external demands from the state and wider society, and amidst criticism of a tendency to seek to exercise control over the work of existing Muslim organizations (see, for example, *Q-News*, June 2004), the MCB's volunteers have remained committed to adapting the liberal public reason of 'democracy', 'the rule of law' and 'race equality' (Modood, 2002; Radcliffe, 2004) to the project of Muslim identity politics.

From Counter-culture to Multicultural Convergence? The Islamic Foundation in Transition

While revealing a good deal about the changing shape of both state policymaking and the cultural capital of Muslim community leaders, the emergence of the MCB provides only limited opportunity for reflection on the Islamic tradition as a resource for public engagement in Britain. The organization periodically convenes meetings of Islamic scholars to advise on important matters but the common currency of its representations to the state and wider society is not, of course, 'scholarship' but the 'sound-bite'.[27] Contestation over Islamically 'legitimate' strategies of adaptation vis-à-vis the non-Muslim state is increasingly conducted in the public sphere 'proper' as witnessed by the disruption of a MCB 'General Election 2005' press conference by 'radicals' rejecting the legitimacy of participation in a non-Islamic political system (*The Times*, 19 April 2005). However, such debates remain most elaborate and intense within the 'diasporic' public sphere (Werbner, 2002), where transnational Islamic movements and their related institutions and organizations compete for influence.

In this regard, the newly urbanized majority of Muslims in Britain have been most influenced by the 'traditionalist' and 'neo-traditionalist', Sufi and *'ulama* based, Barelwi and Deobandi movements of South Asia.[28] Although in theory possessing access to the fullest range of classical Islam's intellectual resources, the religious specialists associated with these two movements have in practice tended to support 'isolationist' (Lewis, 2002: 219) strategies of adaptation to non-Muslim rule in Britain as they did under the Raj (see Birt, this volume). In contrast, a more upwardly mobile, 'Islamist' minority, which includes both the 'radical revolutionaries' associated with movements such as Hizb al-Tahrir and the 'reformists' I want to consider in more detail here, has tended to adopt positions of 'resistance' and 'engagement' respectively (Lewis, 2002: 219).[29]

Since the 1960s and 1970s 'reformist' Islamist trajectories in Britain have been most associated with elite JI-related organizations. JI was formed in pre-partition India during 1941 by the noted theorist of the Islamic State, Sayyid Abu'l-A'la al-Mawdudi (d.1979). In Muslim-majority Pakistan, despite poor electoral performances, JI's cadres are known for being a dedicated, well-organized and 'opportunistic' vanguard, willing to accommodate to prevailing political conditions and structures in pursuit of political power (Nasr, 1994). Similarly in secular Britain, with no prospect of an Islamic State, it was the student and young professional migrants of the JI-related organizations who developed a *da'wa* ('call' or 'mission') strategy based on the creation of a revivalist 'counter-culture' (Lewis, 1994: 110).

A key 'reformist Islamist' player in the *da'wa* enterprise in Britain has been the Islamic Foundation (IF), based at Markfield in rural Leicestershire. However, research on Muslims in Britain reflecting developments in the 1970s, 1980s and into the early 1990s tended to discuss the IF only in limited detail (for example, Andrews, 1993: 71-2). Nevertheless, a scholarly discourse about the institution quickly became established, which can readily be summarized here. Although officially independent and with no formal links to JI, key IF staff during this period often had overlapping membership of JI/JI-related organizations. Indeed, one of the institution's main activities, publishing, was generally concerned with the writings of JI's 'lay intellectuals', especially Mawdudi himself, Khurshid Ahmad (economist, founding Director General of the IF in 1973 and vice-president of JI) and Khurram Murad (d.1996, engineer, Ahmad's successor in 1978 and past vice-president of JI). In keeping with JI's 'revivalist' credentials, IF publications in the 1970s and 1980s routinely presented 'Islam' within a selective (and arguably sectarian) framework, tending to dismiss as innovations (*bid'a*) the alternative epistemologies of Sufism and Shi'ism. Notably, the availability of World Muslim League funding during this period identified the institution with a Saudi Arabian axis network of pan-Islamic organizations. A centre for *da'wa* and the Islamization of knowledge in Britain, the IF proved to be of little interest to Muslims at the grassroots.

In a definitive contribution to this literature, Lewis (1994: 108-112) detected the first suggestions of a questioning of Mawdudi's legacy amongst the youth of JI-related organizations during the late 1970s and early 1980s. Nevertheless, his overall assessment was that the tradition had not: 'at present developed the intellectual resources for living creatively and with good conscience with minority status and relative powerlessness in a pluralist state ... The emphases have been activist rather than reflective and intellectual' (1994: 110). Until recently there has been no attempt to update Lewis' account or comment upon developments during the 1990s, a period of important transformations within 'reformist Islamism' in the Muslim world per se. Indeed, while the ideological project of first generation Islamists such as Mawdudi was highly distinctive, since the mid 1980s and into the 1990s, emblematic movements such as the Ikhwan are now widely understood to have 'democratized', accommodating to the nation-state and institutionalizing within the mainstream of civil society. Roy (1994), for example, regards this as evidence of the 'failure' of political Islam whereas Burgat argues that 'it is the outsider's dominant view of political Islam that has failed, because it has chosen to ignore, if not fight against, the possibility that Islamism could evolve' (2003: 161). In this respect, I want to suggest that 'reformist' developments in 1990s Britain cannot be understood without some reference to trends which circulate on a global scale.

Interestingly, the IF is now beginning to attract the attention of European and American, as well as British, scholars. Peter (2003), for example, has argued that the Rushdie Affair exposed the institution to new opportunities for faith-based public engagement, its activity in this respect having hitherto been confined mainly to interfaith relations. The affair precipitated a crisis in the 'race and ethnicity' paradigm of minority affairs in Britain and into the 1990s the state and public services gradually sought to take Muslims as 'Muslims' more seriously. Moreover, Janson (2003) maintains that new markets for the IF's unique packaging of 'Islam' for English-speaking audiences, for example, school-based Religious Education, also began to consolidate at a time when streams of Saudi funding were running dry following the collapse of oil prices in the late 1980s. Indeed, not unlike the 'professionalization' associated with the UKACIA (and eventually the MCB), the IF began to imitate more 'secular' institutions, exhibiting 'considerably less interest in ... flag waving proclamations of ideological or theological orientation' (Janson, 2003: 170).

During the 1990s and into the 2000s, then, the IF has de-emphasized its original concern for *da'wa* and counter-cultural Islamization, especially in marketing some key ventures. These include a Home Office-endorsed *Cultural Awareness Training* programme on Muslims in Britain for non-Muslim professionals (McLoughlin, 2003), [30] and the *Markfield* Institute of Higher Education (MIHE) which offers postgraduate degrees in Islamic Studies validated by Loughborough University [my emphasis]. With the translation of Mawdudi's work now complete, Janson suggests that the IF's publishing business also exhibits signs of 'diversification' and 'controlled expansion' (2003: 179-180). However, his overall argument is that, while 'socially committed ... [and] actively working against Muslim isolationism', and while adapting to Britain's 'intellectual and commercial pluralism' (2003: 363), ultimately the IF still 'attempts to harness British liberalism for the sake of 'Islamic' particularism', that is, an essentialist 'Sunni revivalist interpretation of Islam', which is advanced as representative of 'Islam' per se (Janson, 2003: 151).

I think a more nuanced assessment can be forwarded here. Mandaville (2001: 132-6), for example, citing members of IF staff as examples, argues that, given the religious and political freedoms of the diaspora, and intensified encounters with Muslim 'others', Islamic intellectuals and activists in the West are increasingly evolving innovative, cosmopolitan and self-critical reformulations of their tradition. Mandaville perhaps overstates the widespread acceptance of such a trend in Britain, for any transformations at the IF are still, in my opinion, very much in transition. Nevertheless, since the late 1990s especially, I do want to argue that a critical mass hospitable to such perspectives has undoubtedly begun to emerge at the institution. The existing literature suggests that while the IF was initially inspired by the tradition of Mawdudi and JI – 'first generation' Islamism – it also reflects the values and experiences of a 'second generation' more aware of the global interdependency of 'Islam' and the 'West' – i.e. Khurshid Ahmad (Esposito and Voll, 2001). My contention is that it is now necessary to speak of a 'third generation' of (diasporic) intellectual-activists who are, moreover, far more reflexive concerning their Islamic lineage than Janson (2003) would seem to allow.

Although their numbers remain small, within the academically oriented 'Islam in Europe' and 'Muslims in Britain' research units of the IF especially, 'thirtysomethings' of British-Asian heritage have been joined by converts to Islam with whom they share similar cultural capital, lived experiences and investments, most especially in terms of confidently embracing and successfully negotiating relationships, education, activism and careers in the interstitial spaces that constitute 'British-Muslim' identity. Some remain well networked in terms of organizations such as the ISB. However, given the largely undocumented 'fragmentation and breaks' within the JI-related tradition during the 1990s, some of ISB's membership can be very much 'out on a limb', with concepts such as 'the Islamic movement' and '*da'wa*' all now 'up for grabs'.[31] Indeed, again like the MCB, other members of staff are more determinedly 'non-affiliated', perhaps reflecting something of the 'the post-*ikhwan*', 'independent Islamist', trend described by Roald (2001: 54). Moreover, even those who identify with a 'neo-traditionalist' heritage, are critical of JI's dismissal of Sufism and want 'reformists' to engage more seriously with the expertise of the *'ulama* (rather than simply making their own 'stabs' at 'indigenizing modernity'), can still find within the IF today an important intellectual 'breathing space away from activism'.[32] A desire to work 'ecumenically' on concerns common to all British-Muslims is being reciprocated.

The argument here, then, is not that 'third generation'/(post) 'reformist Islamism' has displaced its more 'particularistic' (Janson, 2003: 151) forbears at the IF but rather that the two now 'cohabit' in the same space. Director General, Khurshid Ahmad, for example, welcomes the fact that 'it is no longer necessary to import staff' to work at the institution and that a growing 'British-Muslim ethos' is finally 'detaching the institution from Pakistani and Arab culture'.[33] At the same time, however, unlike many of his younger colleagues, Ahmad is still committed to 'Islamization from below' and does not exclude the non-Muslim state from such transformation although, 'the route to the state is through the individual, community and civil society ... there is loyalty to the society but we also to try to improve it'.

Traces of both trends are detectable in a short document concerning the 'duty' of Muslim participation in civil society, prepared by Malik (2000), a practising solicitor, ISB member and former Citizen Organising Foundation trainer based at the IF.[34] Engaging implicitly with New Labour's discourse of civic renewal, Malik begins by arguing that in terms of relations with non-Muslims the Qur'an teaches Muslims 'to uphold justice and equity' for all people 'regardless of their faith, race or gender' (2000: 2-3). All, he maintains, are the 'children of Adam' (2000: 4). Moreover, Muslims are encouraged to follow the example of the prophet Joseph who found the 'scope ... to promote good and prevent harm ... in a non-Muslim(!) government' (2000: 8). Indeed, Malik insists that the Qur'anic concepts of 'good and evil are not defined from some high moral ground' (2000): 8). Rather, that which is *ma'ruf* (good) means simply 'what is common to people or that which is known by common sense' (2000: 8). This puts an overwhelming emphasis on 'common values' as opposed to uniquely 'Islamic values'. Indeed, despite the 'self-interested' concern with 'tribal ancestry' of many mosques in Britain (2000: 3) – something discussed above – Malik suggests that it is only through supporting civil society causes *that do not affect Muslims directly* that they 'will come to know and understand others and allow others to understand them' (2000): 8). Muslims 'must not only learn about citizenship ... but teach others and be an example' (2000: 9), for 'to work collectively' shows the way to empowerment, 'to become powerful influential people in society' (2000: 10).

Here, the adoption of civic consciousness and active citizenship by British-Muslims does not suggest that they blindly adopt or assimilate dominant values. Rather, an emphasis on understanding the political system of Britain promises the possibility of learning the skills to engage in critical dialogue about 'citizenship' and 'integration' in a more pluralist, even post-national, society. Crucially, there is a concern with the 'common' rather than the 'communal' good, co-operation rather than competition, with non-Muslims seen as partners and religious differences what Baumann (1991: 131) would call 'relational rather than absolute'. While still reflecting a 'strategically essentialized' account of what it might mean to be 'a good Muslim', I would argue that Malik is beginning to problematize 'difference multiculturalism' and usefully approach what Baumann (1999: 126) calls 'multicultural convergence', that is, seeking 'the same point of agreement [with others]; but ... from its own point of origin, and by its own route'.

Conclusion

While the structure of the British State is such that religious institutions find a voice in the 'secular' public sphere more readily than in some other European countries, into the 1990s the creation of a 'faith' as well as a 'race' relations industry has both shaped, and itself been influenced by, an emergent Muslim identity politics. Precipitated by the Rushdie Affair especially, the move beyond grassroots representation, first by the UKACIA and then the MCB, has increased the public profile (but, for most Muslims at least, not necessarily the authority) of a national 'community' leadership. For this leadership, the desire for 'engagement' is in part a reflection of new and established middle-class cultural capital and ever increasing personal and professional investments in the 'mainstream' of British society. However, as the contested and incomplete transition from 'counter-cultural da'wa' to 'multicultural convergence' at the IF demonstrates, the 'good' of 'engagement' is legitimated Islamically in quite different ways. Whether attempts by Malik (2000) and others (for example, Ramadan, 1999) to 'translate' 'Islamic' political thought into 'Western' categories will ultimately produce a desecularizing and pluralizing challenge to the hegemony of liberalism (Parekh, 2000) and/or a rationalizing (and secularizing) 'hollowing out' of Islam (Roy, 1994) remains to be seen. In any case, the developments in 'reformist Islamism' considered here suggest the need for a re-imagining of 'political Islam' by Western scholars and policy-makers. Despite the appeal of rejectionism, what Burgat suggests of the re-intellectualization of Islam in the Middle East is increasingly true amongst avowedly 'Muslim' intellectual-activists in Europe: 'democratization and re-Islamization are today following paths that meet at many points' (2003: 138).

References

Ahsan, M.M. and Kidwai, A.R. (eds) (1993), *Sacrilege versus Civility: Muslim Perspectives on The Satanic Verses Affair*, Markfield: The Islamic Foundation.
Andrews, A. (1993), 'Jamaat-i-Islami in the UK', in Barot, R. (ed.), *Religion and Ethnicity: Minorities and Social Change in the Metropolis*, Kampen: Kok Pharos, 68-79.
Bauman, G. (1999), *The Multicultural Riddle*, London: Routledge.
Bevir, M. (2005), *New Labour: A Critique*, London: Routledge.
Birt, J. (2005), 'Lobbying and Marching: British Muslims and the State', in Abbas, T. (ed.), *Muslim Britain*, London: Zed, 92-106.
Bourdieu, P. and Passeron, J. (1977), *Reproduction in Education and Society*, London: Sage.
Denham, J. (2002), *Building Cohesive Communities*, London: Home Office.
Esposito, J. and Voll, J. (2001), *Makers of Contemporary Islam*, Oxford: Oxford UP.

Goes, E. (2000), 'The Third Way and the Politics of Community', conference paper presented to *The Third Way and Beyond*, Sussex University, 2 November.

Husband, C. (1994), 'The Political Context of Muslim Communities' Participation in British Society', in Lewis, B. and Schnapper, D. (eds), *Muslims in Europe*, London: Pinter, 79-97.

Janson, T. (2003), *Your Cradle is Green*, Lund: Lund Studies in History of Religions.

Lewis, P. (1994), *Islamic Britain*, London: I.B. Tauris.

Lewis, P. (2002), *Islamic Britain*, London: I.B. Tauris. Second Edition.

Malik, N. (2000), *Muslim Participation in Civil Society*, London: Citizen Organising Foundation.

Mandaville, P. (2001), *Transnational Muslim Politics*, London: Routledge.

MCB (2002), *The Quest for Sanity: Reflections on September 11 and the Aftermath*, PO Box 52, Wembley, London: Muslim Council of Britain.

McLoughlin, S. (2002), 'Recognising Muslims: Religion, Ethnicity and Identity Politics in Britain', *Cahiers d'études sur la Méditerranée orientale et le monde turco-iranien (CEMOTI)*, 33, 2002, 43-54.

McLoughlin, S. (2003), 'Islam, Citizenship and Civil Society: new Muslim leaderships in the UK', presented to the conference, 'European Muslims and the Secular State in a Comparative Perspective', La Sorbonne, Paris, 30 June–1 July, available at: http://euro-islam.info/PDFs/Final_ICDEI_Symposium.pdf.

McLoughlin, S. (in press), 'Mosques and the Public Space: Conflict and Co-operation in Bradford', *Journal of Ethnic and Migration Studies*, 31 (6).

Modood, T. (ed.) (1997), *Church, State and Religious Minorities*, London: Policy Studies Institute.

Modood, T. (2002), 'The Place of Muslims in British Secular Multiculturalism', in AlSayyad, N. and Castells, M. (eds), *Muslim Europe or Euro-Islam*, Lanham, Maryland: Lexington, 113-130.

Nasr, S.V.R. (1994), *The Vanguard of the Islamic Revolution: The Jama'at-i Islami of Pakistan*, London: I.B. Tauris.

Nielsen, J. (1999), *Towards a European Islam*, Basingstoke: Macmillan Press Ltd.

Nielsen, J. (2001), 'Muslims, the state and the public domain in Britain', in Bonney, R., Bosbach, F. and Brockman, T. (eds), *Religion and Politics in Britain and Germany*, Munich: K.G. Saur, 145-154.

Ouseley, H. (2001), *Community Pride Not Prejudice*, Bradford: Bradford 2020 Vision.

Parekh, B. (2000), *Commission on the Future of Multi-Ethnic Britain*, London: Profile.

Peter, F. (2003), 'Islamic Activism, Interfaith Dialogue and Identity Politics: The Islamic Foundation in Leicester, 1972-2003', in van Kongingsveld, P.S. (ed.), *Proceedings of Leiden Institute for the Study of Religions*, August.

Putnam, R.D. (2000), *Bowling Alone: The Collapse and Revival of American Community*, New York: Simon and Schuster.

Radcliffe, L. (2004), 'A Muslim lobby at Whitehall?', *Islam and Christian-Muslim Relations*, 15(3), 365-386.

Ramadan, T. (1999), *To be a European Muslim*, Markfield: The Islamic Foundation.

Roald, A.S. (2001), *Women in Islam: The Western Experience*, London: Routledge.

Runnymede Trust, The (1997), *Islamophobia: A Challenge for Us All*, London: 133 Aldersgate Street, London, EC1A 4JA.

Taji-Farouki, S. (1996), *A Fundamental Quest: Hizb al-Tahrir and the Search for the Islamic Caliphate*, London: Grey Seal.

UKACIA (1993), *Muslims and the Law in Multi-faith Britain*, London: UKACIA.

Werbner, P. (1991), 'Black and Ethnic Leadership in Britain', in Werbner, P. and Anwar, M. (eds), *Black and Ethnic Leaderships*, London: Routledge, 15-37.

Werbner, P. (2002), *Imagined Diasporas among Manchester Muslims*, Santa Fe: James Currey.

Notes

1 My brief account of the MCB here is based mainly upon a mapping of the organization's website, www.mcb.org.uk. The website houses general information about the MCB, its press releases, a list of affiliates, membership and committee details, news of particular campaigns, weekly updates and back copies of its occasional newsletter, *The Common Good*.

2 I use the term 'Islamist' somewhat tentatively here to suggest a modern interpretation of Islam which is self-consciously ideological and political. 'Reformists' are routinely seen as those exponents of 'political Islam' who seek to 'Islamize' public space gradually through an accommodation to the political process, whereas 'radical revolutionary' Islamists sanction armed uprising in order to capture power.

3 My interest in the IF began when I met two members of its staff at a 'Global Ethics' conference at Glasgow University in September 2001. I was subsequently invited to two events organized by the IF, firstly at the IF itself in May 2002 and then at the British Council in London, June 2003.

4 See, for example, 'British is race slur' (*The Sun*, 10 October 2000), which 'misread' the report's decoupling of Britishness from its racialized connotations of whiteness, and Home Secretary, Jack Straw: 'I do not accept the arguments of those on the nationalist right or the liberal left that Britain as a cohesive whole is dead' (*BBC News Online*, 11 October 2000).

5 These are available at: www.homeoffice.gov.uk/comrace/cohesion/keydocs.html.

6 For an assessment of the relationship between 'communitarianism' and New Labour, see Goes (2000) and Bevir (2005). This is further explored in a lecture by former Home Secretary, David Blunkett, at www.homeoffice.gov.uk/docs2/civilrennewagenda.pdf.

7 Available at: www.official-documents.co.uk/document/cm53/5387/cm5387.pdf.

8 See www.homeoffice.gov.uk/terrorism/index.html.

9 See, for example, the MCB's account of the lobbying process at: www.mcb.org.uk/census2001.pdf.

10 See, www.neighbourhood.gov.uk/page.asp?id=524.

11 See, www.odpm.gov.uk/stellent/group/odpm_urbanpolicy/documents/page/odpm_urbpol_608134.hcsp.

12 See the recommendations of the steering group on the engagement between government and faith communities at: www.homeoffice.gov.uk/docs3/workingtog_faith040329.pdf.

13 For the main 2001 Census data on religion see www.homeoffice.gov.uk/comrace/faith/.

14 Nevertheless, the 2005 Queen's Speech (*BBC News Online*, 17 May 2005) mentioned bills legislating against both Incitement to Religious Hatred and 'religious discrimination' (Equality Bill).

15 However, a number of younger Muslim *'alims* (scholars) in the Deobandi tradition (see note 28), who combine the classical training of al-Azhar university in Egypt with higher degrees from British universities, now speak on community affairs in their localities and work through the MCB on a national level. See Birt, this volume.

16 A national umbrella organization, the Union of Muslim Organisations of the UK and Eire (UMO), had been set up in 1970, but as Nielsen remarks it was 'essentially irrelevant because all the major aspects of government which affected Muslims were based at local level until well into the 1980s' (1999: 40).

17 See www.mcb.org.uk/aim.html.

18 A national newspaper quickly 'promoted' Sacranie to 246th 'most powerful person in Britain' (*The Observer*, 24 October 1999). More recently he has been knighted.

19 Telephone interview with Sher Khan, Chair, MCB Public Affairs Committee, 26 June 2003.

20 Indeed, 'no member body and its branches could have more than five of its members elected to the Central Working Committee' (*The Common Good*, 1(3): 2).

21 See MCB Annual Report 2003-04 at: www.mcb.org.uk/agm2004.pdf.

22 See the Secretary General's Introduction to the MCB Annual Report 2002 at: www.mcb.org.uk.

23 1998, for example, saw Muslims achieve equality with Anglicans, Catholics and Jews when the first state-aided Muslim primary schools were established. In 1999 the first civil service post directed at the Muslim community was announced, an Islamic advisor to the prisons, where Muslim numbers have more than doubled in recent years.

24 See 'press releases' under 'media' at www.mcb.org.uk: 'MCB expresses total condemnation of terrorist attacks' (11 September 2001) and 'MCB opposes War on Afghans – Insists on Justice' (9 October 2001).

25 See Secretary General's Annual Report 2002-03 at: www.mcb.org.uk/2002-3.pdf.

26 Ibid.

27 The Qur'an, 5:32, for example, which establishes the sanctity of life, was widely cited by Muslims in the wake of 9/11 to disassociate Islam from terrorism (MCB, 2002: 29).

28 Lewis makes the succinct distinction between those Islamic movements which seek to 'defend' (the Barelwis), 'reform' (the Deobandis), or 'reject' (Ahl-i Hadis, Jama'at-i Islami) the traditional paradigm of South Asian Islam, exemplified by Sufi pirs (mystical guides, saints) and their shrines (1994: 28).

29 Hizb al-Tahrir (the Liberation Party, founded 1953, Jerusalem) propagates a utopian message of reviving the *ummah* (Islamic community) and liberating those Muslims who live under *kufr* (systems of unbelief in Muslim or non-Muslim countries) by (re)establishing the *khilafah* (Caliphate) and an Islamic state ruled by *shari'ah* (Taji-Farouki, 1996).

30 The approach to this training was described to me as 'warts and all' (personal correspondence with Dilwar Hussain, IF, 3 February 2003).

31 Interview with Dilwar Hussain, IF, 27 October 2003.

32 Interview with Yahya Birt, IF, 27 October 2003.

33 Interview with Khurshid Ahmad, IF, 17 October 2003.

34 The Citizen Organising Foundation promotes broad-based community organizing and the strengthening of civil society, including a role for faith groups. A 'memorandum of understanding' was signed with the IF in 1998.

Chapter 5

Religious Authorities or Political Actors? The Muslim Leaders of the French Representative Body of Islam[1]

Alexandre Caeiro

Introduction

Throughout the Muslim world, the postcolonial state has become a major producer of Islamic knowledge, attempting to counter transnational versions of Islam by producing vernacular religious authorities, institutions and doxas. In an interesting parallel, following the waves of post Second World War Muslim immigration, many European countries have also started to engage in the promotion of national forms of Islam. This is a move epitomised by the famous call for an 'Islam de France', rather than 'en France', as Nicolas Sarkozy, France's Interior Minister (2002-2004) so often emphasised. If it is not immediately clear what 'French Islam' will look like, its broad contours have started to emerge, enunciated here and there by some established, and often non-Muslim, intellectual or politician: French Islam is a *cultural, linguistic, financial, political* and *theological* enterprise. French Muslims will adopt French 'norms', i.e., they will integrate or assimilate; Arabic will be stripped away to the bare minimum, perhaps even eliminated like the Latin of Sunday mass, and Muslim actors and institutions in France will be conversant with Voltaire's language. French Islam will be financed by French Muslims and structured around a single organization, following the hierarchical pattern of the Catholic Church which has modelled French religious (and non-religious) institutions in the modern age. [2] Finally, French Islam will be distinctively 'liberal', its Way or *shari'a* 'bien tempérée à la française' (seasoned the French way),[3] and perhaps, like other things French, turn out to be an example to the world.

The key to this project of 'domestication' (De Galembert, 2001; Bowen, 2004), judging from contemporary French political discourses, is the organization of the Muslim religion into one 'church'. This body will separate the wheat from the chaff, marginalising 'bad' and promoting 'good' Muslims, in an interesting secular reversal of the Islamic injunction to 'enjoin the good and forbid the evil' (*amr bi'l- ma'ruf wa nahy 'an al-munkar*).

This chapter gives an overview of the historical process leading to the institutionalization of Islam in France's regime of laïcité. It provides an account of the major Muslim responses to the demands of the state and the expectations of the wider French society. It then discusses some questions raised by the discrepancy between the juridical, political, and social roles invested upon the Conseil français du culte musulman (CFCM) as it strives to achieve the status of a Muslim authority in France. The conclusion focuses on the prospects for institutionalized Islam in the current religious landscape.

France's Search for Institutional Islam

The progressive sedentarization of Muslims has driven most Western European states to take Islam explicitly into consideration, seeking arrangements and negotiating the modalities of its integration in the public sphere. The processes of the institutionalization of Islam undertaken by many of these states have paradoxically been greatly determined by the demands of the 'host' societies, seemingly replicating pre-established church-state patterns. As Koenig (2004: 93) has argued, both the claims of recognition and the modes of symbolic and organizational incorporation are shaped by different institutional arrangements of political organization, collective identity and religion. Indeed, recent research has confirmed the prominence of national institutions and constraints in the shaping of Muslim religiosities in Europe.[4]

In France, the complex legal-political-social regime of laïcité, erected as a constitutional principle for the first time in 1946, and reiterated in the 1958 Constitution, postulates a strict separation between the church and the state, which, according to Article 2 of the 9 December 1905 law, 'does not recognize, pay, or subsidize any [form of] worship'. Painfully constructed over more than one century, the legal corpus of laïcité was a compromise solution which attempted to heal a divisive political concept (Baubérot, 2000). As Hervieu-Léger (1999: 213) has argued, the outcome, French laïcité, is a 'system of the institutional regulation of the religious' based on a 'denominational definition of religion'. Religions in the public sphere are requested by the state to present a single 'privileged interlocutor'. It is on this basis that they can negotiate the modes of their public recognition (Amiraux, 2003). Confronted with de-regularized practices, the French authorities – and the regime of laïcité – are ill equipped to manage problems of public order triggered by religion.[5]

The institutionalization of Islam in France has been fraught with the difficulties of representing a multi-faceted religion in a context of recent migration, competing political agendas, and shifts in public policy. The main driving force in the process has been the secular state, and the priorities of successive Ministers of the Interior – who are also 'Ministers of Cults' – have helped shape a process marked by laborious balancing acts between the expectations of the state, Muslims and other French actors. At the same time, Muslim leaders have responded in different ways to the demands placed on them by the state, as well as to the expectations of the wider society, often echoing, instrumentalizing, or subverting them for their own purposes.

Given its symbolic weight, the Grande Mosquée de Paris (GMP) has always made strong claims to embody 'the privileged interlocutor' of the French State in matters of Muslim worship. The first mosque in Metropolitan France, the GMP was built during the interwar period in homage to the loyalty of the North African battalions during the Great War. Initially sponsored by the king of Morocco, it was reassigned to Algeria by the French Foreign Minister in 1957, a link that has perpetuated itself to this day (Kepel, 1994; Le Pautremat, 2003). The GMP's historical claims are reinforced by the sociological composition of Muslims in France, where Algerians make up an estimated 43 per cent of the population of Muslim origin. To varying degrees this has made Interior Ministers receptive to the representational claims of its Rectors, from Cheikh Abbas Bencheikh El Hocine to the current incumbent, Dalil Boubakeur. The process of the institutionalization of Islam in France is, to a large extent, the history of the bargaining over the place of the GMP in any future Muslim representative body.

In a climate dominated by fears of international Islamic terrorism, an oscillation in French public policy between including the diversity of Muslims and favouring specific tendencies has shaped the state organization of Islam. One Muslim actor, Soheib Bencheikh, strategically articulated this equation when he described the options facing the Minister of the Interior as he attempted to identify Muslim representatives: 'either privilege a scholarly representation, whose only task is to adapt Islam to France, or try to reflect the diversity of the community, searching for spokespersons for each sensibility'. According to Bencheikh, only the former 'gives Muslim representatives a religious legitimacy and vaccinates the Muslim community against fundamentalism' (*Le Monde*, 9 December 1999).

French Interior Ministers seem to have internalized this tension between the competing forces of 'Representativity' and 'Moderation'. The Framework Agreement, adopted under Daniel Vaillant in May 2001, stipulated that 'the designation of the representatives will be based on a transparent and democratic procedure'.[6] Nevertheless, in order to offset the undesirable effects of such democratic forms of participation, Interior Ministers stretched the limits of laïcité by imposing a number of chosen personalities. Nicolas Sarkozy, in particular, negotiated with Muslim leaders the quota of 'co-opted', as opposed to 'elected' members (including the number of women[7]), who would sit on the administrative council of the future Muslim body.[8]

The discussions around the 'representativity-moderation trade-off' eventually hinged on the position, if any, to be given to the Union des organizations islamiques de France (UOIF). Arguably the most dynamic Muslim organization at the grassroots level, and gathering together over 200 associations, the UOIF is depicted in the French media and academia as 'fundamentalist', 'Islamist' and 'radical'. Its ideological, if not organic, links to the Muslim Brotherhood are seen as a threat to the French Republic. In response, the UOIF has attempted to portray itself as the promoter of an Islam of 'citizenship', contesting the GMP's monopoly on Islamic 'moderation'. A founding member of the European Council for Fatwa and Research (ECFR),[9] the UOIF is one of the few organizations in France systematically engaging with religious texts and thus able to posit itself as a religious authority, rather than as a mere (political) representative of Muslims. The

UOIF has been carefully articulating its political strategies with reference to (a moderately conservative reading of) the Islamic tradition (*fiqh*), underlining that 'living in the West, organizing the Muslim community in France or creating a European Islamic culture is not [itself] blameworthy'. In a widely disseminated document, the *fatwa* commission of the UOIF typically issued a theological justification for its participation in the broad consultative process (*Istichara*) launched in 1999 by J-P. Chevènement, stating that 'the mode of representation of Muslim worship pertains to the sphere of *ijtihad* [personal effort in interpretation]'.[10]

Despite their reservations, Interior Ministers from the mid-1990s onwards have engaged in a policy which could be best described as *containment through engagement*. They have preferred to keep the UOIF 'in', rather than let it fall 'outside', the process, gambling that such a formative political experience would have some lasting effect upon it. The UOIF has in turn tried to distance itself somewhat from its transnational religious authorities (Yusuf al-Qaradawi and Faysal Mawlawi), promoting local figures such as Ahmed Jaballah and Tareq Oubrou as its spiritual reference points instead. Engaged in the politics of recognition, the leadership of the UOIF has adapted the *fatwas* issued collectively at the ECFR to fit the boundaries of legitimate national political discourses, seeking to harmonize *shari'a* and French law rather than enter into a process of bargaining with the state (Caeiro, 2003). The hesitations of the UOIF's leadership concerning the Muslim headscarf controversy in France are symptomatic in this regard.[11]

The electoral system adopted for the Muslim representative body was based on mosque surface area. At one end of the spectrum places of worship below 100m² were allowed one delegate, while at the other end, mosques larger than 800m² were allocated 15 delegates. Given its special relationship to the state, the GMP was assigned 18 delegates. Such a criterion was not exactly *sociologically* neutral. It produced a biased representation of Muslim places of worship and their congregations by disproportionately impacting on the urban-suburban divide: given real estate prices, mosques in cities tend to be smaller than those outside cities. In terms of ethnic affiliation, Arab mosques funded by the Gulf States can afford bigger spaces than those of, say, Sub-Saharan African groups. Regarding age group, 80 per cent of mosques are controlled by the first generation, while the youth socialize mainly in associations. More fundamentally, this measure was controversial since it placed the mosque – and by implication the mosque committee – as the privileged marker of Islamic identity.

The first elections to the CFCM, which took place in April 2003, confirmed the decline of the GMP and the vitality of the UOIF. The biggest winner, however, was the list led by the Fédération nationale des musulmans de France (FNMF), reflecting more accurately the religious sociology of Islam in France. Moroccans invest most in places of worship (40 per cent of *imams* are Moroccan, against 25 per cent Algerian and 13 per cent Turkish) and are more regular in their religious practices. Headed by Mohammed Bechari and supported by the Moroccan consulates, the FNMF proved most skilled at coalition-building, drawing combined strength from ethnic, traditional and literalist Islam, often through the involvement of personalities close to the missionary movement, Tablighi Jama'at.[12] While these results did not impact on the 'top posts', which had been allocated to the three largest federations four months in advance, they nevertheless conferred some legitimacy upon the regional bodies, the privileged interlocutors of the French authorities at the local level.

The build-up to the 2005 elections has highlighted the fragility of the initial balance of power. In September 2004 Boubakeur announced that his GMP would not participate in the elections, since his demand for more favourable electoral criteria had not been met. Then, in February 2005, the FNMF used its dominance in the Muslim body to obtain an indefinite postponing of the elections scheduled for April, a move suggesting that the Fédération is set to suffer a loss of electoral seats. In both cases, only the interventions of the Interior Minister have allowed the CFCM to continue operating under a guise of normality.

Profiles of Muslim Actors

The state institutionalization of Islam in France has also been marked by the competing strategies of Muslim actors. What follows here is a brief sketch of some of the key Muslim personalities involved in this process. The list is far from exhaustive, but these profiles nevertheless represent a concise sociology of Muslim leaders: from the Algerian administrator or the modernist theologian to the Sufi leader or the female social scientist; from the charismatic local *imam* or the rival Muslim representative to the youth association leader or the secular Muslim politician. The first four actors considered here are – or were – members of the CFCM, while the last four are non-institutionalized figures who have kept themselves away, or been excluded from, the state organization of Islam.

Institutional Actors

1. *Dalil Boubakeur* (Algerian) has been Rector of the GMP since 1992.[13] He is the president and spokesperson of the CFCM. This somewhat unusual accumulation of functions already hints at Boubakeur's role: he is the interlocutor of the French State, the acceptable figure for the wider non-Muslim society, put in place by Nicolas Sarkozy. Boubakeur has successfully promoted his Mosquée as a bastion of 'moderate Islam' and 'follower of the Maliki School' which predominates in North Africa.[14] Paid by the Algerian State, to which he is accountable,[15] Boubakeur is a medical doctor and a political representative who, apart from his genealogy, has no claims to religious authority. His position at the CFCM looks fragile once his term of office is completed in 2005.

2. *Soheib Bencheikh* (Algerian) embodies the liberal Islam that the French public so desperately seeks.[16] He is one of the few members of the CFCM with the profile of a theologian, albeit a very modernist one. Bencheikh studied at the Islamic Institute of Algiers and Al-Azhar before completing a doctorate in religious sciences in France. In 1995 the GMP nominated him as Mufti of Marseilles with (unofficial) support from the French State. Bencheikh has set himself the task of

'freeing his community from obscurantism', multiplying the condemnations of Muslim *ostentatious* practices in France and accentuating, in French public discourse, the simplistic dichotomy between 'good' and 'bad' Muslims. During the process of institutionalizing Islam in France he has threatened to resign countless times, a strategy which allows him to simultaneously criticise the Interior Minister and to distance himself from the GMP, while at the same time preserving an official platform for his self-promotion.[17] He became, in April 2003, a 'dissident' figure at the CFCM.

3. *Cheikh Khaled Bentounès* (Algerian) presents a spiritual and modern face of Islam as the leader of the 'Alawi *tariqa* (Sufi order). Having come to France to pursue a business career, Bentounès became the leader of the 'Alawiyya on the death of his father in 1975. He has reconciled this with his professional activities, regularly touring Europe, North Africa and the Middle East, teaching and also engaging in interfaith activities. In response to a manifest demand, Bentounès has recently published a collection of articles and interviews expounding his vision of Islam, France and the world.

4. *Dounia Bouzar* (French) entered the bureau of the CFCM as a replacement for Betoule Fekkar-Lambiotte when the latter resigned in protest at the place given to 'the fundamentalists' (read UOIF) in the future Muslim body. A social worker turned anthropologist, Bouzar was nominated because of her engagement with Muslim youth. She is also one of the rare Muslim voices whose discourse is audible in the French public sphere, where she has attempted to deconstruct essentialist interpretations of Islam (both from within and without), and argued for the need to consider the importance of 'extra-religious variables' in Muslim self-understanding. She resigned in January 2005, declaring that there was no place for her expertise – the reconfiguration of Muslim religiosity in the secular context of France – at the CFCM. Her resignation raises questions about the pertinency of a system of co-option.

Non-institutional Actors

5. *Larbi Kechat* (Algerian) has been Rector of the Adda'wa mosque in the nineteenth arrondissement of Paris since 1989. He is a charismatic leader who combines Islamic scholarship with a university degree in the social sciences. Unlike other Islamic leaders, whose recognition by the state has undermined their legitimacy amongst Muslims, Kechat's refusal to participate in the *Istichara*, despite Chevènement's invitation, has added to his reputation as an independent leader. He is comfortable with the absence of institutionalized Islam, a situation that he has described as closest to the Prophetic ideal.

6. *Dhaou Meskine* (Tunisian) is an *imam* in Clichy-sous-Bois (Greater Paris) and principal of France's first independent Muslim school (La Réussite). Historically a rival of the UOIF, he presented himself as candidate for the CRCM in Ile-de-France but was defeated by the president of the UOIF, Lhaj Thami Breze. Meskine

heads the broadest association of *imams* in France, the Conseil des imams de France. Established in 1992, the organization brings together over 250 *imams* regardless of 'ideology, origin and affiliation'.[18] Meskine has argued that the CFCM should perform an administrative function only; given its lack of scholars, it has no legitimacy to engage in the interpretation of Islam. He has also suggested a possible 'complementarity' between the CFCM and his body, proposing the creation of a national *fatwa* commission through the Conseil des imams de France.

7. *Fouad Imarraine* (French) is an *imam* and leader of the Collectif des musulmans de France (CMF), which has links to the Swiss intellectual Tariq Ramadan. Imarraine has been among the staunchest critics of the French State during the institutionalization of Islam. He has denounced the lack of transparency in the process, the limited role given to the ballot in the composition of the new body, and state interventionism in terms of the nomination of the co-opted individuals. The religious neutrality of the state, according to Imarraine, implies respect for each religion's endogenous principles of organization. If the 'socially-legitimate' definition of laïcité is the arena of a symbolic struggle between competing actors (Baubérot, 2000: 119), Imarraine is proof that Muslims have started to participate in the contest.

8. *Abderrahmane Dahmane* (Algerian) is a former ally, turned opponent, of D. Boubakeur. Close to the centre-right political parties, Dahmane has also criticized the institutionalization of Islam as 'undemocratic' and 'unrepresentative'. He founded the Conseil des démocrates musulmans, a 'secular' counterpoint to the CFCM, which aims to represent Muslims politically in France. The charter of his movement, which echoes in many ways the Declaration of Intent that Chevènement first sent to the Muslim participants as part of the consultative process, consists of an explicit acknowledgement of the principles of Human Rights. Proving that alliances and rivalries are erratic in French Muslim politics, Dahmane and Boubakeur now look set to join forces again 'against the fundamentalists' in a future Council of secular Muslims which is likely to be established under the patronage of Sarkozy's successor, Dominique de Villepin.

And the Future? The CFCM's Contested Role

Apart from the symbolism of providing Islam with a seat at the Republic's table, there has been some confusion about the actual mission of the CFCM. The need to institutionalize France's second largest religion appeared so self-evident that there seems to have been little prior discussion, within and without the Muslim body, about the aims and jurisdiction of the CFCM. Is it a political representative of Muslims at the official level or a religious authority responsible for defining Islam in the French context? Or is it both, or neither?

From a legal perspective, the CFCM is an 'association' of the type defined by the law of 1901, a law, in principle, reserved for non-religious bodies. The aims of the CFCM have been broadly defined in its own internal statutes as follows: i) to defend the dignity and interests of Islam in France; ii) to favour and organize the sharing of information and services between places of worship; iii) to encourage dialogue between religions; and iv) to provide the state with representatives of Muslim places of worship.[19] In addition to these four goals, the Conseils regionaux du culte musulman (CRCM) represent the CFCM at the regional level.

Beyond this juridical definition of the Muslim body, however, there are also latent political and social expectations concerning the role of the CFCM. 'Organized Islam' is widely expected to act – sooner or later – as a religious body, defining the modalities of the adaptation of Islamic normativity to the secular context of France.[20] In the post 9/11 context, as Bonnefoy (2003: 22) has remarked, the distinction between 'good' and 'bad' Muslims has come to permeate all levels of French public institutions, becoming a quasi-scientific category that is employed by political leaders and exploited in the media, structuring mainstream perceptions. The CFCM is expected to contribute to the formalization of 'good Islam' in France, disseminating a liberal doxa and marginalizing radical elements. In other words, the representative body of Muslims in France is being asked to become part of the solution to the problem of a 'socially controversial religion'.[21]

State officials have often echoed this wider societal demand. Whilst Sarkozy argued repeatedly that the CFCM will help create 'a transparent, open, modern, and liberal Islam compatible with the laws of the Republic',[22] Prime-Minister Raffarin, in his inaugural address to the Muslim council, articulated the 'moderate vocation' of the CFCM by asking the Muslim body to be 'the enlightened word of French Islam', in particular 'among the youth'.[23]

Whether the theological adaptation of Islam to the French context is a necessary condition of its institutionalization has been a matter of some debate (Schnapper, 1994; Roy, 1999). However, this is a theme that a number of Muslim actors have been willing to instrumentalize. Boubakeur appealed to the Interior Minister to have, as his guiding principle, 'the option in favour of an Enlightened and liberal Islam' (2003: 99), adding that 'besides problems relating to rituals, [the CFCM] needs to begin to reflect anew on Islamic religious thought ... [becoming] more open to contemporary times and ideas ... [and] continuing the work of the early reformists' (2003: 108-109). Likewise, a number of secular Muslims have recuperated the theme of an Islamic *aggiornamento* for their own purposes.[24]

If the twenty-five regional bodies (CRCM) act in conjunction with local authorities to resolve issues relating to Muslim ritual worship and practice, it is the national body which is supposed to tackle questions of Islamic doctrine. However, unlike its Catholic and Jewish counterparts, the CFCM is not comprised of religious scholars.[25] Its current membership is almost totally made up of mosque managers and technocrats. In 2003 the CFCM did manage to agree the dates for the beginning and end of the month of Ramadan, a divisive issue which had previously undermined the unity of Muslims in France (and beyond). However, the significance of the absence of religious scholars was brought into sharp relief in the wake of the proposal to ban the Muslim headscarf from public schools. The three major federations (GMP, UOIF and FNMF) all agreed that the *hijab* was a religious prescription and so opposed its banning. They were, nevertheless, split on the question of what religious advice to give to Muslims. Three months before the

Stasi commission was due to deliver its report recommending the ban of 'conspicuous religious signs' from public schools (Commission présidée par Bernard Stasi, 2004), on 13 September 2003 Mohammed Bechari announced the setting up of a theological commission within the CFCM to reflect upon the issues. Divided and lacking formal expertise, the commission broke down before it was able to initiate the reflection, never mind delivering the requested *fatwa*. To add insult to injury, Sarkozy went 'on holiday' to Egypt and 'met' Sheikh Tantawi of Al-Azhar in Cairo. In a perfect example of harmony between the wishes of the *mustafti* (*fatwa*-petitioner) and the answer of the *mufti*, Tantawi told the Minister that Muslims in non-Muslim countries cannot be expected to follow the prescription of veiling. This move by the Interior Minister not only undermined the moral authority of the CFCM but also cast doubt on whether the call for a 'French Islam' really means a docile 'state Islam'.

Another sensitive issue is the training of *imams* (see also Birt, this volume). The *imam* in France has been promoted to the status of representative of Islam, a position he does not hold in Muslim majority countries and to which he is most often (and self-consciously) ill-equipped. There is a consensus among state, non-Muslim commentators, and Muslims at large on the desirability of training *imams* that are fluent in French and familiar with the French social context. Accordingly, one of the eleven commissions (eleven 'Herculean tasks', as they are known internally) established by the CFCM soon after its formation was to deal with this issue. This commission, headed by a Moroccan, Abdallah Boussouf (Strasbourg), and an Algerian, Hamza Gharbi (linked to the GMP), is faced with the difficult task of providing practical solutions while at the same time being bound by the internal statutes of the grassroots Muslim associations.[26] The first report of this commission, presented to the CFCM in May 2004, recommended a course focussing on French language and history for *imams* preaching in France. It also suggested the creation of a faculty of Islamic theology and cautiously advised keeping the practical training of would-be *imams* in the hands of private institutes.[27] However, unhappy with the progress of the commission, the Interior Ministry encouraged the formation of a parallel informal body comprising of Muslim and non-Muslim experts in March 2004. In December the Interior ministry announced the provision, as of September 2005, of university courses for would-be *imams* on private law, the constitutional law on public freedom and the history of French institutions. Given the need to manage the internal diversity of the CFCM, it is nevertheless difficult to see a consensual approach to the curricula emerging from the Muslim representative body. In particular, the place to be given to the social sciences alongside the traditional Islamic disciplines is likely to be problematic.

The CFCM is caught between the expectations of the different social and political actors involved in the institutionalization of Islam in France. Muslim actors both within and without the CFCM realize this tension when they argue for a purely administrative mission for the Council. For, in one sense, the CFCM comes ... too late. Muslim organizations in France have already established, with different degrees of success, their own rival *imam*-training institutes, their own *fatwa* commissions and their own *halal* food labels.

The public debate over the CFCM relates to broader issues of Muslim citizenship in France. Throughout the years, and sometimes even simultaneously, public authorities have sent mixed messages. On several occasions, Sarkozy, acting with an urgency which did little to reassure wider French society, made links between 'the international situation', the 'five million Muslims in France' and the 'obvious need' to 'represent' them at the official level. Such a widely shared description of the institutionalization of Islam in France ultimately reposes on an ethnic, rather than a religious, definition of Muslims. Critics blamed Sarkozy for 'constituting, through religion, a public body for the regulation of social problems',[28] of 'placing, in sum, the religious at the heart of the political'.[29] In partisan politics, some considered Sarkozy's personal role in the formation of the CFCM as his only contribution towards pacifying the French *banlieues* and countering high unemployment rates.

Within the Muslim camp many have criticized the CFCM for being 'unrepresentative' and 'undemocratic'. Secular elites of Muslim origin resented the representation of their traditional constituencies at the official level along religious lines. One actor regretted that, during the process of the institutionalization of Islam, 'speech was confiscated by the religious actors'.[30] By privileging the Islamic component of immigrant identity, the state was accused of practising a 'reverse [religious] communitarianism' and of pursuing dubious electoral gains, as well as playing into the hands of the Islamist movements active in the French suburbs.

Perhaps the strongest indication, *ad contrario*, of the inherently political character of the CFCM was the concomitant rise of parallel secular Muslim bodies. The Conseil français des musulmans laïques (CFML), launched in Paris in May 2003, purported to be the Islamic equivalent to the Conseil représentatif des institutions juives de France (CRIF).[31] Its avowed aim was to 'represent the silent majority of French Muslims', excluded from the elections to the CFCM, in a body eager to 'participate in questions of public debate and laïcité'.[32] The CFML, however, was not free from theological undertones, as the presence of Soheib Bencheikh – who thus achieved an unlikely combination of the two posts – and the invitations sent to Boubakeur and Bechari indicated. The CFML was implicitly acting not only as a complement but also as an *alternative* to the CFCM, operating in the same political field. Its un-named enemy was the UOIF, decried as 'fundamentalist' and seen as having too central a role in the CFCM. A statement supporting the banning of Muslim headscarves from public schools ('a necessary refreshing of the 1905 law which takes into consideration the arrival of Islam in France'),[33] adopted in the opening session of the CFML, only seemed to confirm this. When internal divisions paralysed the CFCM in the autumn of 2004, it was almost natural that its secular counterparts would also come to a standstill.

Underlying both Sarkozy's statements and Muslim criticism of his methods was a shared view of the future body as 'representing Muslims', rather than the Muslim religion, at the official level. Thus the French State and a wide spectrum of Muslims converged in placing an impossible burden of representativity upon the CFCM. Such expectations were in contrast to the state's privileged interlocutors from the other main religions, which represent more homogeneous constituencies and tend to be specialized in matters relating to worship.[34] If the demands for greater accountability emanating from Muslims are a testimony to their internalization of democratic forms of political representation, they nevertheless contribute to a reinforcing of a certain Muslim 'exception' to laïcité.[35] Ironically, this comforts the perception that Islam is a foreign religion which does not distinguish between the religious and political spheres.

Conclusion

The main purveyor of legitimacy to the CFCM so far has been the French State. Indeed, its active involvement has ensured that the 'forced marriage' that is the Muslim representative body has not yet ended in premature divorce. This voluntaristic posture of the state is, nevertheless, also the greatest difficulty in the relations between the CFCM and the Muslim grassroots, suspicious of all forms of government control. Beyond the internal rivalries, which will in all likelihood continue to mar the Muslim body, and the discrepancy between its social, juridical and political roles, the CFCM will soon be confronted with the more fundamental challenge of 'de-institutionalization' in its struggle to achieve religious legitimacy amongst Muslims. Conceptualized according to a French historical model of institutional regulation of religion, the CFCM seems at odds with the plurality of Islamic networks and the fluidity of Muslim religiosities in France.

References

Amiraux, V. (2003), 'CFCM: A French Touch?', *ISIM Newsletter*, 12 June, 24-25.

Baubérot, J. (2000), *Histoire de la laïcité en France*, Paris: Presses universitaires de France.

Benbassa, E. (2003), *La République face à ses minorités – les juifs hier, les Musulmans aujourd'hui*, Paris: Fayard/Mille et Une Nuits.

Bencheikh, S. (1998), *Marianne et le Prophète: L'Islam dans la France laïque*, Paris: Grasset.

Bentounès, Ch.K. (2003), *Vivre l'islam: Le soufisme aujourd'hui*, Gordes: Editions du Relié.

Bonnefoy, L. (2003), 'Public Institutions and Islam: A New Stigmatization?', *ISIM Newsletter*, 13 December, 22-23.

Boubakeur, D. (2003), *Non! L'Islam n'est pas une politique*, Entretiens avec Virginie Malabard, Paris: Desclée de Brouwer.

Boubakeur, D. (2004), *L'islam de France sera libéral/Entretiens – Nathalie Dollé*, Paris: AliAS.

Bowen, J. (2004), 'Does French Islam Have Borders? Dilemmas of Domestication in a Global Religious Field', *American Anthropologist*, 106 (1), 43-55.

Caeiro, A. (2003), 'Pan-European Fatwas and National Contexts: Dilemmas of *Ifta'* in Western and Eastern Europe', paper presented at the MSHS/University of Poitiers conference on 'Balkan Muslims and Islam in Western Europe', 14 November, Poitiers, France.

Caeiro, A. (2005), 'Transnational 'Ulama, European Fatwas, and Islamic Authority: A Case Study of the European Council for Fatwa and Research', in van Bruinessen, M. and Allievi, S. (eds), *Producing Islamic Knowledge: Transmission and Dissemination in Western Europe*, London: Routledge, forthcoming.

Césari, J. (1998), *Musulmans et républicains: les jeunes, l'islam et la France*, Brussels: Editions Complexe.

Comission présidée par Bernard Stasi (2004), *Laïcité et République – Rapport au Président de la République*, Paris: La documentation Française.

De Galembert, C. (2001), 'La régulation étatique du religieux à l'épreuve de la globalisation', in Bastian, J-P, Champion, F. and Rousselet, K. (eds), *La globalisation du religieux*, Paris: L'Harmattan.

El Khatib, M. (2003), 'Le processus de mise en place d'instances représentatives de l'islam de France – De Pierre Joxe à Nicolas Sarkozy: 1990-2003', unpublished Masters thesis, Institut d'études politiques: Rennes, France.

Frégosi, F. (1998), 'Les problèmes d'organisation de la religion musulmane en France', *Esprit*, January.

Frégosi, F. (2004), 'L'imam, le conférencier et le jurisconsulte: retour sur trois figures contemporaines du champ religieux en France', *Archives de Sciences sociales des Religions*, 125, January–March, 131-146.

Hervieu-Léger, D. (1999), *Le pèlerin et le converti: La religion en mouvement*, Paris: Flammarion.

Hervieu-Léger, D. (2003), *Catholicisme français: la fin d'un monde*, Paris: Bayard.

Islam de France – revue d'information et de réflexion musulmane, n° 1/8, Paris: Al-Bouraq – Mémoralis.

Kaltenbach, J-H. (1990), 'Quelques réflexions sur la naïveté en droit musulman', in Etienne, B. (ed.), *L'islam en France*, Paris: CNRS.

Kepel, G. (1994), *A l'ouest d'Allah*, Paris: Seuil.

Koenig, M. (2004), 'Öffentliche Konflikte um die Inkorporation muslimischer Minderheiten in Westeuropa – analytische und komparative Perspektiven', *Journal für Konflikt- und Gewaltforschung*, 6, 85-100.

La Médina – le magazine des cultures musulmanes, n°s 1/20, Saint-Denis.

Le Pautremat, P. (2003), *La politique musulmane de la France au XXe siècle: de l'Hexagone aux terres d'Islam*, Paris: Maisonneuve et Larose.

Nordmann, C. (ed.) (2004), *Le foulard islamique en questions*, Paris: Editions Amsterdam.

Peter, F. (2003), 'Training Imams and the Future of Islam in France', *ISIM Newsletter*, 13, December, 20-21.

Roy, O. (1999), *Vers un islam européen*, Paris: Editions Esprit.

Sarkozy, N. (2004), *La République, les religions, l'espérance – entretiens avec Thibaud Collin et Philippe Verdin*, Paris: Les Editions du Cerf.

Schnapper, D. (1994), 'Muslim Communities, Ethnic Minorities and Citizens', in Lewis, B. and Schnapper, D. (eds), *Muslims in Europe*, London: Pinter.

Ternisien, X. (2002), *La France des mosquées*, Paris: Albin Michel.

Zarka, Y.C. (ed.) (2004), *L'Islam en France – Cités*, special issue, Paris: PUF.

Notes

1 I am grateful to Valérie Amiraux and the editors for their comments.
2 Hervieu-Léger (2003) has shown how the hierarchical model of the Catholic Church continued to permeate all French institutions long after their secularization.
3 Kaltenbach (1990: 227).
4 See the network's research online at www.euro-islam.info.

5 This is true of all religious gröups. For a Catholic example, see Hervieu-Léger (1999: 226). Whether this is due to a systemic juridical incapacity or to a lack of political will is open to question.

6 Ministère de l'intérieur, *Accord-cadre sur l'organisation future du culte musulman en France*, 2001.

7 It is ironic that the religiously neutral French State places greater demands on some religious traditions than others. Women are absent from virtually all the main religious bodies in France and their exclusion is a burning issue in French Catholicism and Judaism alike.

8 Sarkozy demanded the inclusion of at least five women in the first general assembly of the CFCM, asked for a 'milder' representative of 'Foi et pratique' (Tablighi Jama'at) in the CFCM's Bureau; he also requested the protection of African and Turkish minorities within the future body. This set of demands, perhaps not surprising from the first senior French politician to actively call for positive discrimination in favour of France's minorities, gave rise to an ironic response from the UOIF, accusing the Minister of encouraging 'communitarianism' among Muslims.

9 This is a pan-European body set up by the Federation of Islamic Organizations of Europe (FIOE) to address the canonical problems associated with the presence of Muslim minorities in Europe (Caeiro, forthcoming).

10 UOIF (2002), *Les bases religieuses de la représentation du culte musulman en France* (Arabic and French).

11 After a member of the UOIF hinted that a law banning the headscarf would be desirable (Le Monde, 14 October 2003), the Union adopted a conciliatory stance during its annual Bourget meeting (Le Monde, 13 April 2004) before issuing a press statement expressing its 'support' for the pupils 'regardless of their decision' to wear or not to wear the headscarf in school.

12 *Libération*, 21 April 2003.

13 See Kepel (1994: 289-293).

14 The reference here to following a specific jurisprudential school or *madhhab*, known as *taqlid*, is a conservative call which is at odds with the advocacy of *ijtihad*, the new interpretative efforts of Muslim scholars. In the case of Boubakeur, it marks an opposition to the eclecticism (*talfiq*) of Islamic reformist movements influenced by the Salafiyya, including both Muslim Brotherhood and Wahhabi discourses.

15 After his poor election results in April 2003, he was called back to Algeria to 'explain himself'.

16 Usually portrayed in the French media as 'enlightened', Bencheikh has also, on occasion, been described as the 'very moderate' ('le très modéré') Mufti of Marseilles (*Courrier de Mantes*, 25 December 2002), suggesting that, in some media representations, the figure of the progressive Muslim thinker is either unthought or unthinkable.

17 Frégosi in Zarka (2004: 98).

18 Personal communication.

19 See 'Projet de statuts du CFCM approuvé par la COMOR le 17 avril 2003' at http://oumma.com/article.php3?id_article=615.

20 Frégosi in Zarka (2004: 106).

21 The phrase is borrowed from F. Messner.

22 *Le Monde*, 8 April 2003.

23 *La Croix*, 6 May 2003.

24 Calling for an 'aggiornamento' pays immediate dividends. The anthropologist Malek Chebel, member of the Mouvement des musulmans laïques de France, was decorated by the French President in May 2004, two months after the publication of his 'Manifesto for

an Enlightened Islam' (Manifeste pour un islam des Lumières – 27 propositions pour réformer l'islam, Hachette Littératures, Paris, 2004). On other secular Muslim movements, see Frégosi in Zarka (2004: 104).

25 The legal basis of the CFCM, as a 1901 non-religious association, seems to preclude any form of theological activity.

26 According to their constitution, the CFCM and the CRCMs cannot interfere in the internal statutes of Muslim organizations – a specificity of the French Muslim body which limits its action severely.

27 At present, a number of these institutes already exist, organized along ideological and national lines, and unlikely to federate the different components of French Islam. The refusal of the Commission to consult the Conseil des imams, the largest body of its kind, does not indicate a general willingness to supersede existing inter-Muslim rivalries.

28 Guénif-Soulaimas in Zarka (2004: 127).

29 *L'Express*, 20 November 2003.

30 Hanifa Chérifi, quoted by *AFP*, 'Des personnalités musulmanes s'organizent pour la défense de la laïcité', 21 May 2003.

31 *La Croix*, 22 May 2003. The CRIF is an umbrella organization of Jewish institutions in France, which includes the Jewish places of worship body, the Consistoire Israélite.

32 *La Croix*, 22 May 2003.

33 *Témoignage chrétien*, 15 January 2004.

34 The Conference of Bishops, as the deputy of the Pope in France, represents institutional Catholicism; the Jewish Consistoire de Paris, controlled by the orthodox and ultra-orthodox tendencies, excludes the conservative and liberal trends of French Judaism.

35 On the colonial origins of the Muslim exception to laïcité, see Frégosi 1998.

Chapter 6

Interests, Identities, and the Public Sphere: Representing Islam in the Netherlands since the 1980s

Thijl Sunier

Introduction

For Muslims all over the world, but particularly in the Western world, 9/11 and successive events have made it very clear that, more than ever before, Islam has become a public issue. As Salvatore and Eickelman rightly state, '[...] Muslims have to confront issues concerning 'public Islam and the common good' in open and public debate' (2004: xi). Muslim representatives and spokesmen must not only be well-informed about rapidly evolving events, public opinions and policies concerning their religion. They must also possess the necessary communication skills to be able to take part in public debate effectively.

The modern media has not only contributed to a 'globalization of Muslim affairs'. It has created new audiences that ask new questions and challenge the traditional production of knowledge by Muslim scholars or *'ulama* (see also Birt, this volume). Eickelman and Anderson have seen in this process a 'reintellectualization of Islamic discourse' (1999: 12). Reintellectualization, they suggest, is rooted in a prioritizing of the current experiences of believers rather than in the conventional exegesis of religious texts. To reach an audience today requires much more than knowing traditional texts and commentaries. Muslim spokespersons must develop sensitivity to what is going on in the minds of contemporary believers, not only in terms of what takes place on a local level, but also on national and transnational levels. It requires the intellectual ability to 'translate' all this into a religious discourse that appeals and makes good sense to an audience.

The idea of 'public Islam' therefore refers to invocations of Islam, not just by traditional religious authorities but also by a range of voices including self-ascribed religious figures, secular intellectuals, women, youth and so on (Salvatore and Eickelman, 2004: xii). Moreover, any understanding of Islam in the West must combine an understanding of the defining features of both these Muslim actors and their associated movements and organizations, as well as the structural contexts of the Western contexts in which they reside. This chapter, then, will give an account of how Muslims have negotiated a public voice in Dutch society in recent decades.[1]

In assessing these developments, three separate, but crucially interrelated dimensions can be distinguished. The first concerns the political agendas of Muslim organizations. Why and how do 'Muslims' organize themselves and what are their objectives and demands vis-à-vis wider society? What sort of leadership exists? The second concerns the construction of identities in specific political contexts. How have Muslim identities developed over recent years and what role has Dutch society played in the construction of these identities? The third concerns the development of debates about the place of Islam in public space. The interrelation of these three dimensions determines, to a large extent, the path of integration into Dutch society. Although they are inextricably linked to one another, they nevertheless constitute separate fields that have their own dynamics. In assessing these three dimensions I will discuss some recent examples of how the presence of Islam has impacted on the political landscape in the Netherlands.

Muslims and Collective Organization: From Ethnicity to Islam

Muslim organizations with both political and non-political goals have been established in the Netherlands not because 'Islam' prescribes this (Nielsen, 1992) but rather because of well-chosen rational strategies by collective actors bounded by specific social and political contexts (compare Eisinger, 1973; Hechter et al., 1982; Jazouli, 1986; McAdam, 1982; McAdam et al., 2001). Initially, Muslim organizational activities were not especially informed by a specific notion of their position in Dutch society. Most Muslims simply considered themselves to be temporary sojourners and most mosques were centres serving 'migrants' and not 'citizens' (Landman, 1992; Sunier, 1996; Rath et al., 1996).

Towards the beginning of the 1980s, however, a turning point was reached. Migrants themselves, but also government, acknowledged that this 'myth of return' was unrealistic. The majority of migrants were in the Netherlands to stay and so, in 1983, the government issued a report in which the outline of a new policy towards their presence was formulated (Ministry of Internal Affairs, 1983: 38-42). The key terms of this policy were permanent residence and integration into Dutch society. Migrant organizations, including Islamic ones, were seen as a possible bridge between the individual migrant and wider society, a potential vehicle for smoothing the process of integration. As a consequence, such organizations were politically and ideologically incorporated into this Dutch brand of 'multiculturalism' (Sunier, 1996). As in Britain, cultural and religious identity became a basic 'right' (compare McLoughlin, this volume), not least because religious 'pillarization' has always been a structuring part of Dutch society. However, the government of the day was primarily concerned with such issues as labour, housing, education, welfare and their implicit final aim was always assimilation.

A sharp increase in the number of Islamic associations in the 1980s can partly be explained against the background of these policies which created the right political and ideological opportunities for Muslim organizations to begin to thrive (Sunier, 1996). Moreover, a new type of leadership emerged: entrepreneurs rather than 'ideologues', whose aim was the mobilization of as many resources as possible for their 'community'. Building up networks with Dutch policymakers and institutions, they acted as interlocutors with the state and wider society. They also emphasized that Islam must be considered the 'natural' form for 'self-organization' amongst Muslim migrants and that only they could 'translate' government policies for their rank-and-file. Moreover, by emphasizing the 'foreign' character of Islam as part of the distinctive ethnic and cultural heritage of specific groups of migrants, they were able to convince policymakers that each group required its own separate resources. As a result, in the 1980s, ethnically based Muslim organizations consolidated at the expense of supra-ethnic pan-Islamic initiatives.

Towards the end of the 1980s, however, several new developments resulted in another key turning point being reached. In terms of 'minority' policy-making, the sanctioning of the preservation of cultural identity, and the prominent role given to migrant organizations in this project, came under increasing pressure. The idea of the 'collective integration' of religious and cultural communities gradually gave way to a more 'individualized' connotation, associated with full-scale integration into society. Subsidies to minority organizations and projects were cut back considerably and they had to look for alternative means of support.

For Muslim organizations and their leadership, the late 1980s and early 1990s also marked a turning point. Young Muslims were gaining increasing influence. Dramatic local-global events such as the Rushdie Affair and the Gulf War, together with changing attitudes towards migrants, led many young Muslims to reconsider their position in Dutch society. In turn, they insisted that their own organizations take more interest in wider societal issues (Sunier, 1996). At this point, there were also several attempts to set up non-ethnic Muslim 'umbrella' organizations. Most important of these was the Foundation for Islam and Citizenship (Stichting Islam en Burgerschap or 'IB') established in 1996. This organization has the objective of improving understanding and sympathy for Islam amongst Dutch citizens by organizing meetings, conferences, courses, issuing press releases and so on.[2] The IB Foundation runs an office and actively takes part in public debates. For example, after the murder of Theo van Gogh (see below), they initiated a meeting to consider how Muslim representatives should deal with public reaction.

Many such actors adopted a strategy of 'pillarization' for Islam, arguing that, as individual citizens, migrants should integrate into society, but, as Muslims, they should have the right to set up their own institutions, just as Catholics and Protestants do. During the 1990s, this new Muslim leadership in the Netherlands treated pillarization simply as part of their rights as Dutch citizens. Indeed, this pillarization of Islam is more or less the political goal of the Platform for Contact between Muslims and Government (Contactorgaan Moslims en Overheid, 'CMO'), founded in February 2004. The immediate reason for the Platform's foundation was the tense situation post 9/11 and during its inaugural ceremony, the chairman expressed the hope that the CMO would establish a stable role as interlocutor of the government.

More important than attempts to set up representative national organizations have been developments at the local level. Before and after 9/11, local negotiations and struggles have been far more significant than the issue of representation on the national level, for it is most often at the local level that crucial interactions and confrontations take place. Representatives negotiate with local administrators about provisions, arrangements and measures that concern the local Muslim population, especially in terms of public services. However, these negotiations only occasionally feature in the media and represent a relatively 'easy job' for Muslim representatives, requiring little in terms of political and rhetorical skills. In some cases, however, local matters develop into national issues with supra-local implications. Simple negotiations about the building of a mosque can become national and even transnational affairs. In the politically tense, post 9/11, context, such situations are more likely to escalate than before.

The so-called 'Wester mosque' in the city of Amsterdam is a good case in point. In the late 1980s a local branch of Milli Görüsh, one of the fastest growing Turkish Islamic association in the Netherlands, bought the premises of a car dealership in the 'Baarsjes' neighbourhood of the city. It provisionally established a mosque complex with a prayer hall, dining facilities, shops and a large hall intended for sports. However, eventually the mosque committee wanted to demolish the existing buildings and replace them with a purpose-built complex. The local municipality was very much against this plan, not simply because it feared the negative response to such a 'foreign' symbol in the neighbourhood, but also because it wanted to use some of the area itself for house building. During the 1990s the two parties were involved in a bitter struggle over the future of the site (Lindo, 1999). Officially, the controversy had to do with the urban planning policies of the local government, but there was also a lot of resentment against Milli Görüsh and its plans amongst the neighbourhood's population. After a long period of negotiations a plan was finally agreed in the early 2000s with the Muslim leadership opting to design its new mosque in the architectural style of the Amsterdam School.

The complex negotiations involved in this case produced a type of Muslim representative whose significance extends far beyond the particular details of this localized dispute. For example, the present director of Milli Görüsh in the Netherlands, Haci Karacaer, became a very well known figure nation-wide. He has taken part in public debates, appeared on television and in magazines on a regular basis. His skill is that he is able to link discourses concerning local urban issues and identities to issues that have national or international significance and vice versa. Indeed, he has managed to create for Milli Görüsh, a movement that only ten years ago was branded 'fundamentalist' by the media, a relatively powerful position in the Netherlands. Their influence now extends far beyond what one would expect in terms of their actual size. By contrast, the much bigger, Diyanet, organization, representing the Turkish Presidency of Religious Affairs, has hardly any role to play in the current fierce debates about Islam in the Netherlands.

Identities and the Changing Political Context of Recognition

The concept of identity, the second of the three dimensions I intend to explore in this chapter, has only recently been 'discovered' by social scientists. Until a few decades ago identity had largely been discarded as a psychological concept that had little to do with culture (Eriksen, 2003). However, this situation is now radically altered and identity and culture often seem to be used interchangeably. Nevertheless, in many early studies of the 1970s and 1980s, especially those concerning Muslims, culture and (religious) identity were too often treated as self-evident and static phenomena. Power, social relations and politics hardly seemed to play a role (see, for example, Vermeulen, 1984; 1995) although, since the 1990s especially (see, for example, Werbner and Anwar, 1991), this has undoubtedly begun to change. The articulation of identities must now be understood as embedded within configurations of power, economic structures and relations of inequality (AlSayyad, 2002). Moreover, within such contexts, politically and socially situated groups such as 'Muslims' do not simply 'achieve' identities of their own choosing. Rather, their identities are also constructed in the context of 'ascription' by dominant discourses.

Various scholars have suggested that identity is closely related to the social organization of difference (Barth, 1969: 10) and developed in dialogue with 'significant others' (Taylor, 1992: 34). Indeed, according to Taylor, identity and the emergence of 'the politics of recognition' are closely related historically. The collapse of the old certainties associated with a pre-modern social hierarchy problematized the concepts of identity and recognition, giving way, by the eighteenth century, to a new concern for being 'true to oneself', for 'authenticity' and equal recognition (1992: 25-36). This was true in both individual and collective terms (the idea of a 'people' or a 'nation' with a 'culture').

Identities are always contested (Baumann, 1996). Two Muslims may adhere to the same religious message which binds them into a community, yet they interpret this message in completely different ways (Cohen, 1985). 'Muslim communities', therefore, rather than being stable groupings, are cross cut by the full range of cleavages that are typical of social life in a complex, urban and industrialized setting. The notion of one 'essential' Islamic community is untenable (compare al-Azmeh, 1994 on the idea of *Islams*) yet, as a political strategy, 'essentialism' is widespread and effective (see also, Jacobsen, this volume).

In the case of the Netherlands, identity and the politics of recognition first emerged as an issue amongst Muslims in the 1980s and 1990s. Under the strong influence of the Christian Democrat Party, which has been in power for many decades, a kind of quasi 'pillarization' policy was adopted.[3] The idea that Muslims (should) constitute a religious pillar is still a very powerful one but, as we have seen, the dominant discourse in the 1980s considered 'Muslim' associations as 'migrant' organizations. Their activities were judged primarily on their ability to assist in the process of integration and 'being Muslim' was still primarily associated with 'being a migrant' and 'being an outsider'. Nevertheless, it was also the 1980s that saw Islam become a public issue. International developments such as the Iranian revolution, the emergence of radical political Islam and, not least, events such as the Rushdie affair, ensured that Islam became a major focus for debate.

As a result, a specific image of Islam became established in public discourse. Islam increasingly became the dominant explanatory factor, not only for the specific (collective) behaviour of Muslims, but also for all kinds of social problems Muslims faced. This 'Islamization' of public discourse about Muslims, lead to a sort of narrowed awareness which suggested that: 'when one wants to know what goes on in the head of a Muslim, then one should study Islam'. All other possible explanations were reduced to 'the Islam factor' (Rath and Sunier, 1994). Although this line of thinking was not to be found explicitly in official documents, it was expressed in numerous newspapers and magazines and informed 'actual' political practice. Where initially migrants were referred to as 'Turks', or 'Moroccans', they were now increasingly bundled together as 'Muslims'.

The image of Islam that was constructed in the Netherlands of the 1980s and 1990s was based on the understanding that Muslims are the least integrated of all migrants. It was felt that, whereas the Netherlands was moving away from religion as a binding force, here was a new group asking for the sort of provision and consideration that had almost entirely disappeared in Dutch society. And this was not just any religion; it was one that was known for its anti-modern character. In such dominant discourse Muslims are seen as passive, fatalistic people who are inward looking. It is for such reasons that they rely so heavily on their faith. For example, a policy report by a local welfare organization in southern Rotterdam, reacting to the increasing influence of the local mosque in the community building process, suggested that '[...] For many Muslims the mosque is the central institution in their lives. This may create problems as their strict norms and values cause an increase in isolation'. The authors concluded that, for this reason, the participation of Muslim leaders in their organization's activities would jeopardize its emancipatory policies.

This image of Islam in the Netherlands was also understood in terms of the biases of Muslim migrants whose origins could be traced to a 'rural background'. Despite the partiality of such commentary, it did allow for the persistence of a certain 'difference' in society (that might well be temporary), providing that certain conditions were fulfilled. Indeed, this discourse suited the majority of Muslims in the 1980s. The 'multicultural' policies adopted were, on the whole, reasonably favourable to Islamic organizations (at least, as migrant organizations). They found it straightforward to convince policymakers that, for example, facilities in their institutions required upgrading so as to meet the standards of wider society. Nevertheless, there was an ongoing concern about the attitude of Muslims and their organizations towards the principles and priorities of the integration program developed by the government.

In the 1990s a new image of Islam made its way into public discourse, linking Muslims in the Netherlands directly to conflict and violence in the Middle East. Muslims were increasingly conceived as a 'fifth column', representing a potential threat to Dutch society. The ongoing debate about growing 'fundamentalism' among migrants, the alleged connections between Muslims 'here' and fundamentalist groups and regimes 'there', and the continuing strong orientation of Muslim diasporas towards their countries of origin, is all part of this image. For example, in his book on Islam in the Netherlands, *Against the Islamization of our Culture*, the politician, Pim Fortuyn (see below), warned of the all too unquestioning acceptance of financial and other ties between Islamic centres in the Netherlands and immigrants' countries of origin (Fortuyn, 1997).

The main difference between the dominant constructions of Islam in the 1980s and the 1990s is that whilst boundaries of difference were once seen as permeable they are not now. The current discourse is highly polarizing and suggests that Muslims will never become 'Dutch citizens' unless they abjure their religion completely. They do not 'fit' into the Dutch nation, since it is not simply the preservation of 'culture' that they aim for, but rather transnational political activism. A lack of 'loyalty' towards the Dutch State is seen as the main problem. Of course, the events of 9/11 have reinforced this image and made it the dominant one, as is the case in almost all the countries of Western Europe. The events not only caused a relative strengthening of this image, but also a revival of the arguments against Islamic institutions such as schools and mosques. For example, even Christian Democrats, traditionally strong defenders of pillarization and of freedom in education, now doubt whether this freedom should be extended to Islamic schools (Sunier, 2004).

Against the background of this heightened sensitivity concerning Islam, the debate about the position of *imams* in the Netherlands has taken a new turn. The majority of *imams* have always been 'imported' from migrants' countries of origins, especially Turkey and Morocco, and even in the 1980s there were attempts to establish training for them. Many politicians thought it important to see what possibilities there were to facilitate such training without discarding the legal separation of religion and state (Landman, 1996: 20). Language and other societal skills were considered important for *imams*, as well as a thorough knowledge of Dutch society, especially in terms of their ability to minister to the growing number of young Muslims born in the Netherlands. All in all, *imams* in the 1980s were considered a potentially useful instrument in fulfilling the integration objectives of the government. Indeed, *imams* trained in Turkey and recruited through the Diyanet have long been considered as an especially effective force against radicalism. However, the enormous diversity amongst Muslims in Dutch society, both ethnic and ideological, always suggested that the legitimacy of any 'new' *imams* trained in the Netherlands would be heavily contested (Landman, 1996).

In the course of the 1990s arguments about integration intensified and the influence of *imams* on young people of Muslim heritage became overstated, with *imams* made 'responsible' for incidents, such as 'gay bashing'. The best example of this in recent years was the so-called 'el-Moumni case'. A Moroccan *imam*, el-Moumni, was interviewed on Dutch television during May 2001 concerning what the Islamic sources said about homosexuality. When he stated that the sources considered it a 'disease', there was a huge public outcry. The *imam*'s statement provided further evidence for those who consider Islam fundamentally incongruent with Dutch values. However, there was a particular 'rough edge' to the debate because, just a few weeks earlier, two young Moroccans had been arrested for attacking homosexuals (*De Volkskrant*, 7 March 2001). In numerous media articles and debates following the interview with the *imam*, a direct link was established to the attacks, despite the fact that, as was argued by others, such youths are not usually regular mosque attenders.

Since 9/11 attention has shifted to *imams* said to preach hatred and anti-western sentiments. The government has gone so far as to stipulate that, from 2007 onwards, the recruitment of *imams* from migrants' countries of origin will be illegal. Muslims themselves have responded with many initiatives to establish educational facilities for *imams*, but the government has little enthusiasm for supporting such initiatives, either financially or materially; any application for funds is rejected by invoking the separation of religion and the state (see Ferrari, this volume). In fact, the hidden agenda of the Dutch government at present is the establishment of training facilities for *imams*, controlled entirely by the state. Many commentators, correctly in my view, consider this a serious violation of the constitutional freedom of religion, not least because the government wants a 'say' in the curriculum of what *imams* will study.

Islam and the Public Sphere

A third dimension relevant to our discussion here concerns the role of Islam in the public sphere. One of the most crucial aspects of developments since the late 1990s is public debate about Islam, not just in the 'neo-liberal' states of Western Europe but also in most Muslim-majority states.[4] Two aspects are especially important. First, public debates about Islam are in fact debates about the relationship between religion and the state, the place of Islam in the nation-state and the very character of those nation-states. This is certainly the case in Europe. Whatever one thinks of the presence of Muslims in the West, it is clear that the presence of Islam challenges the traditional character of European nation-states (Asad, 2002). However, these nation-states are not in any sense already 'accomplished'. Their formative history may extend back more than a century and a half but, as Billig (1995) has shown, even established nation-states must constantly 'reconfirm' and 're-enact' any sense of the 'status quo'. Hegemonic discourses and meta-narratives about the nation-state have to be told and retold, imagined and re-imagined. So, the very idea of Muslims arriving in an already 'completed' nation-state is part of the hegemonic discourse by which Muslims are, *a priori*, excluded from becoming part of the nation as 'Muslims'. The fuss that is made about *imams* saying 'nasty' things about western society, or the fear that 'our' democracies will be 'Islamized' by 'waves' of migrants with an Islamic background (Fortuyn, 1997; Khosrokhavar, 1997), proves, so to speak, the thesis that nation-sates are constantly 'contested' and 'defended'.

An essential aspect of the nation-building process is the construction of the terms by which different groups are included and excluded. The present turmoil about the many 'faces' of Islam, especially the focus on a small radical minority, is mainly an ideological debate about whether Muslims can be part of the nation and, if so, under what terms. It is a debate about the very character of the Dutch nation and it will influence its overall development in the future. More generally, concerns about possible terrorist attacks are conflated with discussions about the religious attitudes of ordinary Muslims.

However, contrary to what 'neo-liberals' claim, the public sphere is not a neutral arena in which all opinions are equally validated. Despite the formal and constitutional right of free speech and the rapid 'democratization of the modern media', the public sphere in the Netherlands is conditioned by unequal power relations. The modern state provides a semi-neutral legal and administrative framework, but as a socio-cultural network the nation is not neutral at all. The question, 'what is 'French' about France?' or 'what is 'Dutch' about the Netherlands?' can only be answered in terms of a particular historical narrative. This calls into question the often sharply drawn distinction between 'civic' nations such as France and 'ethnic' nations such as Germany. Even 'hard core' civic nation-states such as France require a certain degree of common culture, something which is provided mainly by certain formative narratives (Asad, 2002). In such narratives, some groups will occupy centre stage while others will find themselves at the periphery. Likewise, some will be represented in an 'early stage' of the narrative while others will only make their appearance towards its 'end'. In the course of the story of the nation, certain groups will move from the periphery towards the centre, the way that a particular story is told being a defining characteristic of the nation.

Newcomers or outsiders to the debate about the nation introduce new discourses that may disrupt established assumptions. Established participants in the public sphere dispose of a variety of means to counter such intrusions. As in the case of identities, the public sphere is necessarily (and not just contingently) articulated in and through power relations (Asad, 1999). Speech is not only limited by overt legal regulations, but also by implicit discursive conventions. Although all 'voices' can 'speak' in a liberal environment, this does not necessarily imply that they can be 'heard'. With respect to 'religious voices', there is an implicit assumption that a liberal moral and political discourse will be subscribed and applied. Other voices are neutralized or, rather, re-located as being 'outside' the prevailing order of things. In the present debate, for example, it is remarkable how easily that voices which try to 'explain' the motives and drives of terrorists are silenced. Certain opinions are considered more acceptable to the dominant discourse than others.

Debates about Muslims in the Netherlands clearly illustrate the above points. As we have seen, Islam started to become a public issue in Dutch society during the 1980s but a direct link between Islam and issues of national integration came to the fore in the early 1990s (after the Rushdie Affair and the first Gulf War). The first public figure to explicitly raise these issues was Liberal leader, Frits Bolkenstein, in a 1991 speech to the International Liberal Conference in Luzern. In his speech he called on European societies to be aware of the presence of Muslims and to think about how 'we' should relate to Islam and to 'our' own liberal roots (Bolkenstein, 1991). In hindsight, Bolkenstein's address was fairly moderate. Indeed, in a more recent publication he predicts, with typical liberal optimism, that Muslims will eventually be absorbed by modern society (Bolkenstein, 1997: 175).

By relating religion to matters of citizenship, civilization and nation building, Bolkenstein began a debate that was soon to be taken up by others. Towards the end of the 1990s, a growing number of intellectuals started to argue for a deepening and wider dissemination of national awareness and the protection of Dutch cultural identity, both in opposition to the presence of minority 'ethnic' groups and the issue of European unification (see, for example, De Beus, 1998; Scheffer, 2000; Schnabel, 1999; van Praag, 2000). The most explicit reference to Islam in such debates came in a 1997 book by Pim Fortuyn, before he became a maverick politician and was assassinated in 2002. The book was entitled, *Tegen de islamisering van onze cultuur: Nederlandse identiteit als fundament* (*Against the Islamization of our Culture: Dutch Identity as Foundation*).

Such pleas must be understood in terms of a reaction against the sense that many Dutch people were at a loss to define 'What is Dutch about Dutch national culture?' (van Ginkel 1999). Cultural feelings of national belonging had become so 'naturalized' in the Netherlands, it seems, that many thought it hardly worth contemplating. Of course, such a situation also posed dilemmas for 'ethnic' minorities: if they were required to 'integrate' into the nation, what was required of them, what exactly were they to integrate into? How could they hope to become fully-fledged citizens when the rules of the game were unclear and changing all the time?

After 9/11, however, the tone of the debate about Islam and national identity took yet another turn. While most neo-nationalists of the early years of the new millennium were careful about their representations of Islam and religion in general, the attacks on America and subsequent events triggered a much less circumspect response. In 2003, Den Boef, a Stalinist of the former Dutch Communist Party, wrote a book simply entitled, *The Netherlands Secular! Against religious privileges in legislation, rules, practices, habits and attitudes*. Den Boef accuses western scholars of Islam as acting as agents of Islam. Similarly, in the Dutch newspaper, *NRC Handelsblad*, the former Iranian refugee, Afshin Elian, writes almost on a weekly basis about what he considers Dutch society's biggest mistake: allowing Muslims to settle on their own terms. The resonance of Elian's voice in the public debate is enhanced, of course, by the fact that it is generally considered that he is somebody with 'inside knowledge'.

This is even more true of the former Somali refugee, Ayaan Hirsi Ali, who first became known a few years ago when she defected from the Dutch Labour Party and went over to the Liberal Party. After she accused the Prophet Muhammad of being a 'pervert' she was anonymously threatened with death (*Trouw*, 27 January 2003). Since then she has become a public figure who is cited and championed by politicians and the media alike as a role model for the emancipation of Muslim women. Her most recent exploit was a short documentary entitled *Submission* (Channel 3, 29 August 2004), concerning those verses in the Qur'an understood to have negative connotations for women. Interestingly, this provocative documentary aroused hardly any reaction from Muslims. Many thought it not worth the effort to protest, especially in the current climate.

These events took a dramatic turn, however, when the director of the documentary, Theo van Gogh, was murdered on 2 November 2004, apparently by a Dutch youth of Moroccan descent, born and raised in the Netherlands but with contacts in 'radical' circles. The assassination of van Gogh was immediately framed as a 'terrorist assault', not least because van Gogh was well known for his offensive statements about Islam. Indeed, a fierce debate broke out concerning freedom of speech, integration and the place of Islam in Dutch society. The most dangerous aspect of this current debate is that all nuance has completely disappeared and the public sphere is entirely dominated by a sort of 'secular fundamentalist' who seems to welcome every new incident involving Muslims as further proof for their opposition to Islam.

Aside from the sheer hostility which dominates this discourse, two main and inextricably entwined allegations are made. The first is that, instead of formulating clear limits as to what is acceptable and what is not, 'typical Dutch tolerance' has allowed Muslims to set up their institutions (schools, mosques and boards). The second is that these institutions now support all kinds of hideous practices including assaults on gay people, the suppression and circumcision of women, and the creation of terrorist networks. In short, the dominant discourse of the Dutch public sphere currently tends to endorse the view that Muslims have not only shown a lack of 'loyalty' to the Dutch nation (a state from which they benefit economically and politically), but that they have also used the freedom of the Netherlands to threaten the very well-being of that society.

Conclusions

Unlike the Rushdie Affair in the 1980s, the murder of Fortuyn and van Gogh in the 2000s has seen the emergence of Muslim representatives who are well able to counter allegations about Islam using appropriate and effective communication skills. The emerging new media have played a role in this shift but, whereas many critics of Islam still ask Muslims why, as 'outsiders', they do not 'go home', what seems decisive is that an increasing proportion of Muslims articulate their responses and demands as mature citizens. When, in a recent debate with the Christian Democrat Party, a representative of the Arab European League referred to 'the sovereignty of confessional groups', he was implicitly arguing that the time when Muslims simply 'requested' recognition in society was over: 'We no longer ask for something as if we are guests. We demand our place in society as equal citizens, whether you guys like it or not'.

Despite obvious parallels with the situation in other European countries, the developments in the Netherlands are uniquely 'Dutch' in many respects. This 'Dutchness' is revealed in a discourse that conflates issues of 'integration' with 'de-pillarization' and 'de-confessionalization'. As an organizing political principle in Dutch society, pillarization has almost entirely disappeared, but as a narrative it remains extremely powerful (Sunier, 2004). It embodies the idea of a Dutch tolerance towards all kinds of minorities that can be traced back to the seventeenth century when many refugees escaped from Spain. However, at the same time, it is now criticized as the narrative underlying the constituent elements of Dutch 'multicultural' policies in the 1980s. Muslim leaders should be aware of this.

References

Al-Azmeh, A. (1994), *Islams and Modernities*, London: Verso.
AlSayyad, N. and M. Castells (eds) (2002), *Muslim Europe or Euro Islam*, Lanham: Lexington Books.

Asad, T. (1999), 'Religion, Nation-state, Secularsim', in van der Veer, P. and H. Lehman (eds), *Nation and Religion*, Princeton: Princeton University Press, pp. 178-196.

Asad, T. (2002), 'Muslims and European Identity: Can Europe represent Islam?', in Pagden, A. (ed.), *The Idea of Europe*, Cambridge: Cambridge University Press, pp. 209-227.

Barth, F. (ed.) (1969), *Ethnic Groups and Boundaries. The Social Organization of Culture Difference*, London: George Allen and Unwin.

Baumann, G. (1996), *Contesting Culture: Discourses of Identity in Multi-ethnic London*, Cambridge: Cambridge University Press.

Billig, M. (1995), *Banal Nationalism*, London: Sage.

Bolkenstein, F. (1991), *Address to the Liberal International Conference at Luzern*, Den Haag: VVD.

Bolkenstein, F. (1997), *Moslims in de Polder*, Amsterdam: Contact.

Cohen, A.P. (1985), *The Symbolic Construction of Community*, London: Tavistock Publications.

De Beus, J. (1998), *De cultus van Vermijding*, Utrecht: Forum.

Den Boef, A. (2003), *Nederland Seculier!*, Amsterdam: Van Gennep.

Eickelman, D. and J.W. Anderson (eds) (2003), *New Media in the Muslim World: The Emerging Public Sphere*, Bloomington: Indiana UP.

Eisinger, P.K. (1973), 'The Conditions of Protest Behaviour in American Cities', *The American Political Science Review*, 67: 11-28.

Eriksen, T.H. (2003), *Ethnicity and Nationalism: Anthropological Perspectives*, London: Pluto Press. Second edition.

Fortuyn, P. (1997), *Tegen de islamisering van onze cultuur*, Utrecht: Bruna.

Hechter, M. (ed.) (1983), *The Microfoundations of Macrosociology*, Philadelphia: Temple University Press.

Hechter, M., D. Friedman and Appelbaum, M. (1982), 'A theory of Ethnic Collective Action', *International Migration Review*, 16(2), 412-434.

Jazouli, A. (1986), *L'action collective des jeunes Maghrébiens en France*, Paris: l'Harmattan.

Khosrokhavar, F. (1997), *Islam des Jeunes*, Paris: Flammarion.

Landman, N. (1992), *Van Mat tot Minaret*, Amsterdam: VU Uitgeverij.

Landman, N. (1996), *Imamopleiding in Nederland: kansen en knelpunten*, Den Haag: OcenW.

Lindo, F. (1999), *Heilige Wijsheid in Amsterdam*, Amsterdam: Het Spinhuis.

Mandaville, P. (2001), *Transnational Muslim Politics: Reimagining the Muslim Umma*, New York: Routledge.

McAdam, D. (1982), *Political Process and the Development of Black Insurgency 1930-1970*, Chicago: University of Chicago Press.

McAdam, D., S. Tarrow and C. Tilly (2001), *Dynamics of Contention*, Cambridge: Cambridge University Press.

Ministry of Internal Affairs (1983), *Minderhedennota*, Den Haag: BiZa.

Nielsen, J.S. (1992), *Muslims in Western Europe*, Edinburgh: Edinburgh University Press.

Rath, J. and T. Sunier (1994), 'Angst voor de islam in Nederland?, in Bot, W., van der Linden, M. and Went, R. (eds), *Kritiek: Jaarboek voor socialistische discussie en analyse 1993-1994*, Utrecht: Stichting Toestanden, 53-62.

Rath, J., R. Penninx, K. Groenendijk and A. Meyer (1996), *Nederland en zijn Islam*, Amsterdam: Het Spinhuis.

Salvatore, A. and D.F. Eickelman (eds) (2004), *Public Islam and the Common Good*, Leiden: Brill.

Scheffer, P. (2000), 'Het multiculturele drama', *NRC*, 29 January.

Schnabel, P. (1999), *De multiculturele illusie- Een pleidooi voor aanpassing en assimilatie*, Utrecht: Forum.

Sunier, T. (1996), *Islam in beweging: Turkse jongeren en islamitische organisaties*, Amsterdam: Het Spinhuis.

Sunier, T. (1998), 'Islam and the struggle over interests: religious collective action amongst Turkish Muslims in the Netherlands', in Vertovec, S. and Rogers, A. (eds), *Muslim European Youth: Reproducing Ethnicity, Religion, Culture*, Aldershot: Ashgate, 39-59.

Sunier, T. (2004), 'Naar een nieuwe schoolstrijd?', *BMGN*, 119 (4), 610-635.

Taylor, C. (1992), *Multiculturalism: Examining the Politics of Recognition*, Princeton: Princeton University Press.

van Ginkel, R. (1999), *Op zoek naar eigenheid. Denkbeelden en discussies over cultuur en identiteit in Nederland*, Den Haag: Sdu.

van Praag. C. (2000), 'Op zoek naar de grenzen van multicultureel Nederland', *Socialisme en Democratie*, 57 (3), 115-117.

Vermeulen, H. (1984), *Etnische groepen en grenzen: Surinamers, Chinezen en Turken*, Weesp: Het Wereldvenster.

Vermeulen, H. (1995), 'The Concept of Ethnicity, illustrated with examples from the geographical region of Macedonia', in Synak, B. (ed.), *The Ethnic Identities of European Minorities: Theory and Case Studies*, Gdansk: Wydawnictwo Uniwersytetu Gdanskiego, 41-58.

Werbner, P. and M. Anwar (eds) (1991), *Black and Ethnic Leaderships in Britain*, London: Routledge.

Notes

1   According to the latest statistics, there are some 900,000 people in the Netherlands with a Muslim background. They constitute 4.5 per cent of the total population of 16 million. Turks form the largest group, followed by Moroccans, Surinamese, Pakistanis and a few thousand Moluccans. In more recent years, a growing number of Muslims arrived as refugees from various countries such as the former Yugoslavia, Somalia, Iran, Afghanistan and Iraq.

2   See http://www.islamenburgerschap.nl/index1.html.

3   Very recently there have been some voices within the Christian Democrat Party arguing for a revision of 'pillarized' legislation. The dilemma is, of course, that a strict application of the principle of religious equality principle will jeopardize Christian interests as well.

4   For example, new media are playing a decisive role is this development. See Mandaville (2001) and Eickelman and Anderson (2003).

Chapter 7

New Modes of Social Interaction in Italy: Muslim Leaders and Local Society in Tuscany and Venetia

Chantal Saint-Blancat and Fabio Perocco

Introduction

Directly after the events of 9/11, several Muslim strategies of interaction could be observed in the public sphere of Italy. However, this plurality is rarely described or emphasized in mainstream coverage of Islam. During the entire month of October 2001, the press and the main television channels gave voice mainly to 'vocal leaders' such as Boubriki Bouchta, one of Turin's *imams*, or Adel Smith, president of the Union of Italian Muslims. On 5 November 2001, the latter declared, during the popular daily talk-show, 'Porta a Porta' on RAI Channel 1, that 'we should take the crosses off the walls of all public spaces in Italy, because it is not pleasant to see a dead corpse in miniature'. In contrast, no national newspapers or television programmes reported the numerous public appearances of local *imams* in several Northern Italian cities, the 'mosque open days' in Turin or Milan, the many conferences on Islam held during October and November 2001, or the Christian-Islamic summit organized by The Community of Saint Egidio (Rome, 3-4 October 2001). These contradictory accounts of the interaction between Muslims and Italian society are the result of a gradual and insidious social representation of 'Muslim immigration', which has in turn triggered certain vicious circles.

Specific socio-political contexts, or, better, 'backstages' (Goffman, 1974), condition the conduct of both Muslim and Italian actors. This national 'frame' will be discussed in the first part of the chapter. Second, the contrasting picture of interactions between Muslims and Italian society will be examined. A vast majority of Muslims affirm that they encounter no difficulties being Muslim in Italy (Saint-Blancat, 1999: 134). However, this should not imply that all consider Islam as a significant aspect of their 'social capital' as they interact with Italian society. In most cases Muslims seem to opt for a 'privatization of religious behaviour' (Saint-Blancat and Schmidt di Friedberg, 2002; Allam, 2002) and organize mainly as 'Senegalese' or 'Moroccan' workers within the national Trades Unions.

In this chapter, then, attention will focus on the kinds of interactions which would now seem to be determining the future of Muslims' participation and place in the Italian public space. Daily occurrences in Italian towns illustrate that some

Muslims, through conflict, negotiation, adaptation or combinations of these approaches, are trying to reverse the spread of prejudice against them. In Italy, local society responds to them with a mixture of reticence and suspicion, openness and solidarity, with each context of interaction bounded by cultural, political and historical particularities. Interaction is always a 'work in progress' but Muslim actors, be they lay or religious, are clear that they need to regain more control of national public discourses. Such a project of intervention requires the acquisition of competencies so that engagement with Italian institutional and non-institutional actors can be effective. It presupposes that Muslim representatives will learn how to cope with the media, an important dimension of the Italian debate on Islam. It also demands the interiorization of certain codes of behaviour necessary for the creation of trust. This chapter will analyse such matters in case studies of two contrasting local contexts, Tuscany and Venetia,[1] arguing that at the grassroots, Muslim leaders are creating new modes of interaction with wider society in Italy.[2]

The National Framework in Italy and the Construction of 'The Muslim Exception'

Islam in Italy has manifold expressions (Saint-Blancat, 1999). Muslim immigration is multi-national and heterogeneous in terms of migratory projects and practices. Immigrants have come from across northern Africa, the sub-Saharan area, the Balkans, the Middle East and Indo-Pakistan. The most authoritative source, dating from 2002, but before the amnesty involving 700,000 immigrants that same year, estimated that there are around 550,000 Muslims in Italy (excluding minors and converts). This corresponds to approximately 36 per cent of the immigrant population (Caritas, 2003: 219). The heterogeneity of the Muslim presence can also be measured in terms of religiosity, political and ideological orientation, and representation by organizations. Islam in Italy is therefore a complex reality, reproducing in small scale the internal differences of the Muslim world. Compared to other European countries, Muslim immigration into Italy has also been relatively rapid. However, as we shall see, the stabilization of this Muslim population has taken place in a diffuse and flexible manner, adapting to the environmental, economic and socio-cultural variety of the national context which is characterized by regional pluralism.

It was only around the middle of the 1990s that Italy became aware of Islam as an internal phenomenon. This realization contributed to the re-discovery of the country's collective memory of a Catholic identity and to the renewal of debate on unresolved matters such as the relationship between religion and the state (Pace, 1998). For example, in a pastoral letter of September 2000, the Cardinal of Bologna, G. Biffi, invited the government to operate selective immigration on the basis of religion.[3] This was followed by a demonstration organized by Lega Nord, a federalist, xenophobic, sometimes anti-Roman, party and part of the coalition currently in power. The demonstration, on 13 October 2000, was against the founding of a mosque in Lodi, Northern Italy (Saint-Blancat and Schmidt di Friedberg, in press). At the same time, the anti-Muslim positions of Don Baget

Bozzo, Silvio Berlusconi's counsellor, appeared on the front pages of national daily newspapers.[4]

Muslims, then, have gradually become constructed in such a way that makes them the 'exception' in Italian public space. By definition, 'Muslim culture' has become an obstacle to the process of integration, 'the other' of national identity. For a part of the Italian population Islam is a menace to democracy and laicism while, for others, a danger to Catholic identity (Saint-Blancat and Schmidt di Friedberg, 2002: 102). Nevertheless, whichever strategy Muslims adopt, withdrawal or public visibility, they are accused of being 'external' to and 'incompatible' with Italian society.

Various actors contribute to the definition of Islam in public space: opinion makers; political parties; the Church; the media and certain 'vocal leaders'. The Catholic Church, for example, both at the top and the bottom of its hierarchy, exhibits a contradiction in this respect. For years, the Church has been playing a fundamental role as mediator between Islam and Italian society (compare Jonker on Germany, this volume). It is peculiar, then, that certain high ranking representatives have openly advanced positions against Islam, thus infringing one of the golden rules concerning mutual understanding between public religions in secular societies (Casanova, 2000).

Overall, the recognition of Islam as a public religion has not been dealt with very decisively in Italy, with the debate often shifting to more general matters (Pace, 1998), especially the deficit of internal integration that has long been ailing Italy and the frailty of the Republic's founding pacts between liberals, Catholics and socialists. Together these two problems create a general absence of political legitimization.

The media, for its part, has strengthened the perception of Islam as an alien body and a totalizing socio-political order. This creates a sense of hostility, which sometimes gives rise to discrimination on the institutional and popular levels (EUMC, 2002; Open Society Institute, 2002). The voice of Muslims in Italy's public sphere is certainly peripheral and the media does not seek to represent the extent of existing debate among Muslims. Rather, it prefers to 'breed' interlocutors according to stereotypical expectations, thus creating the 'fundamentalist interlocutor'. Since 9/11, for example, the Italian media has represented Islam as essentially an international, and so, foreign phenomenon, enforcing a 'logic of suspicion' which systematically resorts to registers of fear and distance (Hall, 1997; Colombo, 1999).

The absence of a serious political debate about Islam in Italian public space allows hasty judgements to flourish. For the state, there is the risk of becoming 'lured by the petty provocations' (Zincone, 2003) of the 'vocal leaders' mentioned above, leaders who often represent no-one but themselves. Nonetheless, they feed the wildfire of discord. Adel Smith, an Italian citizen converted to Islam, who was recently involved in an Italian 'veil issue' of sorts, is an exemplary case of the media blowing matters all out of proportion. Smith lives in Ofena, a small town in the Abruzzo region. In September 2003 he asked the teachers in the pre-school his children were attending to either remove the crucifix from the classroom or to also exhibit *sura* 112 from the Qur'an. Faced with resistance from the principal, Smith turned to the local judicial authorities and, on 26 October, a judge in L'Aquila (the chief town in the region) passed judgement in his favour. A bitter national debate followed, regarding the relations between the lay state, the church and religious freedom, with indignant reactions from the Vatican and Catholic public opinion in general.

Building Local Social Interactions: Key Figures, Networks, Strategies, Partnerships

Far from the spotlight of such issues, however, 'anonymous' Muslims are silently creating very different sorts of social interactions within their localities. They occupy the social spaces left vacant by the failings of central power, and are able to develop real autonomy and exhibit real enterprise. In the two regional contexts of Tuscany and Venetia examined here, analysis will focus on four dimensions of interaction: i) the formation of Muslim representatives; ii) how they develop social networks and cultural competencies; iii) their communication strategies within the local public space; and iv) the extent to which they succeed in becoming both intermediaries with local society and representatives of their own community.

i) Key Muslim Figures: Continuities and Changes

The first waves of 'Muslim' immigration in the 1980s were amongst students of the middle class, who intended to achieve professional training as engineers, architects or doctors. They were mainly of Somali, Egyptian or Syrian origin and founded the USMI (Union of Italian Muslim Students). Some of these actors are still active in the direction or management of Muslim organizations in Italy and have been crucial in the creation of networks with local institutions, both political and religious. They also provided Muslims with basic needs, such as meeting places or opportunities to learn Italian.

As in Spain, Italian converts (Allievi, 1998) have acted as important mediators between Italian society and Muslim populations. The fact that native converts are citizens, together with their understanding of Italian institutions, partly explains why Italian Muslims are so vocal and constitute more or less the only recognized leadership amongst Muslim organizations today. The leaders of the Union of Islamic Communities and Organizations of Italy (UCOII), the Islamic Religious Community (COREIS) and the Italian Muslim Association (AMI) are all 'Italian' (Schmidt di Friedberg, 2001: 88). Of course, converts present contrasting profiles. Some, such as Hamza Piccardo (secretary of UCOII), or Ali Shutz (who manages the Fondaco dei Mori, a *halal* restaurant, club and library in Milan), are working unrelentingly for a better mutual understanding between Muslims and local communities. Others have contributed to widening the gap between Islam and Italian society through dogmatic overstatements typical of neo-zealots of all faiths. These leaders deliberately employ a provocative style of communication, aimed at hyperbolizing the bounds of difference.

Nowadays, however, the older generation of Muslim immigrants and the Italian converts are tending to be progressively substituted (in particular on a local level) by new figures: factory workers or small trading entrepreneurs, mainly Muslim 'aliens' who are not yet 'naturalized', but tend to consider their Italian born children as citizens. This present generation of new Muslim representatives has one thing in common with their elders. In most cases they still have to assume double functions. They play the traditional role of the *imam*: leading prayers, giving the Friday sermon (*khutba*), teaching Islam to children, presiding over rites of passage and offering religious and juridical advice as far as their competence goes. However, they were, and are, also constantly asked for help regarding numerous social issues: residence permits, housing problems, welfare and labour market opportunities, as well as the Byzantine Italian system of legislation.

Such demands leave little time and space to work on their lack of religious skills, and this begins to explain the feebleness of their credentials and knowledge in the field of theology and religion. Unlike Turks in Germany, Pakistanis in Great Britain, or Moroccans in Belgium, *imams* in Italy do not come from migrants' countries of origin. They are mainly elected informally amongst local Muslims, often because they have a better competence in the Arabic language, some religious knowledge and are fluent in Italian. Moreover, this selection does not generally take place according to the criteria of the Islamic tradition; it has more often to do with the capability of certain Muslim groups to control access to the resources of 'religious welfare', as Dassetto (2003) rightly suggests.

It is very difficult to know what sort of religious training these leaders have received. They tend to be elusive on this question. They could be more properly defined as auto-didactic scholars, who are, nevertheless, acknowledged and respected by those who choose them as leaders. Italian Islam is not institutionalized as in Britain, where Islamic seminaries provide religious education and send some students abroad to Al-Azhar or Medina (Lewis, 2004; Birt, this volume). This lack of theological competence may in the future represent a weakness in the face of the inevitable demands of the younger generations, born, socialized and educated in Italy. The *imam* of the Bassano Del Grappa Islamic Cultural Association in the flourishing Vicenza area, stresses this very clearly:[5]

> We are looking for an *imam*, but it is not easy, we do not want to import him from abroad, we want him to be from this area, we want to raise him here, so that he knows the context. We have one problem: the *imam*.[6]

It would be incorrect here to speak of a generation gap. Rather, the new leaders' personal projects in life (in terms of 'self-building'), combined with certain strategies of social mobility, have led them to their present duties.[7] Some of the most recent arrivals in Italy could not find either professional space or social opportunities to satisfy their ambitions at home. In Italy some will argue that, 'Here I can have my say'.[8] Some have progressively opted for an exclusive religious and community responsibility; others prefer to combine professional activities and their leadership functions. Moreover, political duties and social responsibility do not conflict with possible commercial success and enterprise. On the contrary, they reinforce the credibility of the public figure, both in the eyes of his community and a local culture where professional success is a relevant factor. Local experience is also conceived (even if it is not openly stated) as a preparation for the future in another context, not necessarily Italian. These, then, are 'mobile' leaders and 'glocal' personages.

In other ways, key Muslim figures in Italy may be considered as advanced as the Muslim leadership in the rest of Europe. Considering the relatively recent presence of Islam in Italy, their reaction to social challenges and their strategies of interaction are relatively well advanced. The lack of institutional acknowledgment of Islam lends priority to a role mediating between Muslims and local Italian contexts. This inevitably bears upon the kind of Islamic approach devised by these actors in terms of the framing of conduct, the production of meaning, orthopraxis, or the discourse on the status of women. Some are in favour of rigid and normative observance of the doxa. Others opt instead for a pragmatic understatement, which leaves room for a more flexible interpretation of religious categories. However, representatives do not yet manifest a capability to innovate in the interpretation of holy texts, perhaps the main challenge for European Islam as a whole.

ii) Developing Networks and Competence

Networks and social capital, both resources for individual and collective action, feed the flow of information and mutual trust between social actors and define the contents and the bounds of interchange and mutual expectations (Portes, 1998). Muslims, well aware of the function of these means in accelerating their insertion into Italian society, are creating such resources for themselves. Everyday interaction with local society begins with the gaining of the trust of neighbours, local craftsmen and traders, as prescribed by the Qur'an. Interacting, becoming known and respected, all contribute to the spread of credibility. The creation of networks is a task demanding patience and can only be achieved with time. Younger representatives are adept at understanding the rituals of interaction with Italians and they are able to choose skilfully between various styles of communication, depending on the addressee or on the chosen social field.

The creation of such networks takes place in various stages. First of all a middleman is sought, one who can give the community support: they are usually persons linked with lay or religious charitable workers, or a functionary with whom contact has been sought. A personal relationship of trust is created, perhaps with the school principal, the mayor, the councillor for immigration, or the person in charge of ecumenical and inter-faith dialogue. The next step is from informal interaction to institutionalization of the relationship through official requests, gaining visibility, acknowledgement and legitimacy.

A significant example of the creation of these sorts of interactions is the introduction of a Muslim chaplain to a jail in the Verona province, as related here by the chaplain himself. The *imam* first established contact with the Catholic priest who himself regularly visited the prison:

After six months of waiting, the prison governor granted permission. For three or four months we went to the prison every Friday and did fairly good relief work; around 70 people were attending Friday prayer. Then, suddenly, permission was denied. The official excuse was lack of formal agreement between Muslims and the Italian State. Then we contacted the UCOII President and queried the Ministry of Justice. This denial of permission infringed constitutional rights and so, in this case, a lawyer is to be hired to defend the community and the issue has to become public by means of protest in the national press.

Proof of their capability in this and other ways, then, gives Muslims the opportunity to defend their rights by means of legal action against obvious religious discrimination (see also Amiraux, this volume). The case in question also underlines that a local conflict can quickly achieve a national profile.[9]

Many aspects of Muslim / non-Muslim relations of course remain personal and unofficial. However, they sometimes prove to be as important as legal and official ones. Interaction revolves around a strategy of transparency combined with a rigorous respect for social norms. There is a tendency amongst actors to fearlessly display their difference, but at the same time prove that the existing codes of behaviour are understood, accepted and thus respected. A good example of this is the degree of openness in a Verona mosque: 'We have nothing to hide, enter and see our mosque, better still come and take pictures of us'.[10] This choice for visibility, contrasting with the 'underground Islam' common all over Europe in the 1960s, is spreading into all sorts of social spaces.

Creating social networks and increasing social capital means that Muslim representatives must develop the skills to work with a range of Italian institutions (the City Council, Police or Trades Unions). It means gaining the knowledge and confidence to interact with Christian colleagues or social workers. It also means dealing with issues on all fronts: being able to shift from the juridical resolution of conflict to social mediation. Leadership therefore requires the capability to change register, Goffman's (1974) famous 're-framing'. Today, Muslim public figures in Italy must demolish distrust and undo suspicion through the creation of networks and the employment of a calm yet assertive style of communication.

iii) Strategies of Communication in the Local Public Space

How do representatives create a strategy for visibility in the Italian public space? Which style of communication do they adopt, with whom, when and what are the main difficulties or obstacles they face as part of this process? How do they try to dismantle the social construction of 'the Muslim exception'? According to the *imam*, 'Rachid': 'Communicating means informing, creating relations and being visible, becoming known, reassuring'. Communication is, then, a huge task ranging from maintaining contacts with the media and the Church outside the Muslim community, to communication inside the local community and beyond to regional, national and international Muslim associations. Communication also takes a number of forms, involves the production of flyers for the visit of a 'brother' preacher, to utilizing the World Wide Web, and making public appearances on local television. Styles of communication (and, where appropriate, clothing) are changed depending on the target audience.

Conferences are another important vehicle for public communication, often held in co-operation with different public institutions, from high schools ('we must focus on the youths, there lies our future'), to state and theological universities, as well as the local bishop's see. Such conferences address public opinion as a whole and some are even held in local mosques. An increasingly systematic 'machinery' is therefore in place which attempts to diffuse and make visible more positive images of Islam.

In terms of the differences between the generations, younger Muslim representatives have an easier, more self-assured, and even cynical, approach to the types of relations one should create with the media. They know much better how to deal with journalists, thanks to accelerated experience 'on the ground'. Theirs is an 'active' perspective, which contrasts with the relatively 'passive' attitude of older representatives. Indeed, the general tendency until recently has been towards protecting the community and strengthening its own internal cohesion, rather than turning Muslims into actors involved in the Italian public space. Older representatives preferred to adopt a low profile and neutral positions regarding a public space they found far too politicized and 'mediatized'.[11]

Younger representatives have far fewer doubts in this respect, however. A typical attitude is, 'the media use us, therefore we have to use them'. After 9/11, some maintain that 'it is impossible to remain in silence'. If, on the one hand, 'Islamophobia' has seen Muslims withdraw into themselves, at the same time many younger representatives in particular have felt an urgent need to publicly fight stereotypes:

> The media simply label us. Common people, on the other hand, are divided in two groups depending on their attitude: those who see Muslims as extremists and terrorists; and those who have a more open mindset. Among Italians I see interest and a need for knowledge. We want to utilise this interest to create alliances with the people who have a similar point of view and share a set of values with us.[12]

Similarly, an *imam* in Castelfiorentino (Tuscany) remarks that while the national media often presents an image of Islam associated with terrorism and fanaticism, Muslims have a responsibility to represent themselves more positively:

> we have not presented ourselves well, we have not clearly stated who we are and what we want. It is also our fault, as we have not ourselves explained, showed what Islam is ... Muslims must not be invisible, they must instead ... present themselves well ... [showing] in an orderly and clean manner, that we do not want to be separated from society, but seek integration, being a part of the community in which we live, although pursuing our traditions and maintaining our culture.[13]

In many cases, however, this objective is still very far from being reached. Efforts at communication and public relations activities by some Islamic centres can prove counterproductive and strengthen stereotypes and prejudice against Islam. Frisina, for example, reports on a guided tour of the Misericordioso Mosque which was opened in 1988, in Segrate, a commune on the outskirts of Milan. The tour was intended for primary, junior high and high school pupils. However, the 'authoritarian and dogmatic' communication style of the guide, 'his attitude of superiority' and chosen examples (the authority of the male breadwinner), produced 'a rigid discourse, often impossible for most Italians to understand' (Frisina: 2003: 276-77).

iv) Becoming Partners and Points of Reference

One of the keys to successful communication is taking and adapting to new opportunities. An analysis of the plurality of strategies adopted in such situations can be illustrated by three very brief case studies. The first aims at a progressive institutionalization of relations. The second favours an informal tactic allowing for the integration of Muslims in a wide range of activities amongst local citizens. The third and final strategy considered here privileges a blurring of boundaries by employing a flexible identity which adapts to the demands and/or representations of the local society.

a) The choice of institutionalization The Islamic council of Vicenza is a federalized religious organization on a provincial level. It is extremely active in the field of intra-community cultural and social relations. Six *imams* sit on the council and its overall objective is gaining recognition as a religious community which maintains certain 'peculiarities', although there is also an emphasis on shared values and co-existence. The council has requested two things: the possibility of running multipurpose centres and opening schools for children. The council presents itself as the embodiment of 'moderate' Islam:

> We question ourselves regarding our traditions, the things that have to do with us. We do not question our basic principles, but we are *ready* to reconsider certain traditions which are bound to local context or to ethnicity, but which have nothing to do with Islam ... We have been waiting too long for public bodies to address us. Now we want to be assertive, and we mean to work within the projects of these bodies by suggesting ideas and bringing forth proposals.[14]

b) The informal strategy: how to be a Muslim Italian citizen A key feature of the activities of one of the main figures of the Cornuda Islamic Cultural Centre in the Treviso province, is the flexibility with which he approaches certain boundaries and roles. He often acts and presents himself as an 'immigrant', sometimes as a 'Moroccan', others as a 'charitable worker' or 'cultural mediator', and only exceptionally as 'Muslim'. However, while Islam is routinely left in the background, it has no less importance in reality. Islam is not employed as a means of penetrating public space or in the competition for leadership; rather its main function in social relations is as a referential system of values and meaning. This same person, 'Tariq', is for example, one of the main figures in the association Giovani Senza Frontiere, whose members are drawn from various nationalities, including Italian, and promote socio-cultural activities, such as the founding of an

Intercultural Centre. He also has close contacts with the local 'Caritas' (a major Roman Catholic non-governmental organization), with whom he organizes an important annual intercultural event, attracting around fifteen thousand people. Tariq is also active in the 'Peoples of the Book' association, a group for inter-religious dialogue. In other words, he is active on all fronts, first as an individual and only then as a member of his religious 'community'.

c) 'Deciding not to ride the tiger': the Intercultural Centre of Castelfiorentino[15]
This final case study shows how the space for manoeuvre available to Muslims is often determined by the local social order. After years of co-operation with public bodies to resolve the material problems of immigrants, the Islamic Association of Castelfiorentino has gained the status of 'mediator' by adopting the structure of opportunities offered by the public administration and local institutions. Significantly, the association has accepted the name of 'Intercultural Islamic Centre' conferred by the municipality, arriving at a local but public recognition of Islam. There is an acknowledgement that Islam is manifold, adapted to context, and not separated from the life of the locality. The centre is guided by 'Karim', who knows how institutions think and work, and how to interpret their requests and to comply with their demands. At the same time he manages to persuade immigrants to accept the administration's line of argument. He is a 'broker' (Boissevain, 1974) capable of investing the value of his capital of experience, language skills and networks, to the mutual benefit of the smooth insertion of Muslims in the local social environment.

The three strategies examined above are a symptom of the progressive normalization of Islam in European public space. Furthermore, they illuminate the dynamics at work within Muslim populations. Muslims question what is 'taken for granted' and left unsaid by conventional approaches to religion in European societies. In Europe, the institutional dimension of worship is favoured through the identification of a central authority with the right and duty to regulate religious life in the public sphere: that is to say, the state expects to encounter a Muslim representative who is both legitimate in its eyes and those of all Muslims. The artificial nature of this system, now also a problem for Catholicism (Hervieu-Léger, 2004: 134), leads, in the case of Muslims, to a logic of suspicion. Muslims are routinely challenged in terms of the legitimacy of their (theological-political) model of representation and the extent to which they are (sociologically) representative.

It is not surprising, then, to observe the emergence of a range of ideas about 'representation' and 'community' amongst Muslim representatives. Some, such as 'Ali' from Bassano (Venetia), refuse to frame their activities in terms of being a 'religious minority', perceiving the risk of a 'confessionalization' of Muslims.[16] 'Karim' from Castelfiorentino adopts a similar approach, meaning by 'the Muslim community', 'all Muslim brothers, even those who do not participate, who do not come to the mosque, even those who do not practice'.[17] Those who are not practicing are seen as in error, but they are 'brothers' nevertheless. In contrast, others do prefer to prioritize the religious dimension although they are open to adaptation. 'Malik', head of the Islamic Cultural Centre of Colle Valdesa (Tuscany), states:

Our identity as Muslims here, now, is to preserve our language, our literature, our food, our prayers. It means being a compact community which preserves certain principles ... but at the same time adapts our habits and lifestyles to this reality.[18]

Interestingly, in this respect, Malik has gained permission to conduct wedding ceremonies in the centre, with the couple signing the contract prescribed by Islamic law and the city council authenticating the union for civil purposes with its own official stamp.

Conclusion

The variety and complexity of the situations outlined above are due to the internal plurality of local society and Muslim populations in Italy. Muslim representatives are innovative social actors in these contexts, capable of adjusting flexibly to local socio-economic and political situations. Their strategies of 'bricolage' allow them to concretely face the challenges of integration, while at the same time safeguarding the preservation and transmission of Islamic religious, ethical and cultural capital for those generations of Muslims born in Italy.

In terms of representatives, one is confronted with heterogeneous and largely atypical figures. They are neither religiously learned men nor actual community leaders. They are often anonymous Muslims who daily rework and communicate a public definition of their culture. They are thus forced to negotiate both internal and external boundaries (Saint-Blancat, 2005), mediating the expectations of local society, its stereotypes and its implicit model of co-option, and, at the same time, facing the suspicions, the fears and the hardening of opinion in their own communities. Muslims are not dupes of the dominant discourse in Italy. As Baumann remarks, this 'represents the currency within which they must deal' (1996: 192) with the local and national establishment. Therefore they develop 'discursive competences in close connection with the social facts of everyday life, and they cultivate fine judgements of when to use what discourse in which situation' (Baumann 1996: 204).

Compared to what has taken place in other European societies, such as participation in local political life in Great Britain, or the emergence of an associational 'beurgeoisie' in France, the emergence of a mature Italian Muslim leadership is some way off. The arbitrary nature of Italian immigration policies (Sciortino, 1999; Perocco, 2003b) and the ambiguity of the Italian State concerning any institutional recognition of Islam (Ferrari, 2000), have certainly not helped. Nevertheless, the actors discussed here have come a long way, having created a social space for manoeuvre all of their own. Pragmatic and acrobatic in terms of manipulating religious categories they hardly master, these figures are difficult to classify. However, they do constitute the dynamic fringe in terms of the present processes of interaction between Muslims and local society in Italy. It is difficult to estimate how such interactions will evolve and what the outcomes of this patient daily interfacing will be. In particular, tensions on an international level make the situation especially unpredictable.

References

Allievi, A. (1998), *Les convertis à l'islam: Les nouveaux musulmans d'Europe*, Paris: L'harmattan.

Bagnasco, A. (1999), *Tracce di comunità*, Bologna: Il Mulino.

Baumann, G. (1996), *Contesting Culture*, Cambridge: Cambridge University Press.

Boissevain, J. (1974), *Friends of Friends*, Oxford: Basil Blackwell.

Caritas (2003), *Immigrazione: Dossier statistico 2003*, Roma: Ed. Anterem.

Casanova, J. (2000), *Oltre la secolarizzazione: Le religioni alla riconquista della sfera pubblica*, Bologna: Il Mulino.

Colombo, E. (1999), *Rappresentazioni dell'Altro: Lo straniero nella società occidentale*, Milano: Guerini.

Dassetto, F. (2003), 'Autorité: Représentation et leaders dans l'islam européen', paper presented at the Barcelona Conference, *Les autoritats religioses islàmiques a Europa*, 28 January.

EUMC (2002), *Anti-Islamic reactions in the EU after the terrorist acts against the USA: A collection of country reports from RAXEN national Focal Points: Italy*, Wien, Final Report.

Ferrari, S. (2000), *Musulmani in Italia. La condizione giuridica delle comunità islamiche*, Bologna: Il Mulino.

Frisina, A. (2003), 'Quale islam si propone e quale islam si recepisce? Un'analisi tra le scolaresche italiane. Il caso milanese,' in Colombo, A. and Sciortino, G. (eds), *Stranieri in Italia: Un'immigrazione normale*, Bologna: Il Mulino, 253-279.

Ginsborg, P. and Ramella, F. (1999), *Un'Italia minore: famiglia, istruzione e tradizioni civiche in Valdelsa*, Firenze: Giunti.

Goffman, E. (1974), *Frame Analysis*, New York: Harper and Row.

Hall, S. (1997), *Representation: Cultural Representations and Signifying Practices*, London: Sage.

Hervieu-Léger, D. (2004), 'La dérégulation des religions', *Cités*, hors série, 131-135.

Lewis, P. (2004), 'New Social Roles and Changing Patterns of Authority among British Ulama', *Archives de Sciences Sociales des Religions*, 125, janvier-mars, 169-189.

Open Society Institute (2002), *Monitoraggio della protezione delle minoranze nell'Unione Europea: la situazione dei musulmani in Italia*, Rapporto di ricerca.

Pace, E. (1998), *La nation italienne en crise*, Paris: Bayard.

Perocco, F. (2003a), 'L'islam nella società locale. Un'indagine sugli "stili di riconoscimento della differenza culturale" (Toscana e Veneto)', unpublished PhD thesis, Department of Sociology, University of Padua.

Perocco, F. (2003b), 'L'apartheid italiano', in Basso, P. and Perocco, F. (eds), *Gli immigrati in Europa: Disuguaglianze, razzismo, lotte*, Milano: Franco Angeli, 211-233.

Portes, A. (1998), 'Social Capital: its Origins and Applications in Modern Sociology', *Annual Review of Sociology*, 24, 1-24.

Recchi, E. and Allam, M. (2002), 'L'assimilazione degli immigrati nella società italiana' in Colombo, A. and Sciortino, G. (eds), *Stranieri in Italia: Assimilati ed esclusi*, Bologna: il Mulino, 119-141.

Saint-Blancat, C. (1999), 'Tra identità e fede: una religiosità plurale', in Saint-Blancat, C. (ed.), *L'islam in Italia: Una presenza plurale*, Roma: Edizioni Lavoro, 119-140.

Saint-Blancat, C. (2005), 'L'islam diasporique entre frontières externes et internes' in Michel, P. and Pace, E. (eds), *Itinéraires européens: nation(s) et religion(s) à l'épreuve du pluriel*, Paris: Presses des Sciences Politiques.

Saint-Blancat, C. and Schmidt di Friedberg, O. (2002), 'Mobilisations laïques et religieuses des musulmans en Italie', *Cahiers d'études sur la Mediterranée orientale et le monde turco-iranien*, 33, 91-106.

Saint-Blancat, C. and Schmidt di Friedberg, O. (in press), 'Why are Mosques a problem? Local Politics and Fear of Islam in Northern Italy', *Journal of Ethnic and Migration Studies*, 31 (6).

Schmidt di Friedberg, O. (2001), 'Being Muslim in the Italian Public Sphere: Islamic organizations in Turin and Trieste' in Shahid, W.A.R and van Koningsweld, P.S. (eds), *Religious Freedom and the Neutrality of the State: the Position of Islam in the European Union*, Leuven: Peeters, 87-106.

Sciortino, G. (1999), *Planning in the Dark: The Evolution of the Italian System of Immigration Controls*, in Hammar, T. and Brochmann, G. (eds), *Mechanisms of Immigration Controls*, London: Berg, 233-260.

Trigilia, C. (1986), *Grandi partiti e piccole imprese: Comunisti e democristiani nelle regioni a economia diffusa*, Bologna: Il Mulino.

Wihtol de Wenden, C. and Leveau, R. (2001), *La Beurgeoisie: Les trois âges de la vie associative issue de l'immigration*, Paris: CNRS Editions.

Zincone, G. (2003), 'La Chiesa, lo Stato e la coscienza religiosa?', *La Repubblica*, 31 October.

Notes

1   These two regions have very similar socio-economic structures but different cultural and political cultures. In Venetia, a deeply rooted Catholic culture is prevalent. Social consensus has long been based on the Catholic parish structure, a key actor in the mediation of interests, in the neutralization of conflict, and in the upkeep of cultural hegemony. Certain forms of cultural enclosure and localism can sometimes become transformed into political ideology as in the case of the Lega Nord movement (see below). Since the post-war period, Tuscany, by contrast, has witnessed the consolidation of a socialist political culture, supported by the structures of the communist party and of collateral organizations. The socialist tradition has managed to combine economic growth and public spirit (Trigiglia, 1986; Ginsborg and Ramella, 1999).

2   From April 2002 to July 2003, several in-depth interviews were conducted with Muslim representatives and local authorities. During the same period participant observation was undertaken in mosques and at several meetings between Muslims and local institutions.

3   'We must take seriously the question of saving the specific identity of the nation ... the case of Muslims must be considered with special attention. They have ... a different feast-day, a family Law that is incompatible with ours, an idea of women very remote from ours ... Overall, they have a decidedly fundamentalist view of public life. So, the perfect identification between religion and politics is part of their indubitable and unrenounceable faith, even if usually they wait prudently to proclaim it and assert it to the majority' (Biffi, 2000: 24).

4   For example, 'Muslims do not see Europe as the land of the traveller, but as a place where Jihad, holy war, is licit', *Corriere della Sera*, 17 October 2000.

5   Interview 'Ali', Bassano, 19 December 2002.

6   The problem of training *imams* is a priority all over Europe. See especially Birt, this volume.

7   There is no systematic study of the origins and social trajectories of association leaders in Italy. The very role of '*imam*' is variously defined. In larger Muslim centres, active and

established for more than 10 years, the distribution of duties is more developed and apportioned: an *imam* for the internal management of the mosque (rituals, Qur'anic teaching, cultural and/or relief activities), a figure responsible for public relations, and another (not always permanent) figure with preaching duties. In minor centres the same person fulfils all of the above functions and the perception of his role and the chosen style of communication depend largely on his personality and on the inputs he receives from the locality.

8   Interview 'Rachid', Verona, 24 April 2002.
9   For example, see the paradigmatic case of the mosque dispute in Lodi (Saint-Blancat and Schmidt di Friedberg, in press).
10 Interview 'Rachid', Verona, 24 April 2002.
11 Interview 'Ahmed', Padua, 11 June 2002.
12 Interview 'Hamid', Vicenza, 20 March 2003.
13 Interview 'Karim', Castelfiorentino, 10 November 2002.
14 Interview 'Ali', Bassano, 19 December 2002.
15 We borrow this suggestive expression from Schmidt di Friedberg (2001: 89).
16 Interview 'Ali', Bassano, 19 December 2002.
17 Interview 'Karim', Castelfiorentino, 10 November 2002.
18 Interview 'Malik', Colle Val d'Elsa, 22 May 2003.

Chapter 8

From 'Foreign Workers' to 'Sleepers': The Churches, the State and Germany's 'Discovery' of its Muslim Population

Gerdien Jonker

Introduction

Thanks to the Marshall Plan and the emerging contours of the Cold War, German industry boomed with an unprecedented *wirtschaftswunder* ('The Miracle Years') even before it was free of its Nazi past (Priemel, 2004). By 1952, this situation was prompting the mining and farming sectors to hire contingents of cheap foreign workers on their own initiative. Before long, the German government followed their example and was making official 'foreign worker' agreements with Italy (1955), Greece and Spain (1960), Turkey (1961) and Morocco and Tunisia (1965) (Hisasho, 1998: 42-50; Dietz, 2004: 136).

During this period German politicians wanted simply to acquire the benefits of cheap foreign labour without the additional burdens of making place for yet more migrants in society. The war was lost, the country was in ruins, whole cities had to be rebuilt and millions of returning Germans had themselves to be integrated. Therefore political decision-makers did their utmost to prevent other migrant groups from establishing permanent roots. Until 1965, when new legislation was enforced, decrees regarding non-nationals from the Nazi period remained in place, leaving foreign workers to the whims of their employers. While the new legislation did ameliorate the situation of those from the emerging European Community (EC) countries, as far as Turks, Tunisians and Moroccans were concerned, new 'residence permits' remained strictly tied to 'work permits' and were restricted to just one year. Nevertheless, those who had worked in Germany for more than five years were now allowed to apply for unlimited residency and the right to settle wherever they wished (Staatsangehörigkeitsrecht, 1992: 4).

Remarkably, it was not anticipated that this new opportunity for unlimited residency would encourage foreign workers to reunite their families in Germany. However, by 1970, many Turkish and Moroccan men had turned their backs on the basic dormitories in the *Gastarbeiterlager* and founded family homes.[1] Throughout the 1970s, due to family reunion and other factors, the number of Turkish migrants in Germany grew especially high, reaching 1.5 million. However, their unexpected settlement was generally considered undesirable. The German population, already having misgivings about making space for German refugees, was not ready to accept those who were 'visibly foreign' as well. Workers from rural Turkey especially, seemed to behave in 'foreign ways' and 'looked different'. Indeed, the leading newspapers often let themselves be drawn into propaganda campaigns against the Turks and published sensational articles concerning their assumed 'criminality' and 'sexual threat'. The oil crisis of the 1970s and ensuing unemployment did not improve matters, giving rise to the slogan 'German workers first!' as the growing number of unemployed foreigners were increasingly labelled 'parasites' (Herbert and Huhn, 2001: 201).

Interestingly, during the 1970s and 1980s, and in some ways until 9/11, Turkish and other migrants to Germany from Muslim countries were rarely stigmatized as 'Muslims', by either politicians or by the public at large. However, in 1992, public outrage at the 'cost' of accommodating 'new' 'asylum seekers' resulted in 'pogroms' against older and well established Turkish families. Significantly, these events occurred after the re-unification of Germany, a time when the west of the country was once more struggling to resettle and integrate some 13.5 million people. Many were ethnic Germans, although others were refugees from conflicts in countries such as Lebanon and Palestine (Pohl, 2004a: 11). Indeed, the number of migrants from Muslim countries rose from 2 million (of mainly Turkish origin) in 1990, to 3.5 million in 2002.

Despite these changes the German government was still reluctant to acknowledge that Germany had, *de facto*, become a country of immigration. Indeed, terrorist acts in New York and Madrid, allowed the focus of any perceived 'crisis' or 'threat' to be re-imagined not in terms of those formerly labelled as 'foreign workers' but rather in terms of 'Islam' and of 'Muslims'. The fact that Turks, Bosnians, Iranians and Palestinians had all been unassuming and obliging taxpayers who embraced a predominantly secular outlook was forgotten. The fact that no more than 70 individuals, with around 500 supporters, had apparently been involved with 'international terror networks' was also ignored. Indeed, 9/11 and its aftermath ensured that long expected legislation on 'integration' actually became a major building block of homeland defence against 'Muslim terrorism'.

In what follows, I will discuss the implications of this specifically German response to the politics of immigration and integration in three ways. First, in the absence of much initial interest from the state, I will evaluate the role that the Christian Churches have played as 'mediators' between Muslims and wider society, most especially in terms of their efforts to establish inter-religious dialogue. Second, I will explore why, after 9/11, the state and wider society, as well as some members of the Churches themselves, branded the initiators of such work as 'dewy-eyed' liberals who had naively opened doors to Muslim 'extremists', doors that would have been better kept shut. Third, and finally, I will discuss an example of how the government is now struggling to produce its own 'knowledge' about 'Muslims' in Germany, with reference to the problematic way in which a discussion group dealt with the question of why Muslim women might wear the veil.

The Significance of Christian-Muslim Dialogue in Germany

By the 1970s Germany constituted a largely secularized society and public discussion of religious matters was considered 'matter out of place'. For many intellectuals especially, religion represented an unwanted category of knowledge and there was a general distrust of religious language or any efforts in the direction of inter-religious encounter. Moreover, while social science dedicated a great deal of energy to the study of migration and ethnicity, the impact of these processes in religious terms received very little attention.[2] Unlike other Western European countries, German research on 'Islam in the modern world' did not initially encourage empirical work including work on an emerging European Islam. Political scientists sometimes questioned the opaque structures of Muslim organizations, the inflexibility of their leaders, imponderable international networks, gender inequality or the generation gap. However, instead of discussing these subjects in terms of transformations of traditional Islamic and Muslim self-understanding, they turned them, instead, into a resource for making political judgements about minority communities.

Despite the secularization of German society in the 1970s, both inside and outside the academy, certain public spaces did emerge which were hospitable to interaction with the emerging 'Muslim' presence. In particular, German Churches responded to the influx of Turkish workers and their 'unknown religion' by establishing a number of 'inter-faith' dialogue forums. The German constitution ascribes to both the Protestant and Catholic Churches a status halfway between state and society and the Churches have always sought to translate this status into certain semi-official responsibilities. Therefore, working within a religious frame, the Churches were amongst the first to perceive Turks as 'Muslims' and, moreover, addressed them on equal terms as fellow religious beings.

The implementation of these initiatives was not straightforward, however. A majority of first generation Turkish migrants had deep pride in their own national Republican culture and its founder, Kemal Atatürk. They were raised, and later raised their own children, to respect laicist ideology. While migrants from rural Anatolia were still very much influenced by traditional patterns of religious knowledge and conduct often associated with Sufism, in the world-view of Turkish officialdom, Islam represented a 'backward' tradition to be left behind. However, in their endeavour to establish inter-faith dialogue with Muslims, the Churches did not forge partnerships with laicist Muslims. Rather they established links with lay Sufi movements that did not represent the majority of the Turkish population. These were movements which in Turkey had protested against Kemalist policies of forced modernization and developed an intensive form of piety which became fused with missionary zeal (see Jonker, Chapter 12, this volume).

Representatives of the majority of Turks in Germany warned the Churches against their religious compatriots but this was largely ignored. According to German law the constitution recognizes 'religion' only in terms of 'churches' which are in turn defined as transparent membership organizations with certain bureaucratic features (Luhmann, 2000: 226-50). With this understanding of religion in mind, not surprisingly the Churches identified as partners those Muslim organizations which mirrored their own structures. Having left behind persecution and repression in Turkey, once the Sufi movements were relocated in Germany, they benefited from a new found religious freedom and were amongst the first to institutionalize as private organizations. When the Christians came calling, they were only too willing to oblige.

As far back as the peace treaty of Westphalia in 1648, the German Churches have maintained a tradition of dialogue. This is based upon the widespread conviction that, 'as long as one speaks with others one is protected from violence'.[3] For example, after the Second World War, Jewish-Christian reconciliation circles emerged to re-imagine the established pattern of dialogue in new ways. It was these circles which slowly built up public awareness of what had happened during the war. They worked towards an acknowledgement of 'guilt' at the different levels of German society and, more generally, tried to find some sort of common language 'after Auschwitz'.

Christian-Muslim dialogue in Germany began in 1976 on an entirely different footing. Even with the process of family reunion still underway and Turkish workers only just beginning to organize communal places for prayer, the Churches stepped forward, ready to act in their semi-official capacity as 'go-betweens'. It was the Protestant Church which first took the initiative, inviting the newly emerging Muslim communities to join Die Christlich-Islamische Arbeitsgruppe (ICA) (Christian-Muslim Working Group). This working group was intended to give Christians and Muslims the opportunity to get to know one other and discuss what was of 'common interest'. The idea was not to have individuals act independently but rather to build a communications structure shared between religious representatives from the very outset. It was also agreed that the findings of the working group should not have any official or binding character. Instead, internal recommendations and occasional press releases were to be the instruments with which members would communicate both to their own communities and to wider society. In its wake, local church and mosque communities were expected to initiate their own, local, dialogue circles throughout Germany. The recommendations of the working group were intended as a guide in this respect.[4]

It was in this context that the lay Sufi communities mentioned above moved centre stage while the majority of Muslims were left without representation. The religious character of these lay communities is not in question. However, the Churches did not understand the emphasis on individual responsibility as opposed to hierarchical authority in forms of Sunni Islam. In line with this tradition, Turkish, Bosnian, Kosovan and Palestinian Muslims, all overwhelmingly opted for an easy-going and individual form of religiosity in Germany that, if anything, intensified with old age.

To complicate matters further, expectations differed hugely on both sides. Christians felt that it was their responsibility to act as 'go-betweens' between the government and the foreign workers. They used the working group to gather information about an unknown religion and its influence on an unfamiliar group of people. In contrast, Muslim participants in the working group expected practical help, help that the Churches could not or would not provide. For example, Muslim parents wanted support in their struggles against co-educational sports and biology lessons with directors of education and school principals. Muslim organizations also needed advice on legal matters and practical assistance with finding plots for prayer halls or gaining permission for *halal* slaughter. Therefore, many Christian-Muslim 'encounters' resulted only in disillusion for Muslims, a reaction that Christians did not always understand.[5]

There is a good deal of literature covering these years. However, it involuntarily betrays the focal point of inter-faith dialogue. To give one example, in 1978, the Christian-Muslim Documentation Centre (Christlich-Islamische Begegnungs- und Dokumentationsstelle or CIBEDO) was established in Frankfurt and has since issued a steady stream of information about Islam and the situation of Muslims in Germany. This included accounts of Muslim organizations and institutions, Muslim law and customs, the situation of Muslim women and the question of 'mixed marriages'. At the same time, Christian theological journals identified what they considered common religious characteristics shared with Islam – such as the possession of Holy Scriptures, the belief in a monotheistic deity or the need for mission – and published scholarly discussions on these topics.[6]

Notwithstanding Germany's secular and, sometimes, anti-religious character, Church academies have retained a public function as meeting places for discussion and debate, while their organizing of workshops and summer schools on Islam became another important focus for the production of knowledge about Muslims. However, over the years, only a few Muslims have participated in such proceedings. Once again, representatives of the laicist Muslim majority were not invited but, this time, representatives of pious lay communities could not be convinced to participate. Left to themselves, then, was a relatively small group of individuals who for twenty years or more maintained a commitment to engagement. Although these dialogue partners came to appreciate one another over the years, and sometimes also developed personal friendships, their efforts to build more general trust between Muslims and Christians never really flourished. As one participant put it: 'We all loved one another [but] it was like a head without a body, floating somewhere in the air'.[7]

The dialogue initiative of the ICA, well meant and generally well organized as it was, therefore realized only a fraction of its original plan. One difficulty was that, during 25 years of dialogue, Muslim participants never had the same rootedness in organizations as their Christian partners. At the outset, they were mostly young and had limited education. They knew little of theology, were even less experienced in dialogue and lacked the contextual knowledge necessary to become public actors in German society. In contrast, Christian participants, as a rule, were highly educated theologians, older and more experienced in dialogue, well placed within their organizations and equipped with intimate knowledge of the workings of German society. In other words, the Churches' desire to communicate with Muslims confronted long-standing Christian institutions with the inexperienced representatives of nascent communities. This pattern of structural inequality between Muslim and Christian partners tended to be repeated across the country and consequently, meetings did not take place on a 'level playing field'. The non-binding character of the working groups also presented another obstacle. While the Churches largely put any recommendations to one side,[8] Muslim communities were struggling for survival and found it difficult to prioritize such 'external' matters (Leffers and Thielke, 1999; Best, 1999). Consequently, those Muslims who engaged in dialogue with Christians were largely left to themselves.

As time passed, the majority of Germany's Muslim communities felt misunderstood, isolated in respect of their many problems and, as a consequence, very frustrated (Jonker, 2002b: 9-25). In terms of dialogue, they felt it was predominantly Christian oriented, with even their most pressing needs rarely taken account of. As one *imam* in Berlin, looking back on those early years, explained: 'We did not come here to do theology. All we wanted was work and a little help'.[9]

In the late 1990s, however, the question of dialogue and communication between Muslims and non-Muslims in German society slowly began to change. In the last days of 1998, a new government of Social Democrats and Greens vowed to change integration politics. It set out to i) produce new citizenship legislation where *ius sanguinis* (birth right through blood) was to be complemented with *ius soli* (birth right through land), as well as ii) legislation that would enable the integration of former foreign workers, asylum-seekers and ethnic Germans alike. In order to become better informed about the different migrant organizations and to find ways of co-operating on the matters in hand, for the first time government departments sought to establish official contact with Muslim organizations.

In summer 2000 there were three Muslim umbrella organizations in Germany, several regional *shuras* or Muslim platforms and 2,400 local mosques (Wilamowitz-Möllendorf, 2001). Church academies once more played their role as 'go-betweens' (Fritsch-Oppermann, 1999). In addition, political academies organized their own meetings (Beck, 2001, 2002; Hartmann and Krannich, 2001). The Social Democrats, for their part, established political dialogue circles and platforms, in which, for instance, standards for religious – including Islamic – education were discussed. The Greens organized a series of workshops, in which young Muslims were invited to express their views (Hartmann and Krannich, 2001). Simply because they represented obviously 'religious' organizations, attention once again focussed more or less on the pious lay communities (see Chapter 12, this volume). In all these meetings, the mood alternated between pragmatism and cautious friendliness. Although voices could still be heard warning against 'oil money' and 'the fundamentalist threat', there was something in the air – the sense that a more genuine engagement with Muslims was about to break out.

State, Church and Muslim Responses to 9/11

In the days after the attack on New York's 'twin towers', Germany awoke to the terrible realization that it had been harbouring terrorists. It appeared that the leader of the 9/11 group, 'Muhammad Atta', and a diligent student at the Hamburg Technical University, 'Muhammad Al-Amir', had been one and the same person. The student had been the pride of his professor and had written an excellent paper on urban planning in Aleppo in which he argued that the quality of human life was being distorted by anonymous global forces. His shaken teacher described him as, 'friendly, very intelligent and intellectual, a clear-headed person who was always ready to help out. He smiled a lot.' (Maak, 2001: 1-2). Within a week the police had tracked down two more group members in Hamburg with their trails also leading to the cities of Bochum, Wiesbaden and Frankfurt. All students from Muslim countries were being screened, their fingerprints and photographs of their irises taken, their examination papers scrutinized and their web-sites closed down. It was estimated that approximately one hundred 'sleepers' lived on German soil. These new semantics expressed a new awareness. Borrowed from Bacteriology, the idea of 'sleepers' invoked the image of an infectious disease that had to be isolated and removed for the sake of public health (Briese, 2003: 181-99). It also aptly expressed the feeling of a loss of control. After all, the terrorists of New York and Washington had been studying at German universities without anyone recognizing the imminent danger (NN/3 2001: 2). People wondered, 'how could that have been possible?'.

Almost immediately it was rumoured that the terrorists had been supported by mosque organizations. The media, unfamiliar with the very real differences and diversity within the Muslim population, published lists of Muslim organizations in Germany which failed to distinguish between pious lay communities and groups such as Hamas, Hizbollah and Hizb al-Tahrir. Turkish secular organizations, which had been suspicious of their pious compatriots for some time, declared that the latter were nurturing 'extremist thinking', thereby enflaming the debate. As one of the few institutions that had observed the different groups and knew about their different orientations, the state organization safeguarding the constitution (*Verfassungsschutz*) could have set matters straight. However, for its own reasons, it chose not to. The secular character of the German government, its general lack of knowledge on religious matters and suspicion of using religious language, may all have played a role in the decision. Certainly, empirical research could have explained the structures of Muslim organizations and community life but, apart from a small number of in-depth studies (Heitmeyer, Müller and Schröder, 1997; Alacaioglu, 2000; Lemmen, 2000; Schiffauer, 2000; Nökel, 2000; Tietze, 2001; Jonker, 2002), such a literature was absent.

The Islamic Community of Milli Görüsh ('National View'), a large, Turkish grassroots movement with some 500 well-frequented mosques in Germany, was publicly accused of supporting terrorists. The energetic protests of its president, Mehmed Erbakan, received some echo in the press but his honesty was openly doubted. Indeed, it quickly became an accepted view that 'Milli Görüsh presents itself as a religious community but, under this cloak, in reality it unfolds economic and political activities which raise doubts about its harmlessness' (Rasche, 2001: 7). The tabloid newspapers were also quick to identify other pious communities as possible suspects and it was not long before the credibility of all Muslim organizations in Germany was in doubt. In the face of a 'global terrorist threat', little distinction was made between Islam and Islamism in Germany, with Muslims suddenly represented as a hidden danger.

Public semantics not only coined the idea of 'sleepers'; it also came up with the term 'dewy-eyed' for those Christians who, through their supposedly naïve approach to the Muslim presence, had initiated dialogue with Muslims. Amongst those stigmatized in this way were those Church officials who had drawn Muslim individuals into dialogue. Indeed, almost overnight, even the body of knowledge and experience that the Churches had generated during the many long years of dialogue had lost its validity. Politicians and the media alike unanimously pronounced that they did not know anything about Muslims. The need was felt for a different type of information.

How did the Churches react in this context? One experienced dialogue-initiator phrased it thus:

> In the past, before 11 September, we spoke about private religiosity only. We visited. We explained the functioning of a church or a mosque. We 'sniffed' one another so to speak. We preferred to avoid unsettling questions. After the attacks, however, we have become more challenging. There is this realization: 'What we discuss here is a matter of public interest'. But there are also misgivings. My people nowadays read the Qur'an and state in public that it contains nonsense. They also say that Islam, as a religion, is mischief. In the past, nobody dared to say things like that, but now this is becoming socially acceptable.[10]

The Catholic Bishops' Conference, meeting some weeks after 9/11, officially confirmed the Church's responsibility 'to search for ways to enable true encounter'. It should 'not just develop conflict avoiding strategies' but also 'competence for true dialogue' (NN/1 2001: 5). However, its spokesman, Cardinal Lehmann, summarized the relationship between the two faiths as 'speechless co-existence' (NN/1 2001: 5). Many Christians still faced the world of Islam 'as if it were a bulwark', he stated, thereby implicitly acknowledging the weakness of the dialogue enterprise.

Leaders of the Lutheran Church employed tougher language: 'Our representatives who maintain dialogue with Muslims cannot persist with their dewy-eyed innocence any more. They should make better use of the Protection of the Constitution' (NN/2, 2001: 4). In an internal recommendation, these same representatives, most of whom have been partners in dialogue for 25 long years, are strongly advised 'to first single out terrorist elements' before continuing with the project of dialogue. With Christian-Muslim dialogue now seen as a hopelessly 'romantic', 'cuddly', encounter in the German public sphere, the Protestant initiators of such work were thoroughly shaken by such vilification when they met in January 2002 in order to take stock of their situation.[11]

In the political arena discussions concerning Germany's Muslims have also hardened considerably. There is a new realization that mosque organizations, assumed to be breeding grounds for terrorists, represent only a fraction of the 'normal' Muslim population. Therefore politicians are increasingly listening to the voices of the 'laicist' Muslim majority, whereas the media attempts to uncover the 'secrets' they suspect religious organizations are attempting to hide from the public sphere. This, then, could have been the hour of the average, 'secular', Muslim. However, even the most assimilated citizens of Turkish descent are presently feeling the strain of being 'Muslim' in Germany. One of them, a politician with the Liberal party, has noted:

All German citizens of the Muslim creed find themselves under suspicion. Especially we Muslims of Turkish descent, we are deeply shocked. (...) Did nobody notice there were no terrorists of Turkish descent in the Hamburg group? We are made to pay for the crimes of others and feel utterly helpless. (Daimagüler, 2004: 11)

Unveiling Secrets? Knowledge, Power and Gender Stereotypes

Some months after 9/11, the government began to generate its own knowledge concerning Germany's Muslims. Among the ministries, an internal working group on Islam occupied itself with two concerns: one, strengthening the state's control over Muslim communities and at the same time, two, stimulating dialogue and civil society initiatives.[12] Likewise, political academies framed a new set of tasks for themselves including the collection of information that might be useful to politicians. As one of the actors involved reflected: 'we are searching for Muslim partners who represent their community, experts who are equipped with some spiritual or political authority, people who exercise influence over their communities'. However, as far as he was concerned, such Muslims did not exist – at least not in Germany. It was therefore his ambition to take direct control of influencing Muslim political opinion through the deliberate creation of 'an elite'.[13] However, in all the rounds of discussion that were organized, hardly any Muslims participated.

In Autumn 2002, an academy for political education (which for reasons of discretion must remain unnamed) began to host a discussion group on Islam consisting of an odd mixture of scholarly experts, Church officials and civil servants from one of the ministries keen to 'learn' about Muslims in Germany. Although the outcomes of the endeavours of this group are best described as 'informal', there was certainly an expectation that their 'findings' would be useful for policy and other decision-makers. At that time, a long court case concerning a young Afghan teacher who had applied for the right to wear her headscarf in the classroom was drawing to an end. Indeed, the issue was becoming extremely topical and controversial, with headscarves increasingly seen in the media as 'political weapons'. Therefore, the group decided to begin its reflections on the question of why Muslim women wear the veil.

Against this background the discussion group decided that it needed some sound information on the question of veiling. Therefore the membership decided to invite a secular scholar of Islam from a German university to one of their meetings, someone who happened to be of Middle Eastern descent. It was felt that this scholar could provide an account that would be scholarly and based on an intimate yet unbiased knowledge of 'what Muslims think' on the ground. On the evening in question, the scholar confidently explained to his audience that, according to the Islamic tradition, Muslim men consider 'their women' as 'sexual organs' and so are forced to cover them up. He added that one does not walk down the street with one's private parts uncovered and, glibly, that Muslims all over the world share such ideas.

This explanation met with general consent amongst the audience. For one thing, it confirmed the general suspicion that Muslim women were being oppressed, even when they themselves claimed the opposite. It also confirmed another suspicion, namely that Muslim men treated 'their women' in a way that did not meet Western standards of human rights and democracy. Even the constitution was referred to in questions and comments after the lecture. The 'sexualized' quality of the argument may also have exercised its own effect. Consisting of serious politicians after all, it is amazing that the group did not see the trap they were falling into. Throughout the ages, the characterization of one's opponent as possessing abnormal sexual tastes has been an acknowledged aspect of racial, ethnic and religious stereotyping. However, instead of turning inwards to reflect on their own doubts and fears, the lecturer's talk simply functioned to confirm many of the circle's own suspicions and moral outrage. As one discussion partner told me in private: 'The dirt must be isolated and out on the table'. With these words, the individual expressed his own righteousness, a response that to him legitimated a form of inquisition. It was in this vein that it was agreed to invite some Muslim women to the circle in order to hear their testimonies.

Two months later, three women were invited to a meeting of the group to comment upon the initial lecture. The first, a theologian, claimed that this was the first time she had heard about the 'sexual' argument. The author, she said, had quoted an Islamic tradition judged as having a 'weak' and dubious chain of transmission amongst Muslims. Indeed, she, herself, had never actually heard of the tradition, one which found no confirmation in the Qur'an in any case. For that reason, she suggested, the scholar's arguments should not be taken seriously. She also pointed out to the scholar (who was again present at the meeting) that he was not doing Muslim women in Germany any favours by spreading such a 'mischievous and backward train of thought'. The second woman, head of a women's organization in Berlin, reported that she had done some of her own investigations and had asked women in her organization why they covered their heads. She informed the gathering that the answers she had received ranged from the religious (for example, 'to stand humbly before God') to the worldly (for example, 'to *prevent* them from being treated as sexual objects'). Again, she stressed that she had never heard of the scholar's 'sexual' argument before. The third Muslim woman to speak did not bother with any arguments. She simply observed that the scholar's lecture had been 'bullshit' and 'insulting' and that, moreover, he was fully aware of this fact:

> We are fighting for integration and you are pissing us off. If you would repeat these words in any Berlin mosque community, I am convinced that people would bombard you with their shoes. I have a feeling that you somehow want to protect us, but I can ensure you: we don't need you for that![14]

The three women provoked uproar at the meeting. The suspicions of the audience proved to be stronger than the realities the women had tried to establish. In the ensuing discussion they were repeatedly accused of 'defending their men' and even charged with lying. The evening also proved to be a prelude to a seemingly endless discussion in the media on headscarves and the 'secrets' they 'conceal'. The direction of public discourse on the matter was just another example of how, within a year, the state and wider society's perceptions of Muslims had taken a decisive turn. A chain of rumours and arguments had been set in motion which connected terrorists to Muslim communities, 'Islamism' to 'Islam', Muslim men's treatment of 'their women' to Muslim women hiding 'secrets' under their veils. The impending terrorist threat had finally been anchored.

Conclusions

In the turmoil after the Second World War, foreign workers from outside Europe were brought to Germany to fill the gaps once occupied by slave labour. Theirs was almost a 'non-status' and political decision-makers neglected them accordingly. Foreign workers were not supposed to settle or integrate but more or less by accident family reunion changed this situation. Nevertheless, the idea that foreign workers would one day return home was upheld until the 1990s when parents and the state alike finally realized that German-born children were 'here to stay'. While 'isolation' had long typified the Turkish population, the 'pogroms' that followed German re-unification made it abundantly clear that the country had not accepted this 'foreign' presence. Against this context, Turkish students established migrant organizations that fought discrimination and sought to help their compatriots to integrate. However, such organizations did not address the religious needs of their communities. In public space, Turks were not really identified as 'Muslims' and, indeed, the majority did not wish to be identified as such.

The events of 9/11 turned this fragile equilibrium upside down. Suspicion of 'sleepers' set in motion a change in awareness with Islam suspected of breeding extremism and terrorism. Within the year, migrants from Muslim countries were stigmatized as dangerous people to be feared. However, as Germany had refused to see itself as country of immigration, it did not produce much knowledge about its Muslim population. Religion proved an unpopular subject in scholarship, producing no systematic empirical research on Muslim communities, their organizational structures, theology or religious conduct. Occasionally, the media filled this void with rumours and only church institutions collected information in an organized fashion. However, the information produced by the Churches was not of much interest to other sectors of German society. Politicians have started to generate their own knowledge about Muslims only in the face of perceived danger, creating the present curiosity of the security forces grappling with Islamic theology. The government's longstanding neglect has not helped Muslims integrate in Germany, an ideal that currently seems further away than ever.

References

Alacaioglu, H. (2000), *Deutsche Heimat Islam*, Cologne: Milli Görüsh Eigenverlag.
Beck, M.L. (ed.) (2001), *Der islamische Unterricht in Deutschland – Praxis, Konzepte – Perspektiven. Kolloquium am 16.11.99 im Bundesministerium für Arbeit*, Berlin: Die Bundesausländerbeauftragte.

Beck, M.L. (ed.) (2002), *Vom Dialog zum Kooperation. Fachgespräch am 5.12.2001 im Bundesministerium für Arbeit*, Berlin: Die Bundesausländerbeauftragte.

Best, U. (1999), 'Moscheen und ihre Kontakte nach Außen', Jonker, G. and Kapphan, A. (eds), *Moscheen und islamisches Leben in Berlin*, Berlin: Die Ausländerbeauftragte, 46-52.

Briese, O. (2003), 'Schläfer und Rasterfahndung: Kochs Konzept gesunder Keimträger', Nusser, Tanja et al. (eds), *Rasterfahndungen: Darstellungstechniken, Normierungsverfahren. Wahrnehmungskonstitution*, Bielefeld: transcript, 181-199.

CIBEDO (1978), *Christlich-Islamische Begegnungs- und Dokumentationsstelle*, Frankfurt am Main.

Daimagüler, M. (2004), 'Wort zu Freitag', *Frankfurter Allgemeine Zeitung*, 23 June.

Dietz, B. (2004), 'Arbeitskräftewanderungen nach Deutschland: politische und ökonomische Aspekte', *Strukturprobleme der deutschen und türkischen Wirtschaft und deren Lösung*, hg. von der Konrad Adenauer Stiftung, 136-148.

Eryilmaz, A. and Jamin, M. (1998), *Fremde Heimat: Eine Geschichte der Einwanderung aus der Türkei*, Essen: Klartext Verlag.

Fritsch-Oppermann, S. (1999), *Islam in Deutschland – Eine Religion sucht ihre Einbürgerung*, Loccum: Evangelische Akademie.

Hartmann, T. and Krannich, M. (eds) (2001), *Muslime im säkularen Rechtsstaat*, Berlin: Das Arabische Buch.

Heitmeyer, W., Müller, J. and Schröder, H. (1997), *Verlockender Fundamentalismus. Türkische Jugendliche in Deutschland*, Frankfurt am Main: Suhrkamp.

Herbert, U. and Huhn, K. (2001), 'Guestworkers and Policy on Guest Workers in the Federal Republic: From the Beginning of Recruitment in 1955 until its halt in 1973', in Schissler, H. (ed.), *The Miracle years: A Cultural History of West Germany 1949-1968*, Princeton: Princeton University Press, 187-218.

Hisasho, Y. (1998), 'Wir sind benötigt, aber nicht erwünscht: Zur Geschichte der ausländischen Arbeitnehmer in der Frühphase der Bundesrepublik', in Eryilmaz, A. and Jamin, M. (eds), *Fremde Heimat: Eine Geschichte der Einwanderung*, Essen: Klartext-Verlag, 39-55.

Jonker, G. (2002a), *Eine Wellenlänge zu Gott. Der Verband der Islamischen Kulturzentren in Europa*, Bielefeld: transcript Verlag.

Jonker, G. (2002b), 'Vom Dialog zur Kooperation: Probleme der Kommunikation zwischen Muslimen und der Mehrheitsgesellschaft – Analyse und praktische Beispiele', in Beck, M.L. (ed.), *Vom Dialog zum Kooperation. Fachgespräch am 5.12.2001 im Bundesministerium für Arbeit*, Berlin: Die Bundesausländerbeauftragte, 9-25.

Jonker, G. and Kapphan, A. (eds) (1999), *Moscheen und islamisches Leben in Berlin*, Berlin: Die Ausländerbeauftragte.

Leffers, I. and Thielcke, C. (1999), 'Zwischen Religion und Jugendarbeit: Angebote und Aktivitäten', in Jonker, G. and Kapphan, A. (eds), *Moscheen und islamisches Leben in Berlin*, Berlin: Die Ausländerbeauftragte, 30-35.

Lemmen, T. (2000), *Islamische Organisationen in Deutschland*, Berlin: Friedrich Ebert Stiftung.

Luhmann, N. (2000), *Die Religion der Gesellschaft*, Frankfurt: Suhrkamp.

Maak, N. (2001), 'In einer kleinen Stadt', *Frankfurter Allgemeine Zeitung*, 18 September, Feuilleton, 1-2.

McLoughlin, S. (2005), 'Migration, Diaspora and Transnationalism: Transformations of Religion and Culture in a Globalising Age', in Hinnells, J.R. (ed.), *The Routledge Companion to the Study of Religions*, London and New York: Routledge, pp. 526-549.

NN/1 (author unknown) (2001), 'Den Islam besser kennenlernen', *Frankfurter Allgemeine Zeitung*, 27 September.

NN/2 (author unknown) (2001), 'Evangelische Kirche erwägt kritischere Haltung zum Islam', *Frankfurter Allgemeine Zeitung*, 27 September.

NN/3 (author unknown) (2001), 'Das Netz der Terroristen', *Frankfurter Allgemeine Zeitung*, 29 September.

Nökel, S. (2000), 'Migration', in *Islamisierung und Identitätspolitiken: Zur Bedeutung der Religiosität junger Frauen in Deutschland*, Bielefeld: transcript Verlag.

Pohl, R. (2004a), *Zuwanderungsgesetz: Das 'Gesetz zur Steuerung und Begrenzung der Zuwanderung und zur Regelung des Aufenthalts und der Integration von Unionsbürgern und Ausländern'*, Kiel: Magazin Verlag.

Priemel, K.C. (2004), 'Nur keine Sentimentalitäten, bitte! Bilanzierung einer Firmengechichte: Der Erfolg von Flick', *Frankfurter Allgemeine Zeitung*, 7 August.

Rasche, U. (2001), 'Allah hat einen anderen Plan', *Frankfurter Allgemeine Zeitung*, 13 October.

Schiffauer, W. (2000), *Die Gottesmänner: Türkische Islamisten in Deutschland*, Frankfurt am Main: Suhrkamp.

Staatsangehörigkeitsrecht (1992), *Staatsangehörigkeitsrecht: Gesetze, Verträge, Verordnungen und Verwaltungsvorschriften (Mit einer ausführlichen Einführung von Kay Hailbronner und Günther Renner)*, München: Verlag C.H. Beck. Stand: 1. Juni.

Tietze, N. (2001), *Islamische Identitäten: Formen muslimischer Religiosität bei jungen Männern in Deutschland und Frankreich*, Hamburg: Hamburger Edition.

Wilamowitz-Möllendorf, U. von (ed.) (2001), *Türken in Deutschland*, St. Augustin: Conrad-Adenauer Stiftung.

Notes

1 The term *gastarbeiter* replaced the older term for 'foreign worker', *fremdarbeiter*, around 1965 as the latter held too many associations with the Nazi past. *Lager* or temporary dwellings were erected near factories, sometimes using the old concentration camps built for slave labour. An amazing collection of photographs concerning the living conditions in the *gastarbeiterlager* is published in Eryilmaz and Jamin (1998: 178-194).

2 On the impact of migration, diaspora and transnationalism studies on religious studies, see McLoughlin (2005).

3 Radio interview with Rita Süßmuth, former Chair of the German Bundestag, Deutschland (Radio 7, July 2001).

4 Interview with Christoph Elsas, Protestant member of the ICA since 1979 (7 January 2003).

5 *Ibid.*

6 Among these are the *Berliner Theologische Zeitschrift*, the *Theologische Rundschau*, the *Theologische Beiträge*, the *Herder-Korrespondenz*, the *Una Sancta* and the *Consilium*.

7 'How will dialogue continue?' – Workshop after 9/11 in the Protestant Academy of Loccum (7-9 January 2002).

8 Interview with Elsas, *op.cit.*

9 Interview with Nail Dural (13 May 2003), head *imam* of the Berlin Islamic Federation and a leader of his community since 1981.

10 Interview with Ernst Pulsfort, Spiritual Rector of the Catholic Academy in Berlin (26 January 2003).

11 Interview with Elsas, *op.cit.*

12 Interview with Heidrun Tempel, responsible for Churches and religious communities in the office of the Counsellor (28 January 2003).
13 Interview with 'Paul Bovenschen' (pseudonym), 20 January 2003.
14 The three Muslim women that spoke must also remain unnamed.

Section III
Practising Islam in Secular Contexts: Authority, Religiosity and Identity

Chapter 9

Migration and the Religiosity of Muslim Women in Spain

Gema Martín-Muñoz and Ana López-Sala

Introduction

This chapter presents the results of qualitative research based upon in-depth interviews with immigrant women of Moroccan heritage currently resident in Spain.[1] The Moroccan community is without doubt the most significant Muslim presence in the country. Moreover, smaller groupings, such as the Algerians and Pakistanis, are predominantly male. The research seeks to present Muslim women as active subjects and explore their perceptions of the process of social, cultural and religious adaptation that is taking place as part of their interactions with Spanish society. Fieldwork was conducted in the three regions with the largest concentration of Muslims (Madrid, Catalonia and Andalucía) and a total of 60 women were interviewed. The data presented here reflects the diversity of individual women's experiences and their discourses about religion. Nevertheless, it also reflects a profile that can be more generally identified within the Moroccan community (Khachani, 2000). Moreover, as we shall see, the research provides a deliberate counterpoint to the stereotyped and reductionist images of Islam and Muslims that are currently prevalent in Spain. For this reason, Spain's Catholic heritage and the current non-denominational framework of the Spanish State, requires some brief consideration first of all, as does the integration of Islam and Muslims within such a context.

Catholicism, the Non-denominational State and Islam: The Spanish Context

Spain's democratic Constitution of 1978 established a non-denominational state that was nevertheless compelled to confront a history in which Catholicism had played a significant role in defining official versions of national identity. This identity can be traced back especially to the reign of Isabel and Ferdinand, the so-called 'Catholic Monarchs' (Martín-Muñoz, 1996; Martín Corrales, 2002; Alcantud and Zabbal, 2003). Indeed, significantly for the contemporary context, mainstream historiography has established the idea that 'Spain' itself was a product of the Christian victory over Al-Andalus and of the expulsion of Muslims and Jews from the Iberian Peninsula.

Even more recently, the term *hispanidad* or hispanicity, coined in the early twentieth century, was employed intensively under Franco as one of the main pillars of a shared national identity. It was based upon linguistic and religious unity, upon the Spanish language and Catholicism (Zapata, 2005). Even today, the non-denominational state of Spain has endorsed an agreement with the Holy See securing it significant economic privileges and recognizing the hierarchy of the Catholic Church as a still dominant presence in Spanish society. These privileges include the option given to all Spanish taxpayers to allocate a percentage of their taxes to the Catholic Church. Religion is also present in the state-run public school system; under Socialist Party governments as a subject outside the core curriculum and under right-wing Popular Party governments as part of the curriculum.

Given this privileged relationship with the Church, the Spanish State eventually decided that, in democratic terms, it also had to arrive at agreements with other denominations and religions with deep historical roots in Spain. The aim of such agreements was to ensure rights to freedom of worship. Protestants and Jews both negotiated such accords and in 1992 Spain signed one of the most liberal agreements between the state and Islam in Europe. The Co-operation Agreement between the Spanish State and Spain's Islamic Commission (contained in law 26/92 of November 10) became the first directive to award legal status to Islam in the country since 1492.

The agreement recognizes the status of Islamic religious leaders and *imams*, warrants the legal protection of mosques as places of worship and accepts Muslim unions as common law marriages (although it does not recognize discriminatory practices against women contained within the institution of Muslim marriage, such as polygamy and repudiation). It also allows for Islamic education in state-run schools, the celebration of Muslim feasts and the state's collaboration with the Islamic Commission concerning the preservation and upkeep of Islam's historical and artistic heritage in Spain. A section of the text also contains an important historical testimony, though not without a 'modern' gloss, asserting that Islam 'has a secular tradition in our country, with significant relevance in the shaping of Spanish identity' (Zapata, 2005).

However, the reality is that this agreement was paid only scant attention and, more importantly, it was conceived only for Spanish converts to Islam and for those Muslims who had already attained Spanish nationality. It expressed the political will to make amends for the unfair treatment of Muslims in Al-Andalus yet was signed at a time when the new 'immigrant' Muslim presence had not been consolidated. Significant immigration flows began only in the late 1980s and their religious and social dimensions did not become especially evident until the mid-1990s. As a result, the representatives of the Islamic Commission – two federations formed by converts and 'nationalized' Muslims, the Spanish Federation of Islamic Religious Bodies and the Union of Islamic Communities in Spain, respectively – are quite detached from the realities of Muslim immigrants, and the latter hardly identify with, or feel represented by, the former. In addition, social and political resistance to implementing the terms of the agreement grew considerably as Spaniards' awareness of the new Muslim reality increased. Indeed, today, the accord is effectively meaningless (Moreras, 2003).

The arrival of new immigrants has inevitably begun to challenge the idea of 'Spanish uniformity', especially considering that Muslims (Moroccans in particular) represent the largest percentage of newcomers. The collective 'Moorophobic' memory, built up since the expulsion of the Moors, has become transformed into 'Islamophobic' sentiment. As such, the idea of Muslims as the most prominent 'other' has entered the public discourse of politicians, intellectuals and columnists. The notion of 'desirable immigrants' and 'intruding immigrants', with Muslims representing the latter, has gained widespread currency (SOS Racismo, 2002: 244-252; De Lucas, 2002). Indeed, increasingly there are arguments for a reorientation of demand for immigrant labour towards Latin America and Eastern Europe, because their shared Christian heritage is considered likely to ease integration. [2] Moreover, the Catholic hierarchy has frequently identified the 'threat' that the expansion of other religions could pose to Catholicism in Spain (compare Saint-Blancat and Perocco, this volume).

As a result of this situation, and despite the terms of the Agreement with the Islamic Commission, the practice of Islam in Spain has developed under very precarious and even clandestine conditions. It retains only limited visibility. In most cases, whenever that visibility has emerged as Muslims attempt to integrate their lives into Spanish society, for example, when they attempt to build a mosque, it has been met by feelings of negativity and conflict. The source of such tension is never the mosque in itself, but rather the perceptions that local residents have of the Muslim presence. Instead of interpreting this as the result of new social interactions, it is routinely experienced and expressed in terms of a threat to existing identities and cultures (Martín-Muñoz, 2003: 119-127).

If the 9/11 attacks heightened suspicion of Muslims in Spain as Bin Laden's 'hidden weapons', not surprisingly, it was the 11 March attacks on Madrid in 2004 that triggered most response. Immigrants of Muslim origin and, particularly, their public symbols (prayer rooms, mosques and *imams*) became the focus of intense fears (Moreras, 2005). However, immediately after the attacks, and unlike the United States following 9/11, the immediate reaction was almost serene and there was a general absence of xenophobia. Nevertheless, rather than building on the sentiments of peace, the media and prominent spokespersons of apparently secular Moroccan immigrant organizations quickly set alarm bells ringing with comments about the religious radicalization of Muslim communities in Spain (compare Jonker, Chapter 8, this volume). Ultimately, such interventions have played a crucial role in persuading public opinion that a 'defensive' and 'preventative' stance towards Muslims in Spain is necessary.[3]

The view that more controls on Muslim communities in Spain are needed in the interests of security is gaining ground on the view that defends their integration within the framework of Spain's non-denominational state. However, the political authorities have found themselves suddenly facing the problem of just how to control mosques and *imams* with Islamic ritual practice having been clandestine for so long as Muslims sought social invisibility. Moreover, the authorities' attempts to normalize and give a legal status to Islam are also encumbered by public opinion which opposes, more than ever, the visibility of Muslim places of worship and the equal rights of Muslims before the law. A couple of examples will be instructive.

The decision of Andalucía's regional government to make 6,000 square metres of land available for the building of a mosque in Seville sparked a 'social revolution' amongst local residents (*El País*, *Andalucía*, 5 December 2004). This was the case even though the project was part of a wider government plan to allow four religious denominations to build on public land as a way of effecting the principle of religious non-discrimination. Nevertheless, there were still protests against the building of the mosque in an area of Seville where 5,000 to 7,000 Muslims live and there are currently no mosques. Residents argued that, in a non-denominational state, public land can not be used for the building of a place of worship. However, such a defence of secularism seems only to emerge when Islamic, and not Christian denominations, are involved. Similarly, in 2004, the decision of the Justice Ministry, through the General Secretariat for Religious Affairs, to enforce the law allowing for Islamic education in schools (where ten or more students are Muslim) sparked a very negative reaction. Indeed, in the wake of the 'Islamization' of the issue, the real debate about whether religion should be taught at all in a public system of education has been somewhat ignored.

For the purposes of the present chapter on Muslim women's religiosity, the Spanish approach to the headscarf (*hijab*) in state schools is also worthy of more detailed discussion. Controversy first emerged in February 2002 when a Moroccan girl in a Madrid school insisted on wearing a headscarf in class. Her case triggered a huge debate, especially when compared to the meagre discussion of the violent racist attacks against Moroccan workers in El Ejido during 2000. Following the main pattern of argument deployed in other European countries, mainstream opinion presented the headscarf in terms of a 'threat to our modern cultural values'. More interesting, however, was the reaction of the educational authorities. When another Moroccan girl was expelled from a Catholic school for wearing the headscarf, education authorities forced a state-run school to admit the student, still wearing her *hijab*, to ensure that her education continued. In this case the state did not ignore its obligation to provide all children with an education. However, at no point was the Catholic school – partly funded by the state and, as such, a public entity obliged to admit the children of immigrants – held to account or required to readmit the girl.

Clearly, the continuing impact of Spain's religious heritage in public education is still an issue. Nevertheless, the headscarf debate has remained for the most part in abeyance since 2002, partly because state-funded religious schools use various strategies to prevent the admission of the children of immigrants but also because Muslim girls who wear the headscarf are now well integrated into the state system. It is becoming clear to all that the *hijab* does not affect their learning experience or their relationships with teachers and other students. This does not mean that the debate is now closed, however, since the use of *hijab* among Muslim women still triggers negative social reactions and culturalist interpretations concerning Islam, as we shall see in the interview material to be discussed now.

Difference and Diversity: The Migration Profiles of Muslim Women in Spain

The existence of transnational families and communities is a key factor in determining Moroccan women's decisions to migrate to Spain. Indeed, having relatives or friends who can ease adaptation immediately after arrival is often a determining factor. The desire to enhance professional and educational opportunities is also significant however. Although many women need to undertake low-skilled jobs in the short term, this is often part of a personal project of individual development which embraces expectations of social and professional improvement. Therefore many – especially single and younger – women cite the need to acquire, or improve their level of, education as a factor in deciding to emigrate. Indeed, without doubt, it is the most significant variable in shaping the range of religious discourses outlined in this chapter.

A significant number of the Moroccan women interviewed no longer think of returning to their home country. The option of return is hardly mentioned by young educated women especially. Such attitudes are closely linked to their pessimistic vision of future economic development in Morocco. Moreover, it is this changing and more stable understanding that they are 'here to stay' that underlines the realization that Spain is where they will structure their future lives and those of their children. This has, in turn, fostered expectations of both integration and improved social status. It is in this context that Muslim identity is reasserted, not least because of a desire to transmit Islamic values to the next generation. At the same time, a concern for 'roots' also underlines the fact that women's ties with Morocco are not necessarily weakened. Even those who migrate alone preserve strong family ties with their home country. Nevertheless, given their commitment to a life in Spain, there is an increasingly clear demand for the legal regularization of their immigration status, a demand which reflects the many hurdles that the immigration system imposes upon them.

Contrary to culturalist stereotypes of a homogeneous and monolithic grouping, our fieldwork reinforces the idea of 'Muslim women' as a diverse constituency (Modood, 2000; Martín-Muñoz, 1998; 2002). In particular, it suggests a profile of at least five different categories, which together begin to represent the wide range of Muslim women's experience in Spain. These categories reflect diverse circumstances and experiences of life in Spain and vary with age, marital status, educational level and a rural or urban origin.

First is the category of *entrepreneurial women*, encompassing those who have embarked on the migratory experience alone and who, in some cases, later contemplate family reunification. Within this group we find both: a) young women with university degrees whose migratory project is professional rather than personal; and b) divorced, separated or widowed women whose migratory project is motivated by both economic and family reasons. However, amongst the entrepreneurs it is rare to come across married women with family obligations.

A second category includes *the wives* who join husbands who have lived in Spain for a few years already. This grouping tends to experience most difficulty integrating because their interactions with the outside world are limited and often rely – especially in the early stages – on their husband's and children's mediation. Nevertheless, such women do tend eventually to join the labour market.

A third category of Muslim women in Spain encompasses *the children* of migrant parents, both young girls and teenagers. Although it is unusual, some who are brought to Spain by their parents, stay on with other relatives (usually uncles or other close family members) while their parents return to Morocco. Most are brought to Spain to study or to help out with housework in their relatives' family home.[4]

A fourth, less frequently occurring, category of women are *elderly and dependent members of extended families* who have male or female relatives already settled in Spain. Many grandmothers, for instance, take care of their grandchildren while parents go out to work.

Finally, there are *the students* from Morocco who have travelled to Spain to study for an undergraduate or postgraduate degree. These women have a deeper knowledge of the host society than other segments of the migrant community, and they can be very active, economically as well as socially. Moroccan women registered in Spanish universities have a relatively stable legal status, which they later use as a base for entering the labour market. Moroccan graduates report that things have opened up in this respect in both the public and private sector during the last 3 or 4 years especially. Language schools, overseas trade departments in some companies, tourism, as well as 'social mediation' roles in local authorities and non-governmental organizations, provide new working possibilities. Some also entertain the possibility of self-employment.

Relocating and Transmitting Islam: Migration and Women's Religious Practice

Most of the Muslim women interviewed as part of our research believed that migration had resulted in a relaxation of religious obligations amongst the majority of their compatriots. Despite this, all of the interviewees, except those who were already non-practising, admitted that they remained loyal to their religious obligations in Spain. Indeed, their practices remaining unchanged, a typical response being: 'It's the same here as there, nothing changes, there's no problem'. However, we discovered that attitudes towards religious practice were actually fed by two kinds of discourses that depended largely on i) the length of residence in Spain and ii) the existence of family ties in Spain. As has been the case elsewhere in Europe, the reunification of families as well as the assumption that they are 'here to stay', bolsters communal and public efforts to reconstruct complex universes of meaning associated with customs and traditions.

During the first stages of the migration process most immigrants chose not to vindicate or reassert their religious and cultural worlds. Male workers moving temporarily overseas to improve their living standards formed the bulk of these early migrants (Abu Tarbush, 2002; Aubarell and Zapata, 2003). Today, however, the feeling of permanent settlement in Spain is strong, and this situation has given rise to the question of identity amongst Muslims. There is increased self-awareness, both individually and collectively, of what it might mean to be a future 'citizen' with rights and duties within Spanish society. It is in such spaces that a new religious visibility as well as a new need to ensure freedom of, and recognition for, religion (mosques, cemeteries, *halal* food) has emerged.

Our research suggests that this process of 'identification' with religion is particularly significant amongst women, not only in the public sphere but also in more domestic spaces. Within the family unit, as soon as they become mothers, women are the ones who are most often responsible for the transmission of Islam to the younger generations. Indeed, the degree of women's organization and action in this respect, their ensuring of the existence of the necessary means, instruments and institutions to transmit their Muslim heritage, is a key indicator of the importance of this process. As they normalize their Islamic life in Spain, it is also an indication of the degree of their integration (Spinner-Halev, 2000).

Amongst the Muslim women interviewed the desire to transmit their religious identity to their children is very strong. Of particular relevance is their deep concern about the distancing of some younger women from the framework of rectitude provided by Islam. The transmission of Muslim values, say interviewees, is at present exclusively in their families' hands, especially considering that schools in Spain do not fulfil this function. Therefore, women with children are forwarding a double demand: first that schools reflect the values of their society of origin and, second, that a larger number of meeting places and associations are provided where second generation and migrant children can enhance their understanding of their parents' culture and language. For example, one mother told us:

> Before I didn't care that much about it, but as I see them grow I start hesitating. Because they must know who they are, and that's only possible if we go on holiday, but I would also like it to happen here. The truth is that it feels like two different forces. One tells me we can't return because in economic terms things there are bad ... but here there are many things that can't be.

The reuniting of migrant families therefore presents new demands that must in part be met by the wider society; these are needs that, to an extent, can ultimately foster a more intense relationship with the Spanish environment, for example, in terms of neighbourly relations, where women usually take the initiative.

Our interviewees considered themselves firstly as women and then secondly as Muslims in terms of culture and beliefs. This was a universal rule among all respondents, regardless of educational levels and lifestyles. All abided, to varying degrees, by an orthodox approach to religious practice. Indeed, their continued adherence to Islam's cultural and religious values in the context of migration came to define their identity. In this respect most indicated that their national allegiance was less relevant than being Muslim. Some respondents, who have reflected upon this, explain it in terms of the weakness of citizenship in Morocco. Notably, civic identity was not strong amongst the interviewees, whereas more personalized and substantive values represented in terms of Islam, were.

Regardless of the prevailing discourse on Islam in Spain, for our respondents their Muslim identity was not in conflict with women's development and female emancipation. On the contrary, these two elements coexisted easily. For example, having a profession is seen as compatible with daily religious practice. Therefore we did not observe any conflict between women's different roles but rather a balanced incorporation of different reference points adapted to their new environment. Significantly, the multiplicity of Muslim women's roles and identities would seem to be more of a problem for Spanish society, most especially in terms of the gap between popular stereotypes and everyday realities (Colectivo IOE, 1995; ASEP, 1998).

The women we interviewed reported that they had not encountered any serious difficulties in performing their religious duties in Spain. Most had continued with their daily prayer routines and observed the fast of Ramadan. Certain contradictions emerged throughout the interviews, however, which led us to conclude that while observance of Ramadan remains a common practice, prayers either lose some significance or are 'adapted' in Spain. For example, break-times at work are used for prayers or women 'pray everything at night'. Other respondents say that Spain's long working days and commutes to work prevent them from fulfilling their obligations as strictly as they did in the home country. For them, however, this does not mean a distancing from their beliefs. Other precepts, such as abstaining from drinking alcohol and eating pork, are upheld. Many said that they preferred to eat *halal* meat, but that they have only been able to do so since Muslim butchers opened near their homes.

Overall, most women believe that there are no real obstacles to performing their religious duties in Spain. Nevertheless, increasingly they want their Muslim identity to be acknowledged by wider society, not least to confront Spanish society's 'negation' of it. This is still a 'wavering' discourse but many factors indicate that it will consolidate in the coming years, especially amongst women who arrived in Spain very young and are coming of age in the country. They justify their sporadic patterns of prayer and mosque attendance as a result of their new lifestyles not because life in Spain might have weakened their religious reference points or prevented them from being Muslims. For them, being in Spain simply means experiencing religion in a different way and this is not a source of frustration for them. For example:

> Sometimes I can't study, there's the job, the subway ... but I leave it all to the last minute ... but then I'm tired and don't do it. Ramadan I always, always observe, and never drink alcohol ... now I do things differently, I do more when there's less work, but I feel it the same way, it's the same as over there. I still communicate every day, and what matters is what's deep down and behaving and showing respect.

In some cases, of course, religious practice has intensified, because going to the mosque and praying is considered a means of 'being closer to my country, to my friends and relatives'.

Individualizing Islam: Younger Women, Independence and the Critique of Patriarchy

Moroccan Muslim women's discourses do not therefore reflect some sort of bipolar response to migration in terms of i) retrenchment and the conservation of traditional lifestyles or ii) full-scale assimilation into Spanish society.[5] Instead, for the time being, we observe a fluid process of the reconstruction of identities that combines a negotiation of elements drawn from both native and novel environments. This fluidity clearly captures the degree of social change to which Moroccan women are subject and is especially marked amongst those with higher educational qualifications. These are women who have reflected on what it means to be a Muslim in Spain, something they would not have done in Morocco where being a Muslim is not the subject of 'difference' and so does not foster particular reflection or introspection.

The reality of financially and personally independent Moroccan immigrant women does not, therefore, confirm the widespread assumption that they must have shed their Muslim identities in Spain. On the contrary, independence and Islamic identity coexist amongst most of the young women with university degrees and sometimes also amongst those who do not have degrees. For these kinds of women, adherence to Islam becomes a way of remaining loyal to their 'selves' and forms an important part of their individual identity (see also Fadil, this volume). Contrary to prevailing stereotypes, they do not inevitably accept the patriarchy of their home country where interpretations of Islam are deployed in the service of preserving traditional family structures. Indeed, many of our respondents rejected the social control of women in this way. Moreover, the necessity of acknowledging women as active economic actors is inevitably transforming norms of family structure and women's own perceptions of their roles and rights in society. Therefore, the 'entrepreneurial' women we interviewed were often very critical of those Muslim constituencies and organizations in Europe that call for the defence of tradition and a general separation from European society.

For these women, then, Islam is perceived as a faith, a religious practice and a source of identity, rather than as an immutable lifestyle governed by strict social codes. Those women who have reflected most on this matter say that customs and traditions imposed in Morocco are one thing, while practising Islam as a universal religious faith which embraces all humanity is another. One of our respondents, a businesswoman reflected: 'Islam authorizes women's work, it is not forbidden by the Qur'an. This is only a social habit among Arabs, but it is not true that it is best for women to stay indoors. Islam does not say so'.

Although they do not express it thus, such women are reformulating their reality as Muslim women. However, despite the importance of migration in this dynamic process, such reconstruction was not absent in Morocco where transformations associated with 'modernization' have, of course, their own trajectory. Nevertheless, what is certain is that these transformations become more explicit and intense as interaction with Spanish society begins (Dietz and El-Shohoumi, 2005).

Among younger interviewees, we observed the most autonomous understanding of religious practices and the weakest links to official religious institutions and prayer centres. Although there are exceptions, religion is increasingly perceived in terms of an essentially individual faith in a personalized God rather than in the fulfilment of religious duties and practices imposed by religious institutions, leaders or the family. In fact, the lifestyles of younger Muslim women of Moroccan heritage are not so different from their Spanish peers.

The rejection of religious institutions is widespread amongst younger Muslim women, especially because they consider that these institutions perpetuate sexist views and attitudes. Those who defined their fathers and Moroccan men of their own age as sexist, believed that this male chauvinism is the product of tradition and history, and that 'true' scriptural Islam awards women a status that should not be tainted by mere culture and custom. Two of our younger interviewees, for instance, said that they do not visit the mosque, because it is 'the place of tradition'. At the same time, things may be changing in this respect, as women appear to be increasingly active in some of the new mosques emerging in the Spanish provinces.

Notably, this kind of discourse is not at all apparent amongst older women. It seems to be a generational transformation that is taking place. Indeed, some young Moroccan fathers are also expressing concerns about the need to reconsider Islamic interpretations of women's roles and status, especially when their daughters' futures are in question (Martín-Muñoz, 2003: 133). One woman insisted:

> These things of religion, women having to cover themselves to keep men from looking at them on the streets ... but Islam does not say that either ... I must do the things I must do, such as praying and observing Ramadan ... we must behave, be good and respectful, there are many things in the Qur'an, many things in the future. But it says nothing about me not being allowed to work.

Public Prejudice and Muslim Women's Attitudes to the Headscarf

Despite being generally at ease with their own religious practice in Spain, many of the women interviewed believed that other religious groups – especially the Evangelical and Jewish traditions – were given preferential treatment over Islam. The Spanish administration (especially at the municipal level) may give grants to support social and cultural activities, but it refuses to finance any type of religious activity or practice. Our interviewees were critical of the fact that the administration would only ever support secular, non-denominational associations. Moreover, what now seems like 'religious discrimination' reveals the particular types of integration that administrations are willing to defend. Epistemological paradigms positing cultural and ethnic diversity in secular societies have not always taken the religious dimension of plurality as seriously as they might (Vertovec and Peach, 1997).

Against this context many of our interviewees considered that Spanish society exhibits various prejudices against Muslims which become noticeable when Muslims make their religious identity visible, for example by building a new mosque or wearing a headscarf. Our respondents reported that wearing clothing considered 'Muslim' or 'fundamentalist' sparked hostility especially in public spaces such as the workplace, the market or just around the neighbourhood (Blaschke, 2001). Both women who wore headscarves and those who did not were of this opinion. Spanish attitudes have triggered two different reactions amongst Muslim women: i) the reassertion of the right to wear the headscarf, with far more significance being attributed to this (as a symbol of resistance in the face of rejection) than in Morocco; and ii) the abandonment of traditional Moroccan attire including the headscarf with the adoption of 'western' dress representing an attempt to 'blend in' and avoid stigma.

While permanent settlement often leads to the assertion of Muslim identity, the second of these strategies is most widespread amongst newly arrived, younger women. For this group 'Muslim' visibility can often be seen as an obstacle to establishing new social relations and finding work. This is particularly noticeable amongst women who are employed in the housekeeping, babysitting and care for the elderly sectors. Getting a job was easier, our interviewees said, when traditional attire was not worn. Indeed, in selecting employees, employers seemed to consider the type of clothing worn at interview more important than other factors such as past experience, salary and knowledge of the Spanish language. A woman working as a house-maid reflected:

> I am confronted with many difficulties because of '*hijab*' ... I still eat *halal* meat, I do my prayers ... but I never go out with my scarf on, because everybody stares at me and then no-one wants to hire me. What really matters to them is that you should not wear a scarf, not that you can do the job.

Interpretations of the meaning of 'headscarves' vary considerably amongst the women that wear them. Some say 'it is tradition', others that 'it is a religious duty', and others that 'it is a symbol of Muslim identity'. Notably, none of our respondents defined the headscarf as a symbol of female subservience and, for younger women with higher educational levels, wearing the headscarf did not imply the assertion of patriarchal or discriminatory control over their personal and professional life projects. Younger women, especially those who were born in Spain or arrived when they were still very young, also appeared to be generally more willing to embrace a lifestyle similar to that of other Spaniards, enjoying the opportunities that Spain offers in terms of freedom and education. However, this must be understood within the context of Islam representing a central aspect of their identity. Many young Muslim women, for example, cite examples of young Spaniards who mix tradition with modernity in their lives. It seems, therefore, that many young Muslim women in Spain are already expressing the real possibility of integrating multiple and fluid identities as part of a continuous process of religious and cultural reconstruction.

Conclusion

Attitudes to religion in Spain still stem largely from a sense of national identity with strong links to the country's Catholic heritage. As such, the current model of a non-denominational state makes room for religious expression in the public space. Significant sections of Spanish society contest this situation but, for the time being, there is no consensus on the need for a more thorough secularization. Nevertheless, the idea of secularism is most often invoked in arguments against the public recognition of Islam and Muslims, which raises the troubling question of popular and institutional religious discrimination within Spain. Against this context, our fieldwork reveals something of the diversity that currently exists in terms of the religious practices, interpretations and identities of Muslim women of Moroccan heritage.

The practice of Islam varies among Muslim women depending on their personal situations, their length of their stay in Spain and the extent of their family ties. Nevertheless, extreme reactions, whether total assimilation or isolation from wider society, are not at all representative of the group as a whole. The reuniting of families or having children and the emergence of a second generation fosters attempts to preserve religion, language and culture. For many, religious practice also forms part of their daily routines and personal realities, and they would feel lost without it. Older women tend to explain religion more in terms of tradition, while younger and better educated women interpret the Muslim 'faith' as sources of individual identity and personality that they are unwilling to relinquish. They are also unwilling to accept traditions that assert social and family control over them. Their vision of their faith is personal and direct, and does not allow for subservience or the mediation of male authorities. In this respect, a generational reconstruction of Islam is clearly visible. At the same time, this flexibility in religious understanding deconstructs the prevailing stereotype of Muslim women as subservient to Islam and to Muslim men widespread in Spanish society.

In this respect, respondents attested to the idea that 'Western' lifestyles are not incompatible with allegiance to Islamic faith and Muslim identity. There are few difficulties practising Islam in Spain and those with higher educational levels argue that the main issues should not concern the acceptance of their 'difference' but rather applying the principle of equality. What they want is their Muslim identity to be normalized within the law as just one more element of Spanish society. They also feel that their visibility as Muslims is rejected by certain sections of Spanish society, an 'Islamophobia' which hinders their integration. Therefore, they call for the social acceptance of Islam as and when it becomes visible in daily routines such as the wearing of the *hijab*. Gaining acceptance and respect requires Spaniards to better understand Islam and Moroccan culture. A positive intervention in this respect would be the introduction of such topics into Spain's school curricula.

Finally, it is also noteworthy that the women discussed in this chapter are not playing an active role in immigrant or any other type of community associations. Many say they would like to be involved in such activities and the opportunities for interaction they provide. Setting up associations of Moroccan and Muslim women or encouraging their involvement in associations of Spanish women would foster involvement in civil society and so bolster the processes of integration.

References

Abu Tarbush, J. (2002), *Islam y comunidad islámica en Canarias*, La Laguna: Universidad de La Laguna.
Alcantud, J.A. and Zabbal, F. (eds) (2003), *Histoire de L'Andalousie. Mémoire et Enjeux*, París: L'Archange Minotaure.
AlSayyad, N. (2003), 'Europa musulmana o Euro-Islam: a propósito de los discursos de la identidad y la cultura', in AlSayyad, N. (ed.) *¿Europa musulmana o Euro-Islam?* Madrid: Alianza.
Aparicio, R. (1998), *Identidad y Género: Mujeres magrebíes en Madrid*, Madrid: Dirección Gral. De la Mujer. Comunidad de Madrid.
ASEP (Análisis Sociológicos, Económicos y Políticos, S.A.) (1998), *Actitudes hacia los inmigrantes*, Madrid: OPI.
Aubarell, G. and Zapata, R. (eds) (2003), *Inmigración y procesos de cambio: Europa y el Mediterráneo en un contexto global*, Barcelona: Icaria.
Blaschke, J. (ed.) (2001), *Multilevel discrimination against Muslim Women in Europe*, Berlin: Parabolis.
Colectivo IOE (1995), *Discursos de los Españoles sobre los extranjeros. Paradojas de la alteridad*, Madrid: Centro de Investigaciones Sociológicas.
Colectivo IOE (2001), *Mujer, Inmigración y Trabajo*, Madrid: Ediciones del Ministerio de Trabajo y Asuntos Sociales.
De Lucas, J. (2002), *Inmigrantes ¿cómo los tenemos?*, Madrid: Talasa Ediciones.
Dietz, G. and El-Sohoumi, N. (2005), *Muslim Women in Southern Spain: Stepdaughters of Al-Andalus,* San Diego: Center for Comparative Immigration Studies.
Khachani, M. (ed.) (2000), *Femmes et Migrations*, Rabat: Revue Juridique Politique Economique et Sociale.
Martín Corrales, E. (2002), *La imagen del magrebí en España: Una perspectiva histórica, siglos XVI-XX*, Barcelona: Bellaterra.
Martín-Muñoz, G. (1996), 'Perceptions de l'Islam en Espagne', *Confluences Méditerranée*, 19, 183-196.
Martín-Muñoz, G. (1998), 'The image of Islam and the Arabs in the West. The prevalence of culturalist visions', in Nielsen, J. and Khasawnih, S.A. (eds), *The Arabs and the West: Mutual Images*, Amman: Jordan University Press, 59-72.
Martín-Muñoz, G. (2002), 'The Muslim Women and the West', *Open Democracy*, October.
Martín-Muñoz, G. (ed.) (2003), *Marroquíes en España. Estudio sobre su intergración social*, Madrid: Fundación Repsol.
Modood, T. (2000), 'Anti-essentialism, multiculturalism and the recognition of religious groups', in Kymlicka, W. and Norman, W. (eds), *Citizenship in diverse societies*, New York: Oxford University Press, 175-195.
Moreras, J. (2003), 'Limits and contradictions in the legal recognition of Muslims in Spain', in Shahid, W. and Von Koningsveld, P.S. (eds), *Religious Freedom and the Neutrality of the State: The position of Islam in the European Union*, Leuven: Peeters, pp. 52-64.

Moreras, J. (2005), 'Predicar en tierra ajena: los roles asumidos por los imames en contexto migratorio', Communication introduced in the *4th Congreso sobre la Inmigración en España*, Girona.

SOS Racismo (2002), '¿Sospechosos habituales? La estigmatización de la figura de los musulmanes en España', *Informe annual 2002 sobre el racismo en el Estado Español*.

Spinner-Halev, J. (2000), *Surviving diversity: religion and democratic citizenship*, Baltimore: John Hopkins University Press.

Vertovec, S. and Peach, C. (1997), *Islam in Europe: The Politics of Religion and Community*, London: Macmillan Press.

Zapata-Barrero, R. (2004), *Inmigración, innovación política y cultura de acomodación en España*, Barcelona: Bellaterra/CIDOB.

Zapata-Barrero, R. (2005), 'The Muslim Community and Spanish tradition', in Modood, T., Zapata, R. and Triandafyllidou, A. (eds), *Multiculturalism, Muslims and Citizenship: A European Approach*, London: Routledge.

Notes

1 In Spain, as in Italy, the arrival and settlement of the Muslim community remains a relatively new phenomenon when compared to other European countries. As such, it is still today conceived within the framework of immigration.

2 For example, Enrique Fernández Miranda, government representative for immigration under Popular Party rule spoke in such terms (*El País*, 12 March 2001). Politician and intellectual, Herrero de Miñón, called for immigration based on 'linguistic and cultural affinities' (*El País*, 9 October 1999).

3 When asked what measures should be adopted to combat international terrorism, 34.1 per cent of respondents to a Real Instituto Elcano opinion poll of June 2004 replied that 'it is necessary to enforce tighter controls on Muslim immigrants and mosques'.

4 In our study we did not come across any 'underage' women who arrived in Spain alone, a phenomenon that seems to remain exclusively male.

5 According to our observations, ultra-orthodox retrenchments and isolation from Spanish society result from specific experiences of radical rejection by Spanish society.

Chapter 10

Individualizing Faith, Individualizing Identity: Islam and Young Muslim Women in Belgium

Nadia Fadil

Introduction

Secularization is often used as a root metaphor to describe the Western European modernization process. Several authors have described the different dimensions of the term (for example, Tschannen, 1992; Dobbelaere, 2002). Nevertheless, a central thread running through the literature concerns the ways in which modernity has transformed the social impact of religion. In particular, it is observed that religion no longer has a key role to play in the organization of European societies, having become just one of their many 'subsystems'. Similarly, religion no longer functions as a 'sacred canopy' naturalizing religious affiliation (Berger, 1978) having become instead a question of choice. As Grace Davie puts it, the emphasis now is on *believing* rather than *belonging* (Davie, 2000).

This chapter explores the religiosity of women of Muslim heritage in the secular and modernized context of Belgium.[1] In particular, it is concerned with the individualization of religious faith and practice, which is closely linked to the more general processes of secularization. The individualization of religion can be characterized in terms of certain trends such as the decline of traditional religious authorities (Chaves, 1994) and the manifestation of new forms of adherence (Wilson, 1981) including an eclectic and selective bricolage of religious practice (Dobbelaere, 1999). In this regard, Hervieu-Léger (2000) states that it is not bricolage as such that is modern, but rather 'that they [believers] assert their "right to bricolage" at the same time as the right to "choose" their own beliefs' (1998: 217). For example, it has become socially acceptable to self-consciously combine elements from Zen Buddhism with Christianity, and many Catholics retain their faith while rejecting the Pope's position on contraception. Similarly, in their rich ethnography of American values and mores, Bellah et al. (1985) refer to a respondent named 'Sheila' who called her religion 'Sheilaism', thereby underlining the intuitive and personal approach that dominated her religious quest. Hence, one of the things that seems to be specific about religious practice in a secular environment is that, so to speak, it has become a matter between 'God' and the 'believer' and it is for the believer alone to decide how she or he will practice. In seeking to explore the extent to which individual choice predominates in the religious belief and practice of Muslim women in Belgium, the first part of this chapter explores notions of what it means to be a 'good' Muslim in terms of respondents' conformity to a defined set of practices and rules.

As well as individualization, another, seemingly contradictory, transformation of contemporary religion is the general proliferation of 'affiliation' and 'mobilization' in late modern society (Beyer, 1994; Casanova, 1994). Hervieu-Leger argues that, due to its impersonal and instrumental logic, late modernity has prompted many to seek for more personal and intimate social affiliations, including religious affiliations. Certainly, when speaking of Muslims in Western Europe, an increasing manifestation of Islamic communal identifications can be observed, not least in the public sphere. In the second part of this chapter, then, I will consider the story of one of my respondents, Selma, in particular detail by way of illustrating the relationships between her religious identification and the life-choices she has made.

The Belgian Context: Politics, 'Neutrality' and Public Recognition

This chapter is based on 21 in-depth interviews, conducted during 2000-2001, with young Moroccan Muslim women, aged 16 to 18 years, in the city of Antwerp.[2] The sample presented here has no generalizing pretensions, the aim being, instead, to reflect on different discourses and tendencies, approaches and translations, concerning what Islam might mean for individuals who call themselves 'Muslims'. Regarding the context of these interviews, two remarks should be made.

Firstly, unlike France, Belgium does not follow a system of laïcité but rather attempts to arrive at a less ideological position of 'neutrality'. Different confessions are recognized by law and financed by the state, although the state, in theory, does not intervene in the organization of religion. However, since the recognition of Islam as an official confession in 1974, Muslims have struggled to establish a functional administrative board to organize the financial support given to the Islamic confession. Therefore, after more than two decades of temporary and contested representation, major elections were organized in 1998 in an attempt to finalize an official board for Muslims in Belgium.[3] Its operation, however, was highly problematic and contested, not least because of interference by the state. This resulted in new elections on 10 March 2005 (see Ferrari, and compare Caeiro, this volume).[4]

As to public manifestations of religion, a policy of *laissez-faire* is followed in Belgium, with public services adopting their own positions. In terms of headscarves, for example, this means that each school has the right to choose whether to ban or allow manifestations of religious identity from its buildings.[5] Of the 21 young women interviewed, six wore the headscarf at the time of their interview. None, however, was allowed to wear the headscarf at school.

Secondly, it is worth reporting that the interviews were conducted shortly before and after the municipal elections of November 2000, which saw the extreme-right party, the Vlaams Blok (Flemish Block), become the largest political party in the city of Antwerp, with 33 per cent of votes. Although not explicitly questioned about this, when the question of citizenship was discussed, the Vlaams Blok's victory was raised as an issue by the young women.[6]

To be a Good Muslim: Bricolage, Norms and Individualized Islam?

How do the young women interviewed define what it is to be 'a good Muslim'? Is it someone with 'an Islam of the heart'? What 'content' do they assign to Islam for themselves? Is it an Islam that still responds to certain prescriptions? Several authors such as Babès (1997/2000) and Saint-Blancat (1997) point to a process of individualization in the way that Muslims in Europe practice their faith. For example, Babès observes how the dimension of faith is becoming more important than whether 'they may eat with the left hand or whether saving money [and so accruing interest] is forbidden' (2000: 189) [my translation].

The same sentiments are expressed in the following citation from a conversation with 'Amina' about the difficulties of living an Islamic lifestyle.[7] However, she does not have a very uniform vision of what being a 'good Muslim' might entail:

> Yes, it's difficult, because, actually, there are only a few people who are real Muslims. There are only a few who can say of themselves: 'I'm a *Muslim* Muslim'. I'm Moroccan, I believe in Islam but I don't really pray enough to be considered a real Muslim. They [the real Muslims] live really strictly according to the rules – and that's really difficult – you really need to have a will for it ... But if you believe in your heart, and as long as you think of yourself as a Muslim, and you believe in God, and you find the values of Islam important, then you can call yourself a Muslim. But you don't have to listen to all the others who say: to be a Muslim you have to pray, you have to wear a headscarf – everybody decides it for themselves.[8]

In Amina's reply, we can distinguish two quite different discourses. In the first part of her response, she refers to the difficulty of being a good Muslim, restricting the label of 'real Muslims' to a limited group of people to which she does not seem to belong. In the next sentence, she tries to clarify this by defining a 'real' Muslim as someone who follows a set of practices. She says of 'real Muslims': 'they really live strictly according to the rules – and that's difficult'. Despite her own faith in Islam, her lack of practice restrains her from calling herself a 'Muslim'. She sees Islam as a religious system which one *ought* to follow. Amina's description of her religiosity therefore contrasts with the notion of religious bricolage where a religious system is seen as just one resource from which the individual can 'pick and mix' according to his or her needs. One might conclude, then, that Amina does not experience her religion in a very individualized way as her notion of what makes a good Muslim is associated with a set of rules and is not individually chosen.

In the second part of Amina's response, however, we see a different discourse appearing, a discourse in which 'the self' plays a key part and the 'Islam of the heart' (Babès, 1997/2000) prevails. We must therefore reconsider the idea that Amina's religiosity is not individualized. While in the first part of her answer she clearly emphasizes the necessity of religious practice, in the second part she states that honest intentions (*niyyat*) and ethical principles are important above all else. Furthermore, she insists that every religious practice should be individually chosen. But how might this apparent contradiction between individualized religiosity and a religiosity that insists on obedience to certain prescriptions be observed?

When the voices of other young Muslim women are taken into consideration, what seems at first to be an idiosyncratic interpretation actually emerges as something of a trend, or as 'Btissame' says: 'From the inside I am [a good Muslim], but not from the outside, no. I mean, my clothing and stuff and also having boyfriends and stuff. That's not Islam. There are so many things'.[9] Btissame articulates the religious hybridity that many respondents seemed to experience, distinguishing 'internalized' and 'externalized' dimensions in her definition of a good Muslim. While the first dimension refers to her overall intentions regarding her faith, her *niyyat*, the second refers to her actual practice. Like Amina, though, she insists on the importance of having a strong faith but her lack of practice restrains her from calling herself 'a good Muslim'. For Btissame, both the 'internal' (the faith) and the 'external' (the practice) dimensions are essential if one is to identify as 'a good Muslim'. Failing to fulfil one of these aspects suggests a deficiency.

The dimension of practice is so important in 'Imane's' eyes that her failure to conform made her cry during one of the *khutbas* (sermons) given by the *imam* of her local mosque.

> I'm not a good Muslim, I'm everything but a good Muslim. Sometimes I don't pray out of laziness. What do I do wrong? [thinks] ... sometimes I have boyfriends, and that's not allowed ... yeah, stuff like that. Sometimes I lie – that's also not allowed. I don't wear a headscarf – that's also not allowed ... I mean, when I compare myself with other Muslims. Last week in the mosque, I started to cry. There was an *imam* who really gives himself for Islam; he was reading a part of the Qur'an and I started to cry really hard when I heard that part. I'm just a really bad Muslim; I want to be better.[10]

Imane's perception of religiosity means that her weakness is lived as guilt and sin. The 'sins' that she enumerates illustrate the equal importance of 'ethics' and 'practice': she fails not only in being honest but also in praying five times a day and abstaining from dating. Hence, she does not attempt to legitimate her bricolage. Individual orthopraxis is seen as essential. 'Nora' describes this insight very clearly:

> There are only a few people who practice Islam correctly. Honestly, I've never met anyone who practiced it correctly. [Practising it correctly means] following the rules, all the rules and not just those you like. I chose praying, Ramadan, too, but I don't go to Mecca because it's too expensive. It's no travel brochure, is it?! You don't pick what you like from it.[11]

By using this metaphor of the travel brochure, she contests the very idea of religious bricolage, at least from an Islamic perspective.

There is an apparent duality, then, in the way that these young Muslim women described their religiosity. They all recognized that individual faith is necessary. All insisted on Islamic norms, a world divided in terms of what is *halal* and what is *haram*. Some emphasized mainly the obligatory prayers, others the dietary requirements, but all insisted that one has to practice to be considered a good Muslim. The 'Islam of the heart' is important but not sufficient. Summarizing the different voices heard here, one can not really speak of an individualized religiosity. Although all the young Muslim women insisted on the importance of personal faith and ethics, their discourse did not manifest religious bricolage. Quite the opposite was true and non-practice was seen as 'lacking', a 'sin' accompanied by feelings of guilt for Imane at least.

Although this prescriptive logic seemed to dominate young Muslim women's accounts and all stressed the need to obey prescriptions, they also stressed the importance of choosing individually whether, and to what extent, they 'practiced' and that this should never be socially determined or enforced. In response to the question, 'Do you think you're a bad Muslim if you don't agree with some rules?', Nora replied: 'I don't think so. You try, and as long you try you are Muslim, I think. If you don't agree with something, you have the right not to agree. That's the same for me.' Here, Nora tries to put her earlier thoughts into a wider perspective. She insists that obedience to religious prescriptions must be preceded by individual reflection; one can follow the rules only if one truly concurs with them, if one has really chosen them. This could be interpreted as a manifestation of the discourse of individualization. Individualization is characteristic of a society no longer ruled by 'God, Nature or the System' (Beck and Beck, 2002: 8). The only legitimate choices in a modern society, then, are those made by the subject. However, this does not mean that the individual *actually* makes all his or her own choices: to a greater or lesser extent these are still shaped by social conditioning and social structures. Rather, what individualization refers to is a social semantic where the discourse of 'the self' is predominant 'in people's consciousness' (Beck and Beck, 2002: 203).

Olivier Roy (1999) also describes this emphasis on religious 'individuality' in terms of the conscious choice that the contemporary believer makes to follow the path of Islam. Amongst the young Muslim women interviewed, 'Selma', for example, describes how she considered the headscarf – although a religious obligation – more of a natural step in her overall spiritual quest. In response to the question, 'Do you think that you can be Muslim without a headscarf?', she replied:

> Yes, you can, but I'm going to tell you: if you're really a Muslim, you're going to choose it yourself, to wear a headscarf ... But it's not you who's going to choose but your heart that's going to choose ... it's step by step ... There are some who think 'I'm it' with a headscarf. For me everybody is the same, with or without a scarf ... Muslim, non-Muslim, you can't think that [s]he is better or not ... you make a choice. Forcing, I think, is terrible, but it's you who should choose it yourself. ... It's not about the scarf, that's just appearance. But if you read the Qur'an a lot, then it will come from your heart, and you won't be able to let it go. I've been wearing it already for two years, but I would never be able to let it go. I'm so faithful that I couldn't let go, it has become a part of me, as if without it I would be walking naked.[12]

Selma would seem to problematize any religious act that is the consequence of obligation. However, interestingly, she combines a discourse of the self with a discourse of religious obligation: 'it may be of no importance to you, but for God it is'. According to Selma, wearing a headscarf must be an individual choice but, if one truly and honestly believes, it will seem logical.

Amiraux (2000) observes these same processes amongst her Turkish respondents in Germany, describing them in terms of an affirmation of the genealogical line. Through their emphasis on religious practice they reaffirm their loyalty towards the community, whilst also affirming their autonomy. Thus, by insisting on their autonomy, they also fully inscribe themselves into the mainstream of Western-European discourse. However, this reconstruction of individuality presumes an unavoidable tension between the need to distinguish one's individual 'self' and the necessity of being recognized by a community. Thus, religious practice cannot be individualized to the extent of marginalizing oneself in relation to others and especially one's genealogy. According to Amiraux (2000: 121), it is a balance between religious practice and the autonomy of the self that will be sought after.

One further dimension of the discourse on religious practice typical of the young Muslim women interviewed was a temporal reference to '*later*'. Although most of the women were convinced of the need to obey Islamic prescriptions, they were not ready to do so at the present time. Selma – to whom we shall return in some detail in due course – was one of the exceptions in this respect, making the very conscious choice of living by the prescriptions of her religion. Others, such as Imane and 'Fatiha', were not ready to make that same choice. For example, the idea of doing certain things 'later' became very evident when the topic of the headscarf was raised. When asked, 'Does Islam occupy a great part in your life?', they replied:

> Yes I think so. I mean, I don't wear the headscarf right now, and sometimes I think I'm more Muslim in my heart than those women who do wear the scarf. It's not because they wear the scarf that they're saints ... that they stick to Islam. The headscarf isn't everything; it's the roof on the pillars. If you respect the pillars, and they are solid, then you can put on the roof. I mean, it's good if you respect it from the start. (Imane)

> I'd like to wear a headscarf but the problem is that I'd like to do so many other things in my life, too. I want to sunbathe in my swimsuit, walk with my hair loose. So, I think that mentally maybe I'm ready, but I still want to do other things I couldn't possibly do while wearing a headscarf. (Fatiha)[13]

According to Imane, being a good Muslim can not be achieved suddenly. It is something that has to be built up very self-consciously, with the wearing of a headscarf as the finishing touch, a 'roof' atop the firm 'structure' provided by the five pillars of Islam. For Fatiha, too, the headscarf is ultimately seen as a necessary step in the process of becoming 'a good Muslim'. However, it is not something she is ready to embrace immediately. Wearing it would hamper her in doing things she feels she still wants to do. Indeed, the prospect of taking such a decision is described almost in terms of a conversion that would require an especially modest lifestyle.

Summarizing this initial analysis, it seems that one must conclude that one cannot speak easily of an individualized Islamic religiosity. Though the notion of the self is well developed in the accounts of the young Muslim women discussed here, religious bricolage, seen as a key characteristic of religiosity in a secularized age (Hervieu-Léger, 1998; Dobbelaere, 1999/2000), is not sanctioned or lent legitimacy. The authority of Islam as a system of meanings and norms remains undisputed. Rather, it is engagement with, and entry into, that system that is individualized.

Disengaging Religion and Culture: Islam as a Resource for Contesting Community

The second part of this chapter will explore another aspect of the religious identity of young Muslim women in Belgium. Muslims increasingly self-conscious identification with Islam has been described extensively in the literature on Muslims in Europe (for example, Sunier, 1996; Khosrokhavar, 1996; Vertovec, 1998). Most authors agree that this assertion of Islamic identity involves a disassociation of religious and ethnic identities, with the latter becoming relatively less important. Therefore, while immigration from the Middle East and North Africa means that Islam is still perceived as an 'alien' religion in Western Europe, the argument advanced here is that discourses of Islam are deployed not only to legitimate a new sense of individuality but also to contest and dissociate individuals from established ethno-national communities.

The focus in this section is a more detailed reflection on the accounts of just one young Muslim woman, Selma. In response to the question, 'How did your interest in Islam grow? Did you get it from home?', she replied:

> No, not at all. We used to live amongst Jews and Belgians, but not Muslims. And we were between all those cultures, and my mother, too, she used to be different; she wore those boots and stuff, and I found it weird. I'm somebody who likes to search, and so when I came here [to the place they are living now], there was once a very kind woman I met on the tram, and she started talking with me and telling me about meetings on Islam ... I went once to see what was happening and ... sometimes you just have that kind of people ... whose hearts just open up for those kinds of things ... I don't have enough time [to go now]. I get my knowledge from self-study and stuff. Sometimes there is a bit of Islam at school, but otherwise I do it by myself.

Selma was one of those women who emphasized that her religiosity was the result of individual choice. Here she tells how she 'discovered' Islam not through her parents but by following up a chance encounter. Hinting at her mother's un-Islamic dress, she recalls: 'she used to be different; she wore those boots and stuff'. The most striking thing about her account, then, is that Islam is not so much a part of cultural heritage as an individual quest. It is pursued in terms of active intellectual search and discovery. Moreover, although Selma initially became interested in Islam through an organization, she is now most individually and religiously fulfilled through her own reading.

The tendency towards religion as an intellectual and spiritual quest often seeks to separate the former from the inherited 'cultural practices' of Muslim communities, with the latter often negatively associated with oppressive practices (see also Hashmi, 2000; Cesari, 2002). For example, as Selma maintains:

> So, Islam. They mess it up with culture. It's always the same here: the Moroccan culture is always seen as one and the same as Islam. But that's wrong! You've got to follow Islam, the Moroccan culture, too, but, what is that Moroccan culture like? I'm going to tell you. It influences people to say 'you can do that because you are Muslim'. But it's got nothing to do with Islam at all: here's a Muslim and how they live; and here are the Moroccans, and how they live. Culture and Islam, they mix it together, and people think of us: 'yeah, they're doing it again', or like, women who can't go outside; I also think it's horrible: why can't she [go outside]?! And they're saying: 'it's Islam'. Why should they involve Islam with that? ... You have to see Islam in another way and not just in terms of culture.

This strategy of using Islamic resources as a means for empowerment has been dealt with extensively in the wider literature (Kosrokhavar, 1997; Amiraux, 2000; Göle, 2003). Some even describe an Islamic feminism, describing how, through active re-reading and re-interpretation of religious texts, Muslim women have sought to critique patriarchal accounts (Moghadham, 2002; Badran, 2001). It has already been suggested that Islam becomes a reference point that offers a balance between a discourse of 'the self' and loyalty to religious and ethnic communities. However, the argument here is that this reference to Islam does not only allow for loyalty to the group. It can also create new spaces of, and opportunities for, individual contestation and distancing from religio-ethnic communities. Selma *rejects* such loyalty for its own sake and it is her individuality that appears clearly in the foreground. Rather, a clear absence of explicit communitarian logic marks her discourse. Instead, a more implicit reference to the larger symbolic *umma* of Islam (the community of believers), and especially those who *act* in accordance with the prescriptions of Islam, seems to be her new point of reference:

> Once I was on the tram, and a woman asked us: 'Can you choose your husband by yourself?' I told her: 'Look, Ma'am, according to Islam it is allowed, and my culture also lets me, and it is true that the parents talk to each other, like it's the case for you, too, to ask for the daughter's hand: 'our son is going out with your daughter, in case something would happen, pregnancy or stuff' ... And then the woman was surprised and she didn't know that it was like that. But then, there was that woman [another Muslim] saying: 'yes, but look, for us it is not allowed, it's our father who chooses our husband because these are the best men'. And I was thinking: 'Please, shut up!'. I said: 'Look, Ma'am, our culture is like that, but it's different from Islam'. And then she understood ... And the other woman was irritated and was saying: '[how can] you say that!' I tell her: '... You don't live in Morocco any more, you've got to learn to think and live together. If you don't understand, how are you going to live together?'

Two things stand out in this passage. Firstly, Selma attempts to answer a question from a non-Muslim woman. She clearly differentiates 'religion' from 'culture' in her explanation of 'arranged' marriages. However, another Moroccan woman challenges her and Selma was obviously irritated by her traditional interpretation. Secondly, Selma attaches a very positive image to Islam. She sees this encounter as an opportunity to correct negative representations of her religion, something which she believes is necessary for good relations between Muslims and non-Muslims.

Women like Selma contest not only the way their community practices Islam but also the 'faulty' use of Islamic arguments to legitimate oppressive ways of life. Hence Selma argues for alternative readings of the sources which, in turn, create new spaces for interpretation, practice and individuation. In the following citation the question of marriage between a Muslim woman and a non-Muslim man is re-read against the discovery of a traditional textual source:

> But there are also Moroccan men who marry Belgian women, and that's normal for them, and I think it's wrong. Why can they do it when a woman immediately degrades herself if she does it ... and then you see that a man can convince a woman to convert to Islam ... Yes, it's allowed, but I once read a text, a few months ago, in which a daughter of a friend of the Prophet was married to someone of the same status but he was an unbeliever, and she loved him until he finally converted. He was unbeliever, but she married him.

Selma questions a widely accepted prescription that marriage between Muslim women and non-Muslim men is prohibited. She refers to a *hadith* she has read in which the Prophet tolerated a marriage between a non-Muslim man and a Muslim woman.[14] By supporting her argument in this way, Selma expresses her doubts about the prohibition, although she does not resolutely state that the interpretation is false.

Islamic knowledge would therefore seem to offer 'resources' which can lend legitimacy to processes of individualization. Islam has the potential to empower women to make choices that challenge the customs of ethnic communities. However, women who self-consciously refer to their Islamic identity also emphasize the idea of free will and individual choice in *any* circumstances. Hence, the individualization of religious identity seems also to suggest an individualization of religious practice. In another part of Selma's interview, this sort of affirmation becomes very explicit: for her, the prohibition on Muslim women marrying non-Muslim men should be loosened. A 'devout' Muslim, she argues, would never consider marrying a non-Muslim, for their individual lifestyles and principles would contradict one another. However, for those Muslims who are not 'devout' she argues that, in reality, it would make very little difference (although this assumes the absence of particular ethno-national groups' desire to reproduce themselves):

> They always think it's strange if you marry a Belgian because he's not a Muslim. But if you're a 'real' Muslim, how could you live with someone who's Christian? But yeah, what does it mean to be a Muslim today? You could live with anybody, but if you're really talking about raising Muslim children, then it's hard to raise kids with a Christian. But if you're just a Muslim, you say it but you don't practice it, then it's the same whether you marry a Muslim or a Belgian. As long as you understand each other, that's the most important thing, understanding each other – and then, yes.

For Selma, her religious practice has become a matter of choice. It is not because she is of Muslim background or Moroccan ethnicity that she should practice. Her accounts illustrate how reflection on the question of religious practice can stimulate individualization. Indeed, the difference in this case is not between a Muslim and a non-Muslim, but rather between a practising Muslim and a non-practising Muslim.

Conclusions

This chapter has sought to consider certain aspects of Islamic religiosity in the context of wider discussions about the role of religion in a modernizing society. The main focus has been the extent to which it is possible to observe the emergence of an individualized Islam in the secularizing context of Western Europe. Two approaches to Islamic religiosity were quite evident in the interviews conducted with 21 young Muslim women in Belgium. When asked about the legitimacy of religious bricolage, they maintained that being 'a good Muslim' is not a matter of taste or choice. Though only a few women practised their faith in the way they ideally conceived it, they all shared a conviction that 'a good Muslim' is someone who lives according to certain prescriptions.[15] However, at the same time, a tendency towards individual interpretations that contrasted with conformity to these same religious prescriptions was in evidence. This was manifest in respondents' emphasis on choosing the appropriate moment for 'conformity' to such rules and the relative importance that was accorded to individualized ethics and faith.

While the young women's discourses operated within a religious framework they also exhibited features of de-traditionalization and detachment from a community of origin. Processes of individualization therefore create new spaces of autonomy both within the community (Amiraux, 2000) and that accompany detachment from the community. As the account of Selma illustrates, this detachment from the community did not imply an outright rejection of her ethnic identity as a 'Moroccan'. Rather, it meant the rejection of the idea of loyalty to a specific community and culture simply because it was her inheritance. Indeed, this testifies to the development of a religiosity of believing and a community of choice rather than simply a religiosity of communal belonging (Davie, 2000).

With this understanding in mind, I want to argue that there is a need to focus more clearly on how Muslims individualize themselves *through* Islam rather than how they individualize themselves *from* Islam. Notions such as religious bricolage and 'pick and mix' religiosity (Dobbelaere, 1999) obscure the fact that, for many Muslims within (and without) Western Europe, individualization can be developed within religious frameworks, especially when religion is a significant marker of identity. Individualization, here, is less a matter of religious bricolage and more a matter of inscribing oneself into a religious tradition and finding new opportunities and interpretations within in. In this respect, the active and original ways in which Muslims in Western Europe are making use of Islamic knowledge means that opportunities to discover new and alternative possibilities of religious interpretation, translation and articulation are being created by this process of individualization. However, while some seek their autonomy by emphasizing loyalty to their religious or cultural community, others hold back in this respect, emphasizing instead their own trajectories and choices.

References

Allievi, S. (1999), 'Pour une sociologie des conversions: lorsque des européens deviennent musulmans', *Social Compass*, 46 (3), 283-300.

Amiraux, V. (2000), 'Jeunes musulmanes turques d'Allemagne. Voix et voies d'individuation', in Dassetto, F. (ed.), *Islamic Words: Individuals, Societies and Discourse in Contemporary European Islam*, Paris: Maisonneuve and Larose.

Babes, L. (1997), *L'Islam Positif: La religion des jeunes Musulmans*, Paris: Editions de de l'atelier.

Babes, L. (2000), *L'Islam Intérieur. Passion et désenchantement*, Paris/Beirut: Editions Al-Bouraq.

Badran, M. (2001), 'Understanding Islam, Islamism and Islamic Feminism', in *Journal of Women's History*, 13 (1), 47-52.

Barth, F. (1994), 'Enduring and emerging issues in the analysis of ethnicity', in Vermeulen, H. and Govers, C. (eds), *The Anthropology of Ethnicity*, Amsterdam: Het Spinhuis.

Beck, U. (1998), *Risk Society: Towards a New Modernity*, London: Sage Publications.

Beck, U. and Beck-Gernsheim, E. (2002), *Individualization: Institutionalized Individualism and its Social and Political Consequences*, London: Sage Publications.

Bellah, R.N., Madsen, R., Sullivan, W.M., Swidler, A. and Tipton, S.M. (1985/1996), *Habits of the Heart: Individualism and Commitment in American Life*, Berkeley, Los Angeles and London: University of California Press.

Berger, P.L. (1967), *The Sacred Canopy: Elements of a Sociological Theory of Religion*, New York: Doubleday and Company Inc.

Beyer, P. (1994/2000), *Religion and Globalization*, London: Sage Publications.

Casanova, J. (1994), *Public Religions in the Modern World*, Chicago and London: University of Chicago Press.

Cesari, J. (2002), 'Islam in France: Shaping of a Religious Minority', in Yazbeck Haddad, Y. (ed.), *Muslims in the West: From Sojourners to Citizens*, Oxford: University Press, 39-51.

Chaves, M. (1994), 'Secularization as declining religious authority', *Social Forces*, 72(3): 794-774.

Davie, G. (2000), 'Religion in Modern Britain: Changing Sociological Assumptions', *Sociology*, 34(1): 113-128.

Dobbelaere, K. (1999), 'Towards an integrated perspective of the Processes Related to the Descriptive Concept of Secularization', *Sociology of Religion*, 60 (3): 229-247.

Dobbelaere, K. (2002), *Secularization: An Analysis at Three Levels*, Bruxelles: P.I.E.-Peter Lang.

Göle, N. (2003), *Musulmanes et modernes: Voile et civilisation en Turquie*, Paris: La Découverte.

Hashmi, N. (2000), 'Immigrant Children in Europe: Constructing a Transnational Identity', in Höfert, A. and Salvatore, A. (eds), *Between Europe and Islam: Shaping Modernity in a Transcultural Space*, Brussels: PIE-Peter Lang, 163-173.

Hervieu-Léger, D. (1998), 'The transmission and formation of socio-religious identities in modernity', *International Sociology*, 13 (2): 213-228.

Hervieu-Léger, D. (2000), *Religion as a Chain of Memory*, London: Polity Press.

Khosrokhavar, F. (1997), *L'Islam des jeunes*, Saint-Amand-Montrond: Flammarion. l'Atelier.

Modood, T. and Werbner, P. (1997), *The Politics of Multiculturalism in the New Europe: Racism, Identity and Community*, London and New York: Zed Books.

Moghadam, V.M. (2002), 'Islamic feminism and its discontents: Towards a resolution of the debate', in *Sign: Journal of Women in Culture and Society*, 27(4), 1135-1171.

Panafit, L. (1999), *Quand le droit écrit l'Islam: L'intégration juridique de l'Islam en Belgique*, Bruxelles: Bruylant.

Roy, O. (1999), *Vers un Islam Européen*, Paris: Editions Esprit.

Saint-Blancat, C. (1997), *L'Islam de la diaspora*, Paris: Bayard Editions.

Sunier, T. (1996), *Islam in beweging*, Amsterdam: Het Spinhuis.

Tschannen, O. (1992), *Les théories de la sécularisation*, Geneva, Librairie Droz S.A.

Wilson, B. (1981), *The social impact of new religious movements*, New York: Rose of Sharon Press.

Notes

1 This article is a revised version of the paper presented at the workshop, 'The Production of Islamic Knowledge in Western Europe', Fourth Mediterranean Social and Political Research Meeting, Florence and Montecatini Terme, 19-23 March 2003, organised by the Mediterranean Programme of the Robert Schuman Centre for Advanced Studies at the European University Institute. I am grateful to the organisers of the workshop, the discussant and other participants for their constructive comments.

2 The analysis and reflections contained in this paper are part of an ongoing PhD project on secularization and individualization amongst Maghrebian Muslims.

3 For overviews of the history of the institutional arrangement of Islam, see Panafit (1999).

4 The conflicts after 1998 were related to contestation over elected representatives, the ethnic composition of the board and political interference. The election of 2005 was boycotted by large segments of the Moroccan community, mainly in the region of Brussels, again because of political interference.

5 Civil servants are mostly allowed to wear the headscarf unless they are in contact with some public audience or are acting as a public authority.

6 Today, the party still retains a key position in the city and has increased its influence in the Flemish region generally, having achieved second position in the elections of June 2004 behind a coalition of the Christian-Democrats with a smaller nationalist party. However, the Vlaams Blok changed its name to the Vlaams Belang [Flemish Interest] after it was convicted of racism on 9 November 2004.

7 All names used are pseudonyms.

8 'Amina' interviewed 12 November 2000.

9 'Btissame' interviewed 5 October 2000.

10 'Imane' interviewed 12 February 2001.

11 'Nora' interviewed 2 February 2001.

12 'Selma' interviewed 10 November 2000.

13 'Fatiha' interviewed 25 October 2000.

14 The *hadith* literature refers to the collections of sayings, customs and practices of the Prophet Muhammad. In terms of religious authority, they are considered second only to the Qur'an by Muslims and a major source for Islamic law.

15 This does not mean, however, that the contrary could not be the case. I can only state that I did not encounter it in the 21 interviews conducted.

Chapter 11

The Quest for Authenticity: Islamization Amongst Muslim Youth in Norway

Christine Jacobsen

Introduction

In February 2002 two demonstrations, separated in time only by a couple of days, mobilized Muslims in Oslo.[1] The first was initiated by a small group of highly mediatized young women in the aftermath of several 'scandals' involving forced marriages, female circumcision, and so-called 'honour-killings' in Norway and abroad. The young women accused the Muslim community of not taking women's oppression seriously enough. To varying degrees, they saw Islam, and particularly its 'traditionalist' and 'fundamentalist' interpretations, as obstacles to gender equality and the universal human rights of women. A couple of days later, this critique was met by other Muslims, who claimed that 'culture' and not 'Islam' was at the root of such oppressive practices, and that the latter should be combated by closer attention to essential Islamic principles rather than by their demise. In this second demonstration, harassment of, and campaigning against, Muslims was denounced. Whereas non-Muslim ethnic Norwegians dominated the first event, the second attracted close to a thousand Muslims, representing all the major mosques and Islamic organizations in Oslo. Together the two demonstrations reflect some of the internal religious differences and lines of conflict between young Muslims in Oslo. They also draw attention to the ways in which Islamic religiosity, and particularly the religiosity of Muslim youth and women, has been inextricably entwined with debates about the future of Norway as a multicultural and multi-religious society.

There is evidence of significant transformation, as well as continuity, in the religious identities and practices of young Muslims (Østberg, 2001; Jacobsen, 2002). Two important tendencies in this respect can be referred to as 'privatization' and 'Islamization'. Common to these is the increased emphasis on 'individual reflection' in matters of religion. Muslim identity is increasingly constructed and represented as an individual choice made in the context of other possible choices. The values of 'personal autonomy' and 'authenticity' are central to such representations and to the ethical reflections of young Muslims more generally (Jacobsen, 2002; Leirvik, 2002). As Cesari (1998) shows with regard to the French context, religious individualization may lead both to the view that religious identity and practice is a strictly 'private' affair and to an 'orthodox' reinvestment in the

Islamic tradition which links the individual to a global Islamic *umma* (community). This first tendency implies a 'relativization' of religion, the confinement of religious practice to particular (private) spaces, and a focus on basic religious (and universal) values (that may be considered 'secular'). The second tendency 'normativizes' Islam as a total way of life relevant to politics, law and science as well as to private spaces, and stresses the collective and cultic aspects of religion. Both these tendencies reflect a general propensity among young Muslims in the West towards rationalizing religious prescriptions and proscriptions (Schmidt, 2002). Increased formal literacy among second generation Muslims in the West privileges a 'literate' Islamic worldview and entails a gradual erosion of practices pertaining to so-called 'popular Islam'.

Despite these developments towards constructing and representing Muslim identity as a matter of individual choice, it seems that to a majority of young Muslims, religious identity remains significantly related to a sense of ethnic belonging. References to national and/or ethnic and religious communities remain largely interchangeable, as do references to culture and religion (Østberg, 1998; Jacobsen, 2002). The continued entwining of ethnic and religious belonging is energized not least by the way in which Muslims tend to be categorized as a quasi-ethnic group, representing a 'Muslim culture' that marks the boundary between 'us' (Christian or secular humanist Norwegians) and 'them' (Muslim immigrants or foreigners). Religion is therefore bound up with constructing identity and difference in multiple ways at individual as well as collective levels.

The engagement of individuals with different constructions of Muslim identity and religion varies over time and in particular contexts. In the rest of this chapter, I shall be concerned with the tendency towards 'Islamization' in two Muslim youth and student organizations in Oslo, in particular the importance of essentialist ideas about Islamic 'normativity' and 'authenticity' in their 'identity work'. It is important to note that although the organizations in question have attained a certain public visibility, they attract only a small number of young Muslims, and represent only one among the many different, though overlapping, Islamic tendencies.[2]

The Muslim Youth of Norway and the Muslim Student Society

International labour migration from the late 1960s and subsequent refugee flows have made Islam the second largest religion in Norway (around 2.5 per cent of population). Most Muslims live in Oslo and many maintain only 'nominal' adherence to Islam. Although divided along ethnic, linguistic and denominational lines, mosques and Islamic organizations have long been engaged in various forms of co-operation (Vogt, 2002). The 1990s, especially, saw an increase in this trend, notably under the umbrella of The Islamic Council of Norway (established 1993). The formation of two Muslim youth and student organizations in 1995/6 – The Muslim Youth of Norway (henceforth NMU) and the Muslim Student Society (henceforth MSS) – was also a part of these developments and signalled the 'coming of age' of a new generation of Muslims born and raised in Norway.

As has been noted by several writers on Muslims in Europe, the generational divide is today one of the defining features of Muslim communities. In Norway, the immigrant generation still dominates institutionalized Islam, although young Muslims are increasingly making their voices heard (Vogt, 2000; Jacobsen, 2002). In the NMU and MSS, young Muslims have asserted their leadership in new ways, and have gradually established the authority to speak publicly, both to the Muslim public, for example, in forums like the Islamic Council of Norway, and to the wider public, for example, through inter-faith dialogue and media debates.

This development must be understood in the context of a wider European Muslim landscape, which in the 1990s saw the emergence of a range of Islamic youth and student organizations. The NMU and MSS exhibit many similarities with Muslim youth and student organizations in other European countries, and their founders were notably inspired by the Muslim Youth of Sweden (SUM, previously SMUF) and the Young Muslims UK. The NMU is also a member of the Forum of European Muslim Youth and Student Organizations (FEMYSO).

The NMU and MSS are both centred on educational and social activities. They hold study-circles and seminars, and publish Islamic magazines, in order to enhance their own and other people's knowledge of Islam. In addition, they engage in a broad spectrum of activities ranging from sporting events to trips to Islamic conferences abroad. The organizations reflect the diversity of Muslims in Norway by bringing together youth and students who otherwise affiliate with virtually all of the Muslim national and ethnic communities in Norway,[3] and with different mosques and religious organizations oriented towards Shi'is and Sunnis (including different law schools), Sufism and Salafism. More exceptionally, the NMU and MSS are also gender-mixed.

Although the NMU and MSS include youth from rural/urban, poor/rich, and illiterate/literate family backgrounds, most come from families with higher levels of education than the immigrant Muslim population as a whole. In terms of the higher education that most undertake, the youth themselves may be seen as representing an aspiring middle class. Whereas the NMU caters for youth aged between 12 and 25, MSS members are mainly aged between 18 and 30. A majority have immigrant parents and were either born or raised in Norway, however the organizations also include some ethnic Norwegian converts and foreign students.

The dominant discourse within the NMU and MSS is coloured by contemporary Islamist revivalism in the form that Roald (2001) identifies as 'post-Ikhwan' (that is, an offshoot of the Muslim Brothers),[4] or, in Tariq Ramadan's (1999) terms, 'Salafi-reformism'. Common to Muslims associated with this trend, is the sense that they 'uphold the ikhwān and the salaf notion of "returning to the Koran and the Sunna", the ikhwān idea of Islam as a "rational" religion and the understanding of Islam as a complete way of life' (Roald, 2001: 56). The young Muslims in such organizations construct Islamic identity and practice as a matter of individual choice and personal authenticity. Their revivalist concerns are stimulated by several factors, notably increased formal literacy, and encounters with Muslim as well as non-Muslim others in translocal contexts (Waardenburg, 2000; Mandaville, 2004). Their 'rational' approach to religion entails a critique of 'cultural' practices associated with 'popular Islam'. This entwining of religion with local customs and traditions associated with the parental generation is criticized and a 'normative' vision of 'true Islam', based on religious texts, is presented as a 'purer' alternative. 'Islamic authenticity' has therefore become a primary discourse through which second generation Muslims negotiate and (re)produce identities, norms and values in the complex and ambiguous circumstances of their lives.

A major concern of both the NMU and MSS is to approach questions of *fiqh* in a manner which enables young Muslims to live in Norway in light of Islam: 'Can Muslims engage in national politics?'; 'Should you wear a *hijab* in non-Muslim societies?'; 'How should Muslims relate to the gender conventions of Norwegian society?'; 'Does Islam allow plastic surgery?'; 'Is chatting on the Internet *haram*?'. Neither organization follows a particular Islamic law school, scholar or *imam* in approaching such questions, but the ideas of different, internationally renowned, scholars associated with the 'Islamic Movement', such as Yusuf al-Qaradawi, enjoy considerable popularity.

It is important to stress that this way of locating the NMU and MSS does not imply that the organizations as such, or their individual members, represent one coherent Islamic position. Most of those who attend meetings, especially the younger ones, have little awareness of different theological positions, and are not very familiar with terms such as 'Salafi' and 'Ikhwan'. They (re)articulate reformist discourse at a much more 'experience-near' level in their efforts to 'defend' Islam, to find out what 'true Islam' is, and to live their daily lives as Muslims in a non-Muslim society.

Resisting Majority Culturalism: Disengaging 'True' Islam and Cultural Practice

In Norway, Muslims are often cast as representing a unitary 'Islamic culture', assuming a religious homogeneity that overrides cultural and social differences, including those between different ethnic groups, people of rural and urban origin, rich and poor, educated and illiterate, genders and generations. Such a culturalist understanding of immigrants in general, and Muslims in particular, has become more prominent since the late 1980s (compare Sunier, this volume). It has been coupled to what has been termed a neo-realism in the representation and administration of immigration-related issues which are increasingly regarded as 'problems' to be governed and supervised (Andersson, 2000; Fuglerud, 2001; Gullestad, 2002; Schierup and Ålund, 1991). The state seeks to manage such 'problems' through an ethnocentrically defined policy of 'multiculturalism' (Gressgård, 2002; Gressgård and Jacobsen, 2003). Indeed, recent years have seen several heated debates on 'Muslim problems' and especially those 'gender' issues mentioned at the beginning of this chapter.

When confronted with the construction of such problems as somehow related to 'Muslim culture', the reaction of many researchers, as well as many Muslims, would be that these phenomena have nothing to do with Islam. However, if certain practices are to be excluded from what we call 'Islam', there will necessarily have to be some sort of contest over what Islam *is*. The radical anti-essentialist critique of representations of Islam, which suggests that there are as many *Islams* as there are groups of Muslims becomes problematic in such debates. If Said is correct that all '[...] representations are *eo ipso* implicated, intertwined, embedded, interwoven with a great many other things besides the 'truth', which is itself a representation' (1979: 272), representations of what Islam *is not* are just as problematic and potentially essentializing as representations of what Islam is. We are thus caught in the epistemological dilemma of whether there is an 'Islam' beyond current misrepresentations, or whether its 'reality' is always a construct of particular representations and configurations of power.[5]

In the contemporary identity politics of young Muslims the discourse of authenticity gains its force precisely where the boundaries of what counts as 'true Islam' are defined. Defending Islam from what is experienced as a systematic misrecognition by Norwegian society, and especially the media, has come to be seen as one important part of their religious practice. Countering negative images of Islam in the media, in politics, in the classroom or on the streets – by writing, speaking or setting a good example – is seen as a religious duty as part of the greater *jihad*. For some it becomes more important than observance of the five daily prayers. When asked about his religious practice, 'Abid', an active member of the NMU and MSS, answered in the following way:

> I feel that I have a huge responsibility for defending Islam. Especially after all the shit that happened lately [9/11 and the gender issues mentioned earlier] ... It is my job, I feel, to get rid of the misunderstandings that arise ... It is my responsibility to present another side of Islam. Discussing with people for as little as half an hour I can get rid of a lot of those misunderstandings and get people to become more open ... In the magazine we publish I do this through symbolism. For instance I use pictures of women who are a bit free to illustrate that our girls are not really that oppressed ... To defend Islam is kind of like my *jihad*. But, then again, I often feel somewhat hypocritical when I do things that are against my religion while at the same time defending it. But I've heard that God shows understanding for us growing up here: things are less strict, although we shouldn't take advantage of it, as I feel I sometimes do. You think that you're so smart, and you forget about the fact that God is actually watching.

When talking about his engagement in *da'wa* (the invitation to Islam) and dialogue work, 'Mohammed', a member of the MSS, explains that he usually tries to confront negative stereotypes of Islam by presenting them as 'Pakistani' rather than 'Islamic' problems: 'Pakistanis may be racists, but there is no racism in Islam'; 'Pakistanis may not let their daughters decide whom to marry, but there is no coercion in Islam'. A range of 'problems' can thus be explained in terms of 'cultural tradition' rather than 'authentic Islam'. In deploying such a discourse, young Muslims represent Islam as a transcendent, unchangeable and coherent truth. Its coming-into-being in different localized forms is viewed as a corruption of authenticity.

The attempt to re-constitute Islam separately from its local cultural manifestations is stimulated by an essentialism that seems to mirror the culturalist differentialism of non-Muslims' stereotypes. Both treat Islam as an autonomous subject that 'says' certain things, for example, what Islam 'says' about Muslim girls and wearing *hijab*. However, whereas cultural differentialism assumes a transparent relationship between Islam and the behaviour of actual Muslims, young Muslims themselves contend that 'Islam' is quite different from the way in which some Muslims currently (ab)use it.

Just as Islamic revivalism per se may be seen as partly invigorated by post-colonial resistance to Western hegemony, the embracing of an essentialist Islamic authenticity by young Muslims in Norway (and elsewhere in the non-Muslim world) may in part be understood in terms of resistance to the hegemony of 'majority society' and its dominant paradigms of representing and organizing ethnic and cultural difference. Counter-hegemonic resistance therefore tends to (re)produce the mode of the hegemonic order, in this case through a counter-essentializing of Islam. However, the essentializing practices of young Muslims are effective only to a limited extent in resisting and altering majority representations of Islam. They invite the production of images and counter-images of 'authentic Islam', but without establishing any clear criteria that might authorize a particular construction of authenticity. To authorize their own representations, young Muslims must claim an epistemological position in which some people have a privileged access to 'authentic Islam'. Determining the limits of inclusion and exclusion, insiders and outsiders, the authorized and un-authorized, thus becomes a perennial problem in the essentializing practices of resistance.

The discourse of authenticity allows young Muslims to counter the culturalist representation of Islam as anti-modern, irrational and oppressive. At the same time, this way of dealing with difference presupposes an inauthentic 'other' threatening to defile the purity of 'true Islam'. Whereas many Islamists in the Muslim world conceive of 'the West' as the major threat, young Muslims in the NMU and MSS are more concerned with recovering Islam from its embeddedness in cultural traditions represented by the parental generation. This process of identification and differentiation revolves around dichotomies such as traditional/modern, illiterate/literate, irrational/rational, and rural/urban. The parental generation and occasionally 'the *mullahs*' and 'the *imams*' function as internal 'others', 'cultural Muslims' associated with the traditional, illiterate, irrational and the rural. Young Muslims perceive the parental generation as stuck in customary traditions and unable to recognize Islamic authenticity and its trans-ethnic potential (Schmidt, 2002). The quest for authenticity therefore runs the risk of essentializing and homogenizing its internal and external others, reinforcing the very stereotypes which it aims at deconstructing.

The Culturalist Cartography of Immigration and Nationalizing Muslim Identity

The representation of a homogeneous 'Muslim culture' establishes Muslims as external to the imagined national community of Norway. Popular political discourse increasingly tends to affirm a Christian and humanist cultural heritage as the uniting bond of the Norwegian nation-state, and 'Christian and humanist values' are invoked as the foundation of, and to legitimate, its public institutions

(Borchgrevink, 2002; Leirvik, 2004: 101). This construction of Muslims and Islam as outside the nation is present in the tendency to view ethnic Norwegian converts to Islam as foreigners, or at least as representing a 'foreign culture'. It is also evident in the increased use of the term 'Muslim' as synonymous with 'immigrant' and 'fremmedkulturell' ('of/from an alien culture'). For example, in the debate on whether mosques should be allowed to perform *adhan* (the call to prayer) on Fridays, those against argued that unlike 'Norwegian church bells', the *adhan* was 'foreign to Norwegian society' and a threat to shared Christian culture (*Dagladet*, 22 January 2000; *Aftenposten*, 27 January 2000).

Such debates raise questions about which forms of belonging Muslims may develop in Norway. Young Muslims in the NMU and MSS draw upon two normative models of community in order to challenge this cartography, one based on identification as Norwegian Muslims and the other based on a transnational, multi-ethnic 'Islamic heritage' and identification as part of a global imagined *umma*. These normative models of community may be constructed in different ways, as competing, as overlapping, or as referring simply to different dimensions of identification.

A speech on integration given by the current leader of the NMU at a conference held by the Forum for Municipal Refugee Work (Akram, 2002) illustrates how young Muslims seek to 'nationalize' Muslim identity and establish it as a legitimate part of Norwegian society. Akram begins by presenting himself as a successfully integrated 'immigrant'. While his parents were born and raised in Pakistan, Akram himself was born and raised in Norway. Well knowing that the issue of language is seen by politicians, researchers and people in general as the most significant hindrance to integration, Akram stresses the fact that Norwegian is his first language and that he has a Western-Norwegian dialect.[6] Akram further emphasizes the estrangement he feels during vacations in Pakistan, friendship with ethnic Norwegians, typical student experiences of life in a shared flat, and finally his successful integration into the labour market. He thus challenges stereotypes of 'the immigrant' and demonstrates that he is not only 'well integrated', but also 'successful' judged by Norwegian standards.

Having established himself as a fully integrated Norwegian citizen, Akram claims the universal right to difference guaranteed by his citizenship:

> Like every other person in this country I have my own opinions and I am allowed to make my own choices and decisions. These are my fundamental rights: to freedom of expression, including freedom of religion. These rights, and the rights of minorities to retain their distinctiveness, are essential to any debate on integration, an aspect I think receives too little attention. For what happens to the picture of the well-integrated Athar [Akram's first name] when I confess to being a believing Muslim? (Akram, 2002: 2) [my translation]

Being a believing Muslim, having an 'arranged' marriage and wearing the *hijab* are all examples Akram uses to invoke the basic right a citizen has to freedom of expression, freedom of belief and the right to 'be different' from 'what is common' in Norway. Akram demands to be accepted as *both* a Muslim and a fully integrated Norwegian citizen. The fact that he began his speech with the

Islamic formula – '*Bismillah, al-Rahman, al-Rahim!*' ('In the name of God, the Compassionate, the Merciful!') – translated into Norwegian before a non-Muslim public, aptly illustrates the realization of such an identity.

In politics, the value of 'the national' tends to exceed that of other imagined communities, and minority groups are thus compelled to appeal to 'the national' if they want to be heard (Parker et al., 1992: 8; Gilroy, 1993). This does not imply that identification as 'Norwegian-Muslims' is merely a strategic move towards recognition. There are important ways in which Muslim identity and religiosity is actually transformed 'on the ground' as a consequence of being articulated by people like Akram, in the Norwegian language and with reference to aspects of Norwegian popular culture. The discourse of Islamic authenticity therefore facilitates the formulation of a Norwegian-Muslim identity by essentializing Islam as a subject whose truth lies outside of history, transcending cultural particularisms. It is debateable, however, whether the construction of a Norwegian-Muslim identity which Akram proposes, successfully challenges the construction of Muslims as external to the imagined national community. In so far as Akram sees Muslim beliefs and practices as a part of the distinctiveness that minorities should be allowed to retain – and not a part of what otherwise makes him a fully integrated Norwegian citizen – he seems to uphold the notion of a homogeneous nation in which being Muslim is marked out as 'different' and not part of shared 'sameness'.

Global Imaginaries: The *Umma* as an Alternative Model of Community

Migrants produce new localities and identities such as 'Norwegian-Muslim' but also produce new forms of 'deterritorialized' global belongings. In the case of Islam, 'global belonging' is forcefully expressed in the idea of the *umma*. Imagined in different ways by historically situated actors (Eickelman and Piscatori, 1996), in modern Islamic discourse it often appears as a central normative concept, an appeal for Muslim unity world-wide. Indeed, the contemporary imaginary of Islam is underpinned by a number of processes including international migration, a mass media, new communication technologies, the *da'wa* activities of transnational Islamic movements, and the increasingly global dimension of political conflicts, exemplified by the Rushdie and *hijab* affairs, as well as the so-called 'war on terror'. Furthermore, encounters with Muslim 'others' in translocal contexts where Muslims are ascribed a common identity, reinforces such global imaginaries (Mandaville, 2004).

This cartography of the *umma* represents a 'radical transnationalism', that is, a transnationalism that does not have a spatial grounding in 'a homeland', diasporic community or the like (Lithman, 2004).[7] It structures the self-imagining of young Muslims in the NMU and MSS in several ways. The use of kinship terms to refer to 'sisters' and 'brothers' in Islam regardless of nationality or ethnicity, local demonstrations against the ban on the *hijab* in France and injustices against Muslims elsewhere in the world, all express feelings of connection and solidarity on a global scale. Similarly, the multi-ethnic composition of the organizations locally is also seen as a powerful expression of the global character of Islam.

The transnational imaginary of Islam, especially when it is politicized, can challenge the 'national order of things'. As Asad writes: 'The politicization of religious traditions by Muslim immigrants [...] serves to question the inevitability of the absolute nation-state – of its demands to exclusive loyalty and its totalizing cultural projects' (1993: 266). The interpretation of such challenges, and their potential for transformation, vary considerably however. Bowen interprets the tension between 'demands to develop an Islam proper to France' and 'demands to maintain the translocal orientation of Islam' (2002: 9) as limiting the possibility of settling into and producing new localities. Mandaville (2004), on the other hand, discusses the more positive challenge of a 'form of interstitial identity', a 'third space', and a new mode of 'relating internationally' in which 'the boundaries of political community are constantly open to rearticulation' (2004: 190).

The production of Muslim identities through local and global imaginaries are intimately linked and interlocking processes. Both are energized by culturalist differentialism which constructs Muslims, at a local level, as external to the Norwegian imagined community and, at a global level, as external to the modern, secularized West. Furthermore, global and local (or 'glocal') imaginaries give rise to essentializing responses which invoke a 'core of common values' in policy documents and public discourse on immigrant and minority politics. As such, they reinforce the construction of Muslims as external to the self-imagination of the national community, 'Europe' and 'the West'. The different normative visions of community that young Muslims draw upon in order to 'seize the power of naming difference [itself], and explode the implicit definition of difference as deviance in relation to a norm [...]' (Young, 1990: 171) may both enable and constrain each other, (re)produce and challenge other visions of community, and reinforce and change existing identities and practices.

Islamic Identities and Practices: Questions of the Secular and Secularism

A recurring question in literature on Muslims in Europe has been whether there is an insurmountable antagonism between Islam and secular democracy. As Asad (2003) has noted, the concepts of the secular (as an epistemic category) and secularism (as a political doctrine), which underlie such debates, are poorly defined, and are in need of theoretical as well as empirical clarification. A theoretical clarification is beyond the scope of this article, but the case of Norway illustrates the complex ways in which the categories of 'the religious' and the 'secular' are produced in countries that we refer to as 'modern' and 'secular'. Whereas most European nation states are now 'secular' in the sense that churches are separated from secular institutions of government, Lutheran Christianity remains the religion of the Norwegian State. About 85 per cent of a total population of 4.4 million are members of the church of Norway, and although continuously disputed and challenged, it is increasingly invoked as a foundation for national identity and communal values.

In 1964 the paragraph in the Constitution establishing the Evangelical-Lutheran religion as the public religion of the state was qualified with the provision that 'All inhabitants of the Realm shall enjoy free exercise of religion'. Since then there has gradually been greater accommodation of religious pluralism in Norway. Particular arrangements were developed for 'faith and life stance communities' in order to compensate for the fact that the budget of the Church of Norway is still integrated into municipal and state budgets. One effect of this has been that Islam has been transformed into a 'membership religion', with somewhere between 60 and 70 per cent of those with a Muslim family background registering as members of around 90 Islamic 'faith communities', a few of which have several local congregations. Although the State Church system is being adjusted to take account of the new multi-religious reality, the main socializing institutions of Norway, public kindergartens and schools, still have a legal obligation to provide all pupils with 'a moral and Christian education'. Compulsory religious education, which despite its 'pluralist' intent and disputed confessional basis, also focuses mainly on Christian knowledge with limited possibilities for exemption.

Whereas the relationship between Islam and secular democracy has been at the centre of debates in countries such as France, this has been less the case in Norway. One reason for this is perhaps that the state-supported Christian communitarianism that marks the imagination of the nation gives religion a measure of public respectability (Borchgrevink, 1999). That being said, it is clear that Norwegian politicians, and the Christian Democrats currently in power in particular, attempt to construct their own religiosity as somehow politically neutral in order to fit with the requirements of a secular separation of religion and state. In contrast to this, public discourse often constructs Muslims as unwilling or unable to maintain such a separation. While appeal is sometimes made to the principle of secularism, Islamic symbols and practices such as the *hijab* and the *adhan* are more often problematized as symbols of a 'foreign' religion and culture inherently inimical to women.

Although ambivalent, the 'secular' context of Norway affects the possibilities of Islamic religious practice in important ways. Several cases have recently made clear how the religious freedom of minorities is circumscribed by secular bureaucratic regulations, and the inability of the system to cope with forms of religiosity other than Protestantism. The question of *adhan* was treated politically in terms of public health regulations on noise. Similarly, the provision of *halal* meat has been virtually impossible since it has been dealt with politically in terms of animal protection and food control rather than as a question of religious freedom. Other issues include attempts to prohibit the circumcision of boys on medical grounds and the privileging of health and security over religious freedom when it comes to headscarves.

As Borchgrevink has noted, the particular form which secularity takes in Norway:

> [...] produces a configuration which is hard to understand: a religious indifference which simultaneously allows Christian interests to impose themselves relatively without restriction; something unprincipled and unreflective, preventing anticipation and perhaps accommodating a mixture of arrogance and sloppiness on the part of the majority. (2002: 21-22) [my translation]

Within this complex configuration, mixing a state-supported Christian communitarian vision of national community with an unreflective secularity in state bureaucratic institutions, Muslims in Norway have engaged in alliances with different actors in order to secure rights to religious freedom. Partners for co-operation have included humanist secularists, elements within the Christian community, as well as other religious minority groupings. The NMU and the MSS have been especially active in respect of 'Muslim rights'. They have worked to obtain prayer spaces and *halal* meat in colleges and universities, supported the establishment of private Muslim schools, sought to obtain rights of exemption from Christian/religious education in schools, and lobbied against the discrimination of women who wear the *hijab*.

Norwegian Muslims are thus positioned in-between attempts to secure the legitimacy of religion in public space and attempts at limiting the dominance of Protestant Christianity so as to include other religious and non-religious worldviews. The attempts of young Muslims like Athar Akram to base their claims to religious freedom on a dissociation of 'religion' and 'culture' which privileges an individualized and universalist attachment to Islam and refutes its embeddedness in particular local cultures, is important in the political quest for recognition. In terms of rights to which Norwegian Muslims may appeal, rights to individual religious freedom are better protected by international agreements on universal human rights than rights concerning the retention of one's cultural distinctiveness.

Conclusion

The major conclusion to be drawn from the foregoing discussion is that researchers should be mindful of the power struggles involved in the construction of 'Muslims in Europe' as a field of academic research. Several authors have noted the need to de-essentialize representations of Islam, and suggested that we speak about 'Islams' instead (El-Zien, 1977; Al-Azmeh, 1993). This allows commentators to specify which type of Islam is being spoken about at what particular moment in time (Said, 2002: 1). In view of the analysis I have presented we may conclude that moving beyond essentialism, by speaking of 'Islams' rather than 'Islam', may not be so straightforward. This is so not only because the notion of 'Islams' would be offensive to Muslims, but also for important analytical and theoretical reasons.

Firstly, theoretical efforts to de-essentialize Islam should not lead researchers to overlook the importance of essentializing practices in different kinds of identity work at an empirical level. As I have argued, essentialist representations of Islam, portraying it as a unified, homogeneous and continuous totality, are intrinsic to the identity work of the young Muslims in my study. Encounters with both Muslim and non-Muslim 'others' in a plural city like Oslo energize debates about 'true' Islam. Attempts to deal with (cultural and social) difference with reference to 'true Islam', apparently purified of its cultural particularisms, may be seen as a form of resistance to culturalist differentialism and nationalist cartographies of immigration.

A pluralization of 'Islams' also risks simply displacing rather than resolving the problem of essentialism (Fuss, 1990). If modelled, as Said proposes – 'Each region and people who came under its sway developed its own kind of Islam' (2002: 1) – the notion of 'Islams' could easily end up doing little more than reproduce the (arguably) essentialist assumptions of much 'culture-talk' in anthropology (Borofsky, 1994). The propensity of researchers to talk about 'French Islam', 'Swedish Islam' and so on should, in my opinion, be problematized, as they may imply unreflective assumptions about national cultural homogeneity.

The internal heterogeneity of organizations like the NMU and MSS inevitably raises theoretical questions about what 'difference' makes a difference (i.e. nationality, ethnicity, locality, gender, generation, age, class, denomination). Should we be concerned with a particular form of Islam in i) a particular location (and, if so, at what level? Oslo's Islam, Norwegian Islam, Euro-Islam or even global Islam?); or ii) of a particular ethnic group (Norwegian-Pakistani Islam, Norwegian-Turkish Islam); or iii) of a social group (women's and men's Islam, YUMMIES' Islam,[8] young people's Islam); or iv) of a particular movement through space (travelling Islam, diaspora Islam, migratory Islam). The problem of such categorizations is that they tend to overlook the intersection of differences of several kinds, intersections which produce, and are produced by, complex patterns of exclusion and inclusion, identification and differentiation.

A theoretical de-essentialization of Islam should have empirical heterogeneity as its starting point. We should ask which circumstances make it possible and intelligible to construct different versions of Islam. When it comes to Muslims in Europe we should investigate the particular modern constructions of the religious versus the secular, modernity versus tradition, rationality versus irrationality, distinctions which make it possible to represent Islam and Muslims in Europe in particular ways. The production of 'the religious' and 'the secular' as epistemic categories and political ideologies is a complex historical process that may not be reduced to a question of whether Islam (as an attribute of 'foreigners') is incommensurable with secular democracy (as an attribute of 'indigenous' Norwegian society). As I have shown, the religiousness of young Muslims in Norway shapes and is shaped by the ways in which categories such as 'religion', 'culture' and 'modernity' are constructed in contemporary Norway and beyond.

References

Akram, A. (2002), 'Assimilering integrert i integreringsdebatten', *Utrop*, 2 December.
Al-Azmeh, A. (1993), *Islams and Modernities*, London: Verso.
Andersson, M. (2000), *All Five Fingers are not the Same*, Bergen: Report 1/2000 IMER Norway/Bergen/Centre for Social Science Research, University of Bergen.
Asad, T. (1993), *Genealogies of Religion: Discipline and Reasons of Power in Christianity and Islam*, Baltimore: Johns Hopkins University Press.
Asad, T. (2003), *Formations of the Secular: Christianity, Islam, Modernity*, Stanford: Stanford University Press.
Borchgrevink, T. (1999), *Multikulturalisme: tribalisme – bløff – kompromiss? Debatter om det flerkulturelle samfunn*, Report 99: 3, Oslo: Institute of Social Research.

Borchgrevink, T. (2002), 'Makten eller æren: Kristendom og felleskultur i det flerreligiøse Norge', in G. Brochmann, T. Borchgrevink and J. Rogstad (eds), *Sand i maskineriet: Makt og demokrati i det flerkulturell Norge*, Oslo: Gyldendal Akademisk.

Borofsky, R. (ed.) (1994), *Assessing Cultural Anthropology*, New York: McGraw Hill Inc.

Bowen, J.R. (2002), 'Islam in/of France': Dilemmas of Translocality', Mai, www.ceri-sciences-po.org.

Cesari, J. (1998), *Musulmans et républicains: Les jeunes, l'islam et la France*, Paris: Éditions Complexe.

Eickelman, D.F. and Piscatori, J. (1996), *Muslim Politics*, Princeton and New Jersey: Princeton University Press.

El-Zien, A.H. (1977), 'Beyond Ideology and Theology: the Search for an Anthropology of Islam', *Annual Review of Anthropology*, VI, 2227-54.

Fuglerud, Ø. (2001), *Migrasjonsforstålse: flytteprosesser, rasisme og globalisering*, Oslo: Universitetsforlaget.

Fuss, D. (1990), *Essentially Speaking: Feminism, Nature and Difference*, New York: Routledge.

Gilroy, P. (1993), *Small Acts: Thoughts on the Politics of Black Culture*, London and New York: Serpent's Tail.

Gressgård, R. (2002), *Dilemmaet mellom likeverdighet og særegenhet som ramme for multikulturell dialog*, Doctoral thesis, Faculty of Social Sciences: The University of Bergen.

Gressgård, R. and Jacobsen, C.M. (2003), 'Questions of Gender in a Multicultural Society', *NORA Nordic Journal of Women's Studies*, 2 (11), 69-77.

Gullestad, M. (2003), 'Muhammed Atta and I: Identification, Discrimination and the Formation of Sleepers', *European Journal of Cultural Studies*, 6 (4), 529-548.

Jacobsen, C.M. (2001), 'Young, Muslim and Woman, Norwegian Style', *NIKK magasin*, 3, 23-25.

Jacobsen, C.M. (2002), *Tilhørighetens mange former: Unge muslimer i Norge*, Oslo: Unipax.

Jacobsen, C.M. (2004), 'Negotiating Gender: Discourse and Practice Among Young Muslims in Oslo', in *Tidsskrift for Kirke Religion og Samfunn*, 17 (1), 5-28.

Leirvik, O. (2002), *Islamsk etikk – ei idéhistorie*, Oslo: Universitetsforlaget.

Leirvik, O. (2004), 'Christian-Muslim Relations in a State Church Situation: Politics of Religion and Interfaith Dialogue', in Malik, J. (ed.), *Muslims in Europe: From the Margin to the Centre*, Münster: LIT Verlag.

Mandaville, P. (2004), *Transnational Muslim Politics: Reimagining the Umma*, London and New York: Routledge.

Østberg, S. (2001), *Pakistani Children in Norway: Islamic Nurture in a Secular Context*, Leeds: Community Religions Project Monograph Series, Department of Theology and Religious Studies, University of Leeds.

Parker, A., Russo, M., Sommer, D. and Yaeger, P. (1992), *Nationalisms and Sexualities*, New York and London: Routledge.

Ramadan, T. (1999), *To Be a European Muslim: A Study of Islamic Sources in the European Context*, Leicester: Islamic Foundation.

Roald, A.S. (2001), *Women in Islam: The Western Experience*, London and New York: Routledge.

Said, E.W. (1979), *Orientalism*, New York: Vintage.

Said, E.W. (2002), 'Impossible Histories: Why the Many Islams Cannot be Simplified', *Harper's Magazine*, July.

Schierup, C. and Ålund, A. (1991), *Paradoxes of Multiculturalism: Essays on Swedish Society*, Aldershot: Avebury.

Schmidt, G. (2002), 'Dialectics of Authenticity: Examples of Ethnification of Islam Among Young Muslims in Sweden and the United States', *The Muslim World*, 92 (1/2), Spring, 1-18.

Vogt, K. (2000), *Islam på norsk. Moskeer og islamske organisasjoner i Norge*, Oslo: Cappelen.

Vogt, K. (2002), 'Integration through Islam? Muslims in Norway', in Haddad, Y. (ed.), *Muslims in the West: From Sojourners to Citizens*, Oxford: Oxford University Press.

Waardenburg, J. (2000), 'Normative Islam in Europe', in Dassetto, F. *Paroles d'islam: Individus, sociétés et discours dans l'islam européen contemporain*, Paris: Maisonneuve Larose.

Young, I.M. (1990), *Justice and the Politics of Difference*, Princeton and New Jersey: Princeton University Press.

Notes

1   The immediate precursor to these demonstrations was the 'honour killing' of a Swedish-Kurdish woman, Fadime Sahindal. Although Sahindal's family appear not to have been Muslim, in Norway her death provoked criticism of the Muslim community who were suspected of sympathizing with the use of extreme measures in safeguarding women's 'honour'. This debate was preceded by others on female circumcision in 2000 and 'forced marriages' in 1997.

2   This chapter is based upon a five-year period of anthropological fieldwork in Oslo, including intensive participant observation and interviews.

3   The composition of the organizations shifts over time, but when I began my fieldwork in 1999, there were 11 different national backgrounds represented in NMU: Pakistani, Moroccan, Tunisian, Afghan, Somali, Turkish, Bosnian, Chechen, Iranian, Iraqi and Norwegian.

4   Several young Muslims used terms such as 'Salafi', 'Ikhwan' and, more rarely, 'Wahhabi' to position themselves and others. Patterns of co-operation with other organizations and mosques, as well as the religious orientations of some of the founders, further serve to establish the NMU and MSS within this tendency.

5   This question remains unresolved in Said's (1979) deconstruction of Orientalism.

6   In Norway, having a specific local dialect is considered an important part of a person's identity and belonging.

7   This should not, of course, suggest that it is not localized.

8   Al-Azmeh (1993: 9) uses this term for 'Young Upwardly-Mobile Muslims'.

Chapter 12

The Transformation of a Sufi Order into a Lay Community: The Süleymanci Movement in Germany and Beyond

Gerdien Jonker

Introduction

This chapter explores Sufi piety and devotion in Europe with a focus on Turkish lay communities. Like all Sufi orders in Turkey, the three main lay communities to establish themselves in Germany – the Islamic Community of Milli Görüsh, the Jamaatunnur (Nurcu) and the Islamic Cultural Centres (Süleymanci) – lead an existence that is, of necessity, in opposition to the Turkish State. In 1923, when Kemal Atatürk founded the Turkish Republic on the principles of republicanism, populism, laicism and revolution, he radically effaced any religious influence on matters of state. He abolished the Sufi orders, closed their centres and razed many mosques to the ground. The religious elite were either 'retired' or jailed and the use of Arabic as a liturgical language was eradicated. It took the Turkish government another 30 years to install a state-controlled form of worship, so-called laicist Islam.[1] Meanwhile, the demolishing of the religious infrastructure of the country created a crisis amongst the rural population of Anatolia and beyond, robbing them of their main social compass and resource for knowledge (Mardin, 1989: ix).

Into this void, several Naqshbandi *sheikhs* (Sufi masters), Said Nursi and Süleyman Hilmi Tunahan among them, secretly began their efforts to preserve religious knowledge and translate traditional order rules into broader community patterns (Nereid, 1997; Jonker, 2002). Through the 1940s and 1950s their endeavours saw the growth of religious movements that protested at forced modernization and clung to a heritage of 'Islamic civilization' through the revival of Qur'anic ritual practices and Sufi devotions. When state-controlled worship was finally introduced it was met with fierce competition from these pious lay communities.

The struggle over laicist Islam in Turkey coincided with a large-scale migration to Europe that involved workers of rural origins especially. In 1961, the German and Turkish governments signed an official agreement for the hire of Turkish workers and between this date and 1973, when the agreement officially ended, some one million Turks migrated (Yano, 1998: 168). As early as 1963, the Turkish Sufi orders and the religious movements deriving from them – the

Süleymanci, Jamaatunnur and Milli Görüsh – all established centres in Germany (Schiffauer, 2000: 80-89; Jonker, 2002: 119-123).

Religious systems are not primordial entities. Rather, through the handing down of a corpus of rites, narratives and texts, they produce new constructions and selective (re)imaginings that respond to changing circumstances and institutional expectations, at both local and global levels (Beyer, 1998: 90). The resettlement of Milli Görüsh, Jamaatunnur and Süleymanci in Europe represents a good case in point. It is my argument here that all three constitute a form of religious organization that is new to the Muslim world, namely, lay communities. The main characteristics of lay communities include an intensity of religious practice in combination with the worldly aims of *hizmet* (service) and *da'wa* (missionary activity). There are differences between the communities, of course. Whereas Jamaatunnur and Süleymanci focus on Sufi piety to the exclusion of political aspirations, Milli Görüsh represents a version of 'Islamism' combined with Sufi practice.

This chapter continues in the next section with an overview of the Sufi orders in Germany. Thereafter, I will outline the concept of the 'Sufi lay community' with a case study of the Süleymanci organization. Reporting on the findings of fieldwork and historical research, I describe how the Naqshbandi order became transformed into a modern missionary organization responsive to the new context of Europe. Crucial to the evolution of the Naqshbandi order in this way has been the re-centring of its main forms of communicating with the divine, in terms of the rite of 'remembrance of God' (*dhikr*) and the 'imitation' of the Prophet. In this contribution, I will focus mainly on the latter. Finally, I will sketch out how it is today that many Süleymanci members disapprove of traditional Naqshbandi Sufi devotions.

Sufi Piety in Germany: An Overview

The first overview of the branches of the Sufi orders established in Germany was published relatively late (Dornbrach, 1991). The author, himself a *sheikh* of the Mevlevi Order, mentions the presence of eleven Sunni and Shi'i orders. The Sunni orders Dornbrach mentions are the Naqshbandi, Qadiri, Rifa'i, Mevlevi, Cerrahi, Burhani, Darqawi, Safini and 'Alawi. The two Shi'i orders are the Nimutullahi and the Bektashi. Dornbrach also classifies as Sufi orders the Turkish lay communities that were founded by Naqshbandi preachers, making explicit mention of the Süleymanci.

Dornbrach's work has generally served as a point of reference for other scholarly descriptions (Schleßmann, 1991: 143; Keller, 1991: 359-90; Spuler-Stegemann, 1998: 134-46). To his list of orders, evidence of the Chishti, Shadhili and Tijani orders, as well as the Turkish devotional network surrounding Said Nursi (Jamaatunnur) and the followers of Fethullah Gülen, were added (Spuler-Stegemann, 1998: 141-3). However, some scholars decided not to research what they identified as 'foreign Sufi orders', preferring to concentrate only on those adopted by 'native Germans' instead (Schleßmann, 1999: 12-21). Thus, information on the Burhani, Mevlevi, Naqshbandi-Haqqani and 'Alawi orders is most prevalent, as these orders dominate amongst European converts.

The information offered in these writings never extends beyond short description, however. Similarly, the Christian-Islamic Dialogue journal (Christlich-Islamische Begegnungs- und Dokumentationsstelle or CIBEDO) offers space for religious actors, institutions and movements to represent themselves. However, during the last 20 years the orders have made only sparing use of this opportunity (CIBEDO, 1981: 3-21; 1983: 3-19; 1999: 113). As yet, problem-oriented research that looks at, for instance, societal bases and recruitment patterns, transnational networks, modes of female participation or the tension between charisma and institutionalization, has hardly been undertaken (Hüttermann, 2003, is an exception).

The number of Muslims involved in Sufi devotion in Germany is also open to conjecture. In 1991, Schleßmann estimated their numbers at approximately 1000, whereas Keller suggests 10,000 for the whole of Western Europe (Schleßmann, 1991: 145; Keller, 1991: 366). However, the Mevlevi *sheikh*, Dornbrach, has claimed that between ten and 15 per cent of Turkish Muslims in Germany, and 20 per cent of German Muslims, belong to one Sufi community or another, which suggests numbers of above 300,000 (Dornbrach, 1991). My own research during 1997 and 1998 on Muslim religious life in Berlin confirms Dornbrach's claim (Jonker and Kapphan, 1999). Among the 70 Sunni and Shi'i prayer halls, our research team noted one Rifa'i, two Qadiri, one Burhani and two Naqshbandi-Khalidi *khaniqat* ('houses'). These constituted relatively small communities with no more than 800 members in total. However, in addition to these, the nine Süleymanci mosques and six 'Nur' centres also organized *halqas* (circles) and *dhikr* gatherings, sometimes as often as four times a week. In ten out of 14 Milli Görüsh mosques collective *dhikr* gatherings took place every Saturday night, with both men and women participating together. In addition, female *hocas* (teachers) frequently organized women-only *halqas* and offered courses on Sufism.

All in all, 33 Berlin *tekkes* (lodges), *medreses* (study centres) and prayer-halls – representing more than a third of organized Islamic religious life in the city – were in some way or other regularly involved in forms of Sufi devotion. The research team also frequently heard stories about prayer circles and related therapy sessions that were organized in private households, but it was not possible to include these in our calculations. It thus remains difficult to give a concrete figure for the number of participants overall. However, the 15 per cent *sheikh* Dornbrach suggested in 1991 would seem a sound estimate. Since many migrants who settled in Berlin originally came from Anatolia, the heartland of Turkish Sufism, the character of settlement and communal organization has been somewhat different to other German cities. Nevertheless, Berlin in many ways exemplifies devotional patterns in Muslim communities all over Germany.

Of all Germany's Muslims, 75 per cent originate from Turkey, with Milli Görüsh and Süleymanci now being the country's largest Islamic organizations. The Naqshbandi and Qadiri orders are less visible but still have a strong presence, as do the Chishti-Qadiri and Qadiri-Rifa'i orders, which have genealogies that include many Turkish saints. Next to these Sunnis, 30 per cent of Turkish migrants to Germany are of Alevi descent and, among this Shi'i grouping, Bektashi and other, much more heterodox forms of Sufi devotion, prevail.

Spiritual Hierarchy to Worldly Collective: Lay Communities and their Modern Mission

The idea of 'lay communities' as a new category of Sufi self-organization can be justified in a number of ways (Jonker, 2002b). Firstly, after the prohibition of the orders in Kemalist Turkey, the government replaced Sufi and other forms of religious expertise with its own theological training that generated professionals in state office. As a consequence, it is experts with modern, secular backgrounds that officially represent Turkish Islam today. The founders of the Turkish Sufi lay communities kept their distance from these state theologians as a matter of course. More surprisingly, they also abolished their own 'divine' authority as *sheikhs*. The Naqshbandi *sheikh*, Said Nursi, for instance re-directed the attention of his followers from his sacred person to the Qur'an and wrote 6500 pages of inspired Qur'anic commentary (*tafsir manevi*) to assist them. Another, Naqshbandi *sheikh*, Süleyman Hilmi Tunahan, of whom more later, offered his followers introductory courses in Arabic, Qur'anic recitation and Islamic law so that men and women, mostly uneducated peasants, could perform their religious duties and services independently in the villages. Some thirty years later, two other Naqsbandi *sheikhs*, Mehmed Zaid Kotku and Necmettin Erbakan, suggested that their followers attempt to realize *din ve dawla* (religion and state) within the Turkish political system. Together, in their zeal to rescue the religious tradition that was being suppressed by the secularizing Turkish State, these *sheikhs* transformed their own authority into broad-based communal movements with a collective missionary vocation. So it was then that the religious empowerment of the masses remained a Naqshbandi phenomenon because, as will be explained further below, this order had set the stage for such transformations and renewal long before the modern Turkish crisis occurred.

Secondly, the phenomenon of lay communities is a product of modernity. At their core is the modern idea of society being an object that can be renewed. Most Christian lay communities emerged in spontaneous protest against religious laxity, against political oppression or both (Eisenstadt, 1998: 46). What both Christian and Muslim organizations of this type have in common is their organization around a specific religious cause. For Christian lay communities, this cause was often shaped by welfare or missionary goals. For Sufi lay communities, both in Turkey and in the West, their cause has been defined in terms of rescuing the religious message from state intervention. They seek to accomplish this goal through exemplary and explicit religious conduct (Süleymanci), through the organization of religious education and the printing of religious books (Nurcu), as well as through forms of political organization (Milli Görüsh). Members of Sufi lay communities are, as a rule, engaged believers who are willing to dedicate a substantial part, or even all, of their lives to the worldly aims of their cause.

Thirdly, although still an important element of religious life, the pursuit of the spiritual in these movements is no longer central. Spirituality, the reception of divine grace and the ensuing liberation of the soul, are considered instrumental to the main organizing principle which is the renewal of society in general and the 'laxity' of believers in particular. As suggested above, the engagement of members in a closely-knit and more or less egalitarian community has replaced a more hierarchical approach to spirituality typical of tradition. The lay communities promote a more pedagogical model instead, with members teaching one another. The cohesion of the community has replaced the certainty of a hierarchical model of authority, but without losing sight of the goal of ultimately attaining divine grace.

Finally, it should be acknowledged that the transfer from spiritual to more worldly causes, and from hierarchical to more shared learning structures, has also produced new uncertainties. Many Christian lay communities that were once built upon religious conduct eventually lost sight of their religious core and eventually became secular organizations. Muslim lay communities are well aware of this danger, and have justified dramatic changes in organizational or missionary strategy as an attempt to deal with this problem. A history of the lay Süleymanci Islamic Cultural Centres (ICC) of Germany will serve to illustrate how such changes may come about.

The Süleymanci Movement in Turkey, Germany and Beyond

Key Moments in Süleymanci History

Five particular years mark significant moments in the recent history of the Süleymanci movement: 1959; 1973; 1979; 1994; and 2000.[2] In 1959, the preacher Süleyman Hilmi Tunahan died in Istanbul, leaving behind some 100 students. These were rural peasants with hardly any education whom he had taught to read and recite the Qur'an and to perform religious services in their villages. Süleyman had been a Naqshbandi-Mudjadiddi *sheikh* but, due to the abolition of the Sufi orders during Turkey's forced modernization, he refused to maintain the branch of the order he represented or to appoint a deputy or *khalifa*. So it was that he became the last in a spiritual chain (*silsile*) descending from Sheikh Ahmad Sirhindi (d. 1624) in Sirhind, via Sheikh Ghulam Ali (d. 1824) and Sheikh Ahmed Sa'id Faruqi (d. 1860) in Dehli, to a largely unknown Mujaddadi branch in Medina at the end of the nineteenth century. The chain transferred to Istanbul in the 1920s.

By the time Süleyman died, however, all traditional Sufi orders were being persecuted and knowledge of the Islamic sciences was in danger of disappearing. Before his demise, Süleyman had instructed his students that, while they were to discontinue the order branch in response to this situation, they should seek to hold on to its central ideas. Süleyman's son-in-law, Kemal Kacar, proceeded to transform his master's work into a modern preaching organization with a bureaucratic structure that would ultimately extend world-wide. Because Süleyman had forbidden him to succeed him as 'gate' to the order's chain, Kacar re-orientated the community's main source of spiritual guidance towards the letters of Ahmed Sirhindi instead. These changes resulted in the emergence of what I have proposed calling a Sufi 'lay community'.

In 1973 Turkish labour migration to Germany came to a halt. However, for different reasons that same year was significant for the Süleymanci movement overseas because 'The Islamic Cultural Centres' (ICC) organization was established with a central office in Cologne. Süleyman's followers had established 150 prayer halls amongst Turkish migrants in Germany, each with its own centre for the study of the Qur'an and the Islamic sciences attached. The ICC united these institutions under one umbrella with the aim of furthering the study of Islam. The internal structure of the organization revolves around local prayer circles (*halqas*) which function simultaneously as places of meditation, study and solidarity. Members also regularly perform missionary activities together.

The next year of significance for the Süleymanci movement to be considered here was 1979. This was the year when the ICC went to court in Germany to demand the right to be acknowledged as a religious community comparable to the majority churches. Turkish laicist organizations in Germany and representatives of the Turkish State vigorously objected to this plan and produced a number of 'stories' to incriminate the ICC. In view of its rigid hierarchy, they accused the organization of fascist tendencies and its founder of having sympathized with the Nazi regime. As a result, German trade unions, churches and the government became suspicious of the aims of the ICC. The ICC's devotional life, both the emphasis on *Imitatio Muhammedi* (discussed below) and the performance of silent *dhikr*, was interpreted as a sign of secrecy that concealed unlawful activity against the German State. Due to these incriminating stories and the general appearance and demeanour of members, the judge presiding over the case rejected the ICC's demands (Jonker, 2002a: 81-111). In the years that followed, the organization retired from public life, ceasing to communicate with the outside world and preferring to concentrate on the establishing of additional centres whose number rose to 300.

In 1994, however, the new director of the Süleymanci in Europe, Dr. Nurettin Akman, decided upon a different course. He argued that, for the younger generation, the aim of achieving acceptance in German society should be equally as important as the aim of spreading the faith. The director therefore encouraged young people born in Germany to occupy prominent posts within the organization and contacts with churches were (re)established locally, with dialogue circles springing up in many locations. The ICC also established the first Islamic Academy in Germany, which quickly became considered as its main opening to the non-Muslim world. Within the Süleymanci movement these activities were known as 'normalization' and officially declared part of the *da'wa* project.

When Kemal Kacar died in Istanbul during 2000, Süleyman's grandson, Ahmed Arif Denizolgun, took his place as leader of the Süleymanci organization world-wide. However, as soon as he took office, the course on which the ICC had embarked in Europe was altered. The aim of the organization, Ahmed Arif declared, should be to rescue the souls of Turkish children and engagement with European society was not a priority in this respect. Therefore he removed the younger generation from the key positions they had come to occupy and, instead of entering into dialogue with wider society, a newly appointed (and much older) management was urged to establish Islamic boarding schools. 'The children' needed to be 'saved from bad influences' and 'Europe' constituted just about the worst influence going (Jonker, 2002a: 111-47).

Structure and Organisation of the Movement

Today, the ICC has 350 centres all over Western Europe, as well as some branches in the United States and Australia. However, the majority of these (299 centres) are concentrated in Germany. The German organization has 20,000 registered members but, as a rule, each member represents an entire family, which raises the number of people active in the organization to approximately 60-80,000. Members call themselves *üye*, differentiating themselves from the *cemaat*, the general Muslim public that is the object of the organization's *da'wa* activity and makes use of its facilities. However, not every *üye* is a member of a prayer circle. Those who participate in a *halqa* are called *ihwan* or 'personnel'. Once admitted, they take an oath to perform *dhikr* for the rest of their lives and to remain active in the organization. Tellingly, given the lay orientation of the movement, another name for members is *tevziat fuzuat*, 'civil servants'. It was this term that Süleyman once used to describe the assignment he had given to his students. Sending them home to their villages, he ordered them to become 'civil servants' in the service of Muhammad as distinct from the 'civil servants' the Turkish State employed to 'administer' the religious duties of its people. For members, the name of *tevziat fuzuat* is still held in high esteem, encouraging its bearers in their conviction that they have a special – divinely inspired – mission in life (Jonker, 2002a: 67-8).

To fulfil their mission of rescuing Islamic faith amongst Muslims through more widespread study of the Qur'an and the Islamic sciences, the ICC developed a dual organizational structure, consisting of 'spiritual' and 'economic' sectors. The spiritual sector includes vocational religious training for *hocas* or teachers, which is organized separately for men and women and taught in the movement's local centres. After three years and a series of examinations, during which students must demonstrate adequate knowledge of the Islamic sciences, they receive their *ijaza* (licence) and officially become a *hoca*. Having qualified, graduates are then sent back to their places of birth, mostly German cities where volunteers assist them in educating children in the reading and reciting of the Qur'an. These classes also generate new recruits for vocational training. The *hocas* teach Turkish children whose parents are affiliated with a range of mosques, but especially those associated with Milli Görüsh and Turkish State organized mosques. Indeed, new recruitment to the movement often takes place through these children, who encourage younger brothers and sisters to attend and even convince their parents to become members.

Whenever expansion becomes necessary and the community decides to open new premises, the economic sector comes into its own. Whereas the local *üye* must take responsibility for the funding of new initiatives, the organization's economists and lawyers offer a support infrastructure that includes help with interpreting building regulations, negotiations with banks, the organizing of security services and the provision of telephone contracts (Jonker, 2002a: 124-6). Although the ICC is a hierarchical organization with a leader, to facilitate its mission, it has accepted a certain degree of internal differentiation and professionalization. The lawyers, economists and architects that the organization employs carry full responsibility within their own fields of expertise. During the period of 'opening up' towards wider society in Germany new experts appeared, both in 'inter-religious dialogue' and 'intellectual' or 'cultural work'.

The Persistence of Charismatic Leadership in a Lay Community

In Germany, local spiritual leaders supervise the work of the *hocas* and they, in turn, are controlled by the European directorate. However, the movement's leader in Istanbul has final spiritual authority. Although the institution of the *sheikh* was abolished in the Süleymanci movement, the Istanbul leader's authority rests not only upon organizational 'know-how' but also *maneviat* or 'spirituality'. Given the origins of the movement, this is very interesting. The former leader of the Süleymanci, Kemal Kacar, is said to have received this quality from Süleyman himself. Moreover, Süleyman's grandson is now believed to be imbued with *maneviat* from two sources: the blessing of Kacar on his deathbed and his blood tie to the movement's founder. Ironically, members claim that the possession of *maneviat* is indispensable for the success of the organization. It is seen as what makes children learn and parents enthusiastic; it helps the *ihwan* stay loyal to their cause and the *üye* – and even the *cemaat* – to spend lavishly on funding movement activities. Members say that possession of *maneviat* does not give the leader the power of a *sheikh* – he can never be the 'gate' to the *silsile* – but it undoubtedly transforms him into a very special person indeed (Jonker, 2002a: 136-42).

There seems, then, to be a contradiction within the Süleymanci organization. As suggested above, it claims not to be a Sufi order and its leader is not a *sheikh*. However, the organization has in fact preserved the main feature of a Sufi order – the receipt of divine inspiration through a chain of spiritual forbears and the presence of a leader who acts as a 'gate' to spiritual knowledge. Süleymanci members who participate in *dhikr* focus their concentration on a photograph of the founder. As might be expected, his grave in Istanbul is also a focus for visitation. However, because the Turkish government still suspects the Süleymanci of anti-republican ideas, pilgrims are instructed to visit only in small groups, recite only a short Qur'anic prayer, stay for no longer than ten minutes and generally act as 'inoffensively' as possible. Nevertheless, many claim to have experienced Süleyman's presence at the grave, receiving inner peace and moments of intense insight. Indeed, photographs of Süleyman's grave are the most exhibited pictures within the community.

This persistence of Süleyman's charisma puts the present leader in a rather difficult position. The community expects him to behave charismatically and as a source of grace, but he can not become a *sheikh* because no living person can act as a 'gate' or intermediary in Süleyman's place. This tension was very evident when, in 2000, Kemal Kacar died and Süleyman's grandson took his place. The latter was presented as an able administrator and, indeed, the changes he proposed were all of an administrative nature. Yet a ripple of speculation went through the local communities in Germany: 'does Ahmed Arif possess *maneviat*?'; 'are his decisions actually inspired?'. Stories of dreams and miracles also circulated in which the new leader was very prominent and it was clear to me that believers wanted him to be something more than a university-trained professional. In order to accept him as their leader, Ahmed Arif's decisions seemed to require this additional proof of divine guidance (Jonker, 2002a: 140).

Imitating Muhammad: The Roots of the Süleymanci Disposition

Male students of Süleymanci heritage, whether twenty or seventy years old, whether in Istanbul or Cologne, Amsterdam, Vienna, or Boston, all resemble one another in terms of a distinctive appearance and shared conduct. They dress formally in a grey flannel or dark blue suit, preferably with a waistcoat. This is coupled with a white striped shirt and striped tie, with elegant cuff links and tie-pin to match. Hair is worn short and faces are clean-shaven. Some wear a small moustache, but I never seen a full beard. Their speech is formal, polite and unobtrusive and the way they move might be called 'ceremonial'. Moreover, whenever these men are not in direct communication with someone, their gaze turns to the floor and their faces take on an inward-looking expression.

To the interested observer and dialogue partner, Süleymanci members appear to be in meditative control of their movements, their speech, their emotions and even their breathing. However, to the less interested journalist or politician their manner seems to radiate an air of secrecy and elitist consciousness which in the past has provoked accusations of 'camouflage', 'militancy' and 'occult doctrine' (Jonker, 2002a: 81-111). Indeed, back in 1979, it was this conduct, combined with the rumours set in motion by their opponents, that created an unfavourable impression when the movement petitioned the German legal system for formal recognition.

At an early stage of our acquaintance, the leader of the Berlin ICC community explained to me that they – the students of Süleyman – followed the Prophet in terms of their personal conduct. As most practising Muslims seek to imitate the conduct of Muhammad, this was not exactly a new insight. However, it quickly became clear to me that the Süleymanci follow a method of 'imitation' that is different to most other Muslims. To illustrate their approach, my respondent quoted some of the *khalimat qudsiye* to me, the rules laid down by the Naqshbandi order in the fourteenth century. Among these, he stressed 'awareness of the feet', 'awareness of the breath' and 'solitude in company' as particularly important.[3]

This is an interesting explanation of the Süleymanci disposition in more than one respect. The *khalimat qudsiye* contain eleven rules which, for the most part, are concerned with reconstructing the memory of the primordial bond between God and Man (Ter Haar, 1992: 47-57).[4] Of these, those quoted to me seemed only to concentrate on the initial 'bodily' stages of spiritual progression. The explanation I was given also seemed to transfer rules that in some other time and place had aimed at self-annihilation and *Unio Mystica* (mystical union) to the firmer ground of personal conduct. Such interpretations were confirmed by my respondents who stressed time and again that students of Süleyman take a much more sober approach to spirituality than some mystics of bye-gone ages:

In earlier times, there were *tekkes* everywhere. One could hear *suhbats* [religious conversations] in many places and *sheikh* and *mürid* [pupil] stayed together for a long time. We don't do that anymore. Now, [religious] education is performed collectively. Thanks to a sober view of Sufism, we now possess a modern organization with a spiritual connection.[5]

Instead of seeking mystical experiences, then, Süleymanci focus on their personal conduct: 'we try to refine whatever we undertake. We polish it and make it as beautiful as possible'.[6]

It took some time before I realized that this last quotation originates from Shah Wali Ullah (d. 1763), a Naqshbandi-Mujaddadi *sheikh* of Delhi. However, having done so, I knew that I had stumbled upon a reinterpretation of the old *Tariqat-i Muhammediya* (the Way of Muhammad). The *Tariqat-i Muhammediya*, a school of thought that once flourished in India, proposes the imitation of the Prophet as a way to reach mystical union. The attainment of this goal was intimately connected to the exact application of the *shari'a* in one's life (Schimmel, 1981: 194). Therefore, during the eighteenth and nineteenth centuries, *sheikhs* in the Naqshbandi-Mujaddadi lineage were much given to making delicate observations concerning all aspects of the Prophet's life, 'all he had said, done and silently approved of', as the *hadith* tradition claims. Because the *Tariqat-i Muhammediya* stresses the 'polishing' of even the simplest details of one's personal conduct, students came to think of themselves as direct representatives of the Prophet. For some, the emphasis on refinement of personal conduct also allowed them to remain aloof from the political response to colonialism in British India that began to take hold during the nineteenth century (see Birt, this volume). Indeed, saints of the spiritual chain that Süleyman represented have routinely preferred to turn inwards rather than be driven by the profound social changes around them (Fußfeld, 1981: 198-236).

A hundred years later, and thousands of miles away from India, the preacher Süleyman encouraged his students in Istanbul to become 'civil servants' in sober service of Muhammad. Against the control that the modernizing Turkish Republic exercized over religion, this statement represented a direct challenge to the state. In 1954 civil servants were commissioned to organize Turkish religious life but Süleyman dared to establish an alternative type of 'civil servant', commissioned by no one but the Prophet himself. However, in this political setting, the stress on personal conduct guided by *shari'a* was not intended to produce withdrawal from worldly affairs. On the contrary, the preacher and his students, through 'polishing' the details of the Prophet's life in their own conduct, expressed their dissent from what they considered to be a catastrophic political development.

The idea of a 'modern organization with a spiritual connection' was therefore primarily a response to Turkish secularization. Its institutionalization as a lay community with a *da'wa* mission, however, took place some time later and in a different setting. The European framework in which this was accomplished presented a fundamentally different set of institutional expectations. As a result, further re-imaginings of the tradition were required to adapt to this new context.

The way that young women members of the ICC interpret their mission today may serve as a brief illustration of this.

Female students of Süleymanci heritage realize the *Imitatio Muhammedi* in ways that mirror the conduct described above, but sometimes surpassing that of their male counterparts. Like the men, they dress and speak modestly and unobtrusively. Twenty years ago, they appeared in public without covering their heads, so as not to attract attention in a non-Muslim environment. Today they simply wear a scarf knotted under the chin, refusing the Islamic fashion of concealing the hair underneath. Like the men, they turn their gaze to the floor and use every spare moment for prayer. What is more, these women constantly make *suhbat* amongst themselves, something the men are not in the habit of doing. This means that whenever they have a moment together, while waiting in line or for classes to begin, they will choose a verse from the Qur'an and seek to apply its content to their own situation:

> Of course we could speak of different matters, tell each other all sorts of things, but no, we do it as the Prophet once did. Our Prophet passed on his knowledge like this, his friends memorized it and recounted it to others and so on, and now I hear it and memorize it and also recount it to others. That is a good feeling. We are the People of the Way [*Ahl-i Sünnet*]. We always want to act just as the Prophet did. We want to know exactly the same things he knew.[7]

With the help of this method Süleymanci women investigate their space, its potentiality and its perimeter. Their collective interpretation of an *ayet* (Qur'anic verse) is their way of defining their role within the religious community and beyond. In addition to being 'civil servants', this serves as a means to free them from being treated as mere symbols of the movement. Instead, women are active participants in religious communication:

> The other day somebody quoted 'Obey whom is set above Thee'. Making *qiyas* [analogy] with that one immediately made clear that Kemal Kacar is set above us all. So, we obey him. Nurettin Abi [Dr. Nurettin Akman] is responsible for Europe. He is our boss and we do what he tells us. Okay. But I am the leader of the [female] training. What I decide in here, others have to respect. That's why we meet in the women's congregation every other week. And what we do not discuss in there is discussed over the telephone later. That is why the telephone rings incessantly. This is my territory![8]

Shils (1981) describes traditions as guiding patterns for the re-enactment of the past. Whether past and present superficially appear to have much in common is less important than whether those who form part of the tradition recognize its 'essence' and perceive some sort of continuity with the past. In the wide berth of the Islamic tradition of imitating the Prophet, there are many resources which suggest themselves for potential 're-enactment'. However, the choices that are actually made are dictated, of course, by the needs of the present time. What the men and women of the Süleymanci considered here are looking for are strands of religious knowledge which can fortify their mission in the best ways possible.

They are not explicitly in search of a method to appease 'the heart' and ascend to mystical union. However, their *halqas* do keep open the lifeline to God and 'inspiration' can occur when it is most unexpected. Through these *halqas*, it is the organization as such, and not the individual that is in possession of the 'spiritual connection'. And even though the recent decisions of the Süleymanci's new leader have been extremely hard on young European members, this remains an important reason for remaining within the organization.

Conclusion

Labour migration to Western Europe also saw the Turkish struggle over the place of religion in public life travel to countries such as Germany. However, due to the slowness of the Turkish government in developing any religious alternatives, the Sufi orders were amongst the first to institutionalize. Religious freedom enabled them to establish branches and develop several brands of Sufi lay communities. When, in 1983, religious representatives of the Turkish State were finally installed in Germany, Milli Görüsh, Jamaatunnur and the ICC were already well on the way to becoming recognized as the legitimate representatives of organized Islam.[9] All have a tradition of Naqshbandi piety and *sheikhs* who distanced themselves from their order to rescue religious knowledge for the common people. Likewise, all produce pious and active members with a common missionary goal. In the eyes of these activists, forced modernization in Turkey did away with all spiritual values and methods for obtaining grace. Migration saw their fierce reaction spread to Europe before it had fully institutionalized, and so Western European frameworks have imprinted on their present organizational shape. The result of all this I have termed 'Sufi lay communities'.

The contemporary situation seems to be far removed from the origins of the Naqshbandi order, and indeed, the eleven holy rules that gave the order its distinctive profile in the fourteenth century have been abandoned by the Süleymanci with the exception of just three. Yet, over the centuries, the evolution of the order has pointed towards this particular development. The link must be traced from Bukhara to Delhi, to Medina, to Istanbul and on to Cologne. At each historical and geographical stage, the societal and political frame necessitated a different focus, which in turn transformed the order. Its beacon, Sheikh Ahmed Sirhindi, had already set a course towards a much more 'sober' ideal in the seventeenth century. His decision that, having been lost in God, a mystic's ultimate goal should be the return to reality, was the starting point for the *Tariqat-i Muhammediya*. In his wake, generations of holy men tried to 'polish' their lives as best as they could, perfecting their imitation of the Prophet. Finally, in the twentieth century, this religious endeavour became a victim of the republican zeal that sought to modernize Turkish society.

The example of the Süleymanci has also showed that their cause is no simple continuation of the past. For three generations now, they have decided to dedicate their lives to the spreading of the Qur'an, the preservation and continuation of the Islamic sciences and the adaptation of its core religious terminology to the languages of Western Europe. Personal conduct based on imitation of the Prophet legitimates and serves this aim, but it can no longer become an aim in itself. The requirements of the present, as the Süleymanci perceive them, dictate a different approach. As has been suggested here, religious systems are not primordial entities. Rather, following Shils, they are guiding patterns for the re-enactment of the past in the present. Modernity was the context within which the transformation described in this chapter began and it has resulted in lay communities prone to secularization, itself is a modern phenomenon.

References

Beyer, P. (1998), 'Globalizing Systems, Global Cultural Models and Religion(s)', *International Sociology*, 13/1, 90-143.

Dornbrach, H. (1991), *Islamische Ordensgemeinschaften in Deutschland*, Trebbus: Sufi-Archiv Deutschland e.V.

Eisenstadt, S.N. (1998), *Die Antinomien der Moderne*, Frankfurt: Suhrkamp Verlag.

Fusfeld, W.E. (1981), *The Shaping of Sufi Leadership in Delhi: The Naqshbandiyya-Mujaddadiyya, 1750 to 1920*, Pennsylvania: The University of Pennsylvania Press.

Hüttermann, J. (2003), *Sufitum in Deutschland*, Bielefeld: transcript Verlag.

Jonker, G. (2002a), *Eine Wellenlänge zu Gott: Der Verband der Islamischen Kulturzentren in Europa*, Bielefeld: transcript Verlag.

Jonker, G. (2002b), 'Muslim Lay Communities between Turkey and Germany', in Malik, J. (ed.), *Muslims in Europe: From the Margin to the Centre*, Münster: LIT Verlag, 61-75.

Jonker, G. and Kapphan, A. (1999), *Moscheen und islamisches Leben in Berlin*, Berlin: Die Ausländerbeauftragte.

Keller, K.K. (1991), 'Soufisme en Europe', in Waardenburg, J. (ed.), *Scholarly Approaches to Religion: Inter-religious Perceptions and Islam*, Bern: Peter Lang, 359-390.

Luhmann, N. (2000), *Die Religion der Gesellschaft*, Frankfurt: Suhrkamp Verlag.

Mardin, S. (1989), *Religion and Social Change in Modern Turkey: The Case of Bedüizzaman Said Nursi*, New York: New York University Press.

Nereid, C.T. (1997), *In the Light of Said Nursi: Turkish Nationalism and the Religious Alternative*, Bergen: Centre for Middle Eastern and Islamic Studies.

Schiffauer, W. (2000), *Die Gottesmänner: Turkische Islamisten in Deutschland*, Frankfurt: Suhrkamp Verlag.

Schimmel, A. (1981), *Und Muhammed ist sein Prophet: Die Verehrung des Propheten in der islamischen Frömmigkeit*, München: Diederichs Verlag.

Schleßmann, L. (1991), *Sufismus in Deutschland*, Geographia Religionum, Vol. 7.

Schleßmann, L. (1999), 'Sufi-Gemeinschaften in Deutschland', *CIBEDO*, 13, 12-22.

Shils, E. (1981), *Tradition*, Chicago: The Chicago University Press.

Spuler-Stegemann, U. (1998), *Muslime in Deutschland*, Freiburg: Herder Verlag.

Ter Haar, J.G.J. (1992), *Follower and Heir of the Prophet: Shaykh Ahmad Sirhindi (1564-1624) as Mystic*, Leiden: Het Oosters Instituut.

Yano, H. (1998), 'Zur Geschichte der ausländischen Arbeitnehmer in der Frühphase der Bundesrepublik', in Jamin, M. (ed.), *Fremde Heimat: Eine Geschichte der Einwanderung aus der Türkei*, Essen: Klartext Verlag, 39-55.

Yavuz, H.M. and Esposito, J.L. (eds) (2003), *Turkish Islam and the Secular State: The Gülen Movement*, Syracuse: The Syracuse Press.

Notes

1 Laicism is state control of religious matters. It should not be confused with secularism which is both separation of state and religion and individualization of religious participation. Only French and Turkish governments have adopted laicism in order to control the organization of religion in their countries.

2 This section is based on four years of fieldwork with Süleymanci communities in Europe. The empirical findings are published in full in German (Jonker, 2002a).

3 Head of the Berlin ICC administration and 44 years old at the time of interview (3 November 1998).

4 (1) *Hush dar dam*: Control of breath; (2) *Nazar bar qadam*: Control of feet; (3) *Safar dar watan*: Voyage to the spiritual country; (4) *Khalwat dar anjuman*: Solitude in company; (5) *Yad kard*: The act of remembering; (6) *Baz gasht*: The return of memory; (7) *Nigah dasht*: The protection of memory; (8) *Yad dasht*: The retaining of memory; (9) *Wuquf-i qalbi*: Control of the heart; (10) *Wuquf-i zamani*: Control of time; (11) *Wuquf-i adadi*: Control of numbers.

5 Librarian of the German ICC central office in Cologne and 36 years old at the time of interview (4 July 1999).

6 Head of the Berlin ICC Administration, *op. cit.*

7 Head of female training in Cologne and 24 years old at the time of interview (14 April 1999).

8 Head of female training, *op.cit.*

9 The histories of the Jamaatunnur and Milli Görüsh in Europe have yet to be written. A student of Said Nursi, the preacher Fethullah Gülen, also set up an independent organization called the Gülen movement. Whereas the Jamaatunnur concentrates on spreading the writings of Said Nursi, the Gülen movement is active in (secular) education (Yavuz and Esposito, 2003).

Chapter 13

Locating the British *Imam*: The Deobandi *'Ulama* between Contested Authority and Public Policy Post-9/11

Jonathan Birt

Introduction

Britain's long and intimate relationship with the Indian subcontinent has resulted in the most decisive fact of British Islam: that its major historical continuities derive from the postcolonial fruits of this encounter. Three-quarters of her 1.6 million Muslims are of 'South Asian' heritage, with the major populations being Pakistani (658,000), Bangladeshi (260,000) and Indian (132,000).[1] This chapter focuses on the development of an important Sunni theological tendency (*maslak*) in Britain, that of the Deobandis, in terms of recasting its message of reform, taking up new social and official roles available to its religious leadership, and experiencing greater attention, both benign and hostile, after 9/11.

The Origins and Development of the Deoband Movement in India and the UK

The Deobandi movement emerged among reformist *'ulama* in north India of the 1860s, who were committed to preserving traditional scholarship and learning. To this end, they created a network of financially-independent seminaries, separate from the traditional but diminishing sources of aristocratic patronage, which were designed for mass education, borrowed selectively from Western models, and made full use of print and mail to forge trans-local solidarities. Islam in the Deobandi reform model was 'neo-traditional', no longer *sui generis*, but in an expanded world, oppositional in character, defining itself against popular Sufi custom, other *'ulama*, Hindus and the British. It was rationalizing in the Weberian sense: self-conscious, systematic and based on abstract principles. The reform message looked to scriptural proofs as opposed to local custom to appeal to Muslim ethnic groups across an India that was opening up to mass communications and transport. It encouraged a pattern of self-reliance and personal responsibility; in other words, a form of moral rearmament emerged with the ending of Muslim rule. Alongside this greater reflexivity came disenchantment, particularly with effacing the centrality of intercessory Sufi saints, and a politics of religious difference that in the Deobandi case focused on the individual, and not upon the emerging modern state as was the case with the Jama'at-i Islami (see McLoughlin, this volume). The drive for independence from British rule in the 1920s led to the development of three strands among Deobandis: a wing that looked to restore Muslim rule through a new Muslim homeland; another that backed a 'composite nationalism' in a secular India; and a third, pietist, mystical and anti-political trend, exemplified by its global outreach movement, the Tablighi Jama'at. In sum, if not strictly speaking modernist in its outlook, the 'traditional' Deobandi movement was modernizing in important ways (Masud, 2000; Metcalf, 1982, 1999; Zaman, 2002).

This inward turn produced an *'ulama*-led movement that was always ready to recognize, well before decolonialization, a *de facto* division between secular public order and the private religious sphere. Therefore it has functioned perfectly well as a minority in a liberal democratic context, although this did not preclude a return to formal political involvement in Pakistan or Afghanistan. Nonetheless, aloof from formal politics, Deobandis have generally sought personal goals of the attainment of piety and religious self-knowledge. They have also largely confronted other Muslims rather than the 'West' (Metcalf, 2002) with the latter seen as a source of corruption to Muslim individuals rather than a supranational entity to be resisted through collective political action.

Contrary to Werner Schiffauer's (1988) model of a structural shift in religious consciousness, from majority Muslim rural contexts to minority urban ones, the Deoband movement had thus already achieved an accommodation with modernity, individualism and minority status. Continuities of development, rather than drastic rupture in the post-migration context, therefore become more pertinent. Despite Deoband's greater 'mobility', however, the irony of migration to the ex-colonial metropole has been the transformation of Deoband's North Indian cosmopolitanism into a South Asian parochialism in the multi-ethnic British context. The main challenges for the movement have been firstly to appeal to a younger British-born constituency that is actively disembedding 'pure' religion from what is seen as the composite religio-cultural Islam offered by their parents, and secondly to respond to emergent Salafi and Islamist critiques of following religious scholarship (*taqlid*) and failing to take Islamic politics seriously (Birt, 2005).[2]

The core support for the movement in Britain has come from Indian Muslim communities (chiefly Gujarati and East African Asian), whether for its *'ulama* or for Tabligh, which have been instrumental in its rapid institutionalization. The centres of Deobandi influence reflect the urban concentrations of these ethnic Muslim sub-groups in the mill-towns of the North-West (Bolton, Preston and Blackburn), Leicester in the East Midlands, Dewsbury and Batley in West Yorkshire, and some London boroughs. The Deoband movement has always worked to a pattern of reform that is primarily concerned with the moral transformation of the individual, not society. It creates networks of grassroots support through Tabligh and *imamate* preaching (Tayob, 1999) that accept its reformist message and support *'ulama*-controlled Islamic education, which institutionalizes the movement's influence. The paradox arises, however, that in order to create these networks, the reformers have to answer, and often adapt to, pockets of resistance to their message from the Muslim community at large. Two examples, taken from the cities of Leicester and Birmingham respectively, represent different stages in this pattern of reform.

Deobandi Reform in the British Context

If Muslim Leicester today is a Deobandi centre of learning, a node for the dissemination of the movement's message, in which the *'ulama* are now able to determine the scope and direction of further Islamization, it was not so in the 1970s when they were peripheral. The key to this centrality is attaining the control of Islamic educational institutions. Leicester, with a population of 31,000 Muslims (59 per cent of whom are of Indian heritage), boasts 130 registered *'ulama* (a quarter of whom are British-trained), over 20 mosques, numerous supplementary schools and eight Muslim faith schools including three seminaries. The movement is able to capture young Muslims through the supplementary schools and potentially offer religious and secular education from the ages of 5-18 and beyond. The rampant sectarianism that typified Birmingham and London, particularly in the 1990s, has been largely absent in Leicester. Mild criticism is voiced instead by younger *'ulama* who have wanted to move into new social roles and activities like chaplaincy, interfaith, media, youth work and even political lobbying more quickly than the establishment *'ulama* in the city would like.

By contrast with Leicester, Birmingham is a Deobandi outpost. Its 140,000 Muslims are dominated by Pakistanis (Mirpuris and Punjabis, around 97,000) – linked mostly to the South Asian Sufi orders that opposed Deobandi reform – along with large Bangladeshi and historic Yemeni communities. As a meeting point between the established South Asian groups of the pioneer generation, and the newer Arab-based movements like the Salafis and Hizb al-Tahrir that began to spread from London in the early 1990s, the city has gained a reputation for fierce sectarianism. Therefore the Deoband message has had to compete in a maelstrom of religious argument, which, in a youthful population, has tended to strengthen the appeal of oppositional and radicalized discourses. Young Deobandi *'ulama*, with less than 4 per cent of the local Muslim population being of Indian heritage, have had to create networks outside established Gujarati ones.

The rhetoric and positioning of Shaykh Riyadhul Haq (b. 1971), the *khatib imam* of Birmingham Central Mosque (1991-2003), and a graduate of a British seminary, reflects this context. He is a self-conscious pioneer, struggling to bring the reform message to an often sceptical, even cynical Muslim constituency. *Wa'z* (admonitory preaching) in English is central, its goal being to establish a basic love and attachment to God and His Prophet and an aversion to un-Islamic influences; in general, his approach is fundamentally responsive to Salafi and Islamist critiques. Specifically South Asian cultural and religious references are downplayed, presumed to be parochial, in recognition of the limitations of the older style of Deobandi preaching still common in Urdu, Gujarati and Sylheti. This is also reflected in the preference for Saudi-style Arab dress among his followers, including the black *burqa* and *niqab* for women, assumed to be closer to the

Prophetic norm. The severe Salafi critique of unsanctioned religious practice (*bid'a*) has undermined the implicit authority of scholarly learning; instead, every proposition in religion must be proven by 'sound' textual evidence (*dalil*). In response, studies in *hadith* (narratives of the sayings and doings of the Prophet) have been removed from the formal context of scholarly transmission in the seminary to mass education in the mosque. Shaykh Riyadh has undertaken a learned commentary of an abridged edition of al-Bukhari, the most canonical *hadith* collection, which is also widely disseminated through audiocassettes and through downloadable audio files on the Internet to a global English-speaking constituency (see www.shariah-institute.org).

In a Muslim youth culture where Sufism is heavily contested, Shaykh Riyadh has taken care to recast his particular Sufi tradition – as a designated Sufi *shaykh* of the Sabri-Chishti sub-order – in the universal language of the *sunna* (the Prophetic norm). When teaching the *Risala Qushayriyya*, the primary Chishti teaching text, to his 'students' (noticeably not 'disciples' or *muridin*), significant numbers of whom were ex-Salafis, he had to remove any proposition that could not be proven by explicit textual evidence from the Qur'an and *sunna*. Thus even the reformed Sufism of nineteenth century India moves closer to a mere inward praxis (*tazkiyat al-nafs*). With the rise of popular pan-Islamist rhetoric, he has, uniquely among his peers, ventured to comment publicly and trenchantly on the 'war on terrorism', while always taking care to emphasize the need to protest within the norms of democratic dissent. For example, he encouraged his followers to participate in the anti-war marches (2001-2003), an involvement considered unlawful by radical Islamists like Hizb al-Tahrir (see Taji-Farouki, 1996). However, the thrust of his post-9/11 commentary, to take an example from a 2002 speech entitled 'Steadfastness in the days of *fitna* [discord]', seeks to reinforce personal adherence to scriptural norms at a time when social pressure might lead to assimilation into Western lifestyles. The war on terrorism is linked eschatologically with the Qur'anic model of prophetic witness and undergoing hardship for the sake of faith: 'Nothing has really changed. The persecution of the Muslims ... enmity, hostility, hatred of the *umma* ... ridicule and vilification of Islam [is] part of a constant battle between *haqq* and *batil*, truth and falsehood, which did not start on 9/11 but [was] present from the beginning [of Islam]' (Birt and Lewis, forthcoming).

In his sermons, Shaykh Riyadh makes almost no explicit reference to the virtues of the Deoband elders, a staple element by contrast in 'centres' like Leicester, but instead refers to primary texts and the classical Sunni *'ulama*, especially the traditionists (*al-muhaddithun*), who are widely accepted by most Sunnis. His Anglophone following which is both national and global (through the Internet, an audio cassette ministry, and preaching tours) appeals to young Muslims across ethnic and sectarian lines, including Pakistanis, Bangladeshis, Arabs, Africans and Turks. Such pioneers among the younger Deobandi *'ulama* can be critical of their peers, who have, in their view, taken the easier option of preaching to the converted, many preferring to remain underemployed in the Deoband 'centres'. There is little time in Birmingham for the niceties of 'engagement': more pressing is the work of basic reform and creating primary networks of support outside the movement's core constituency. Already at the heart of Gujarati communities, young *'ulama* from these Deoband 'centres' are not afraid to tackle pressing social and religious issues within their own communities like drugs, underachievement in education and isolationist mentalities. Unlike those concerned with the basic message of reform, they would not conflate integration with assimilation, and so do engage in outreach activities.

As the Deobandi reform movement works from particular locales, unlike the Islamists, it rarely addresses the national stage, as its chief interests are more inwardly directed towards universalizing its appeal among all British Muslims. The annual Youth Tarbiya [Rectification] Conference held since 1998 at a rural location in the Midlands has provided the first national platform for young Deobandi *'ulama*. It was begun to counteract the Salafi polemic, but more importantly to endorse a younger generation of leaders who are able to take the reform message to new constituencies in a radically altered context. Yet in the addresses made at these conferences, there is as yet no consensus on how to universalize the appeal of the reform message, whether the priority is moral reform or upward mobility, or whether to engage with or retreat from the complexities of wider society.

Developments in Deobandi Seminaries

In Britain, despite the politicization of a few younger Deobandi *'ulama*, it is the anti-political trend that has become predominant: firstly through the spread of the Deobandi-affiliated worldwide outreach movement, the Tablighi Jama'at, whose European headquarters at Dewsbury also houses an important seminary; and secondly through the influence of Britain's 'mother seminary', the Dar al-'Ulum al-'Arabiya al-Islamiya (founded 1975) near Bury in Lancashire, commonly referred to simply as 'Bury'. 'Bury' directly or indirectly controls the ethos and curricula of half of Britain's seventeen Deobandi seminaries (*dar al-'ulum*). Its rector, Shaykh Yusuf Motala (b. 1946), remains faithful to his teacher and Sufi guide, Muhammad Zakariya al-Khandhalwi (d. 1982), the chief influence upon the Tabligh movement in the late twentieth century and a noted *hadith* commentator and doyen of the Mazahirul 'Ulum Saharanpur in northern India. Of Saharanpur, Metcalf says: 'in size and influence ... second only to Deoband itself ... [it] came to be considered less intellectual and more Sufi in orientation than Deoband' (1982: 128, 133). Approximately 140 students graduate from Britain's 26 seminaries annually, 80 per cent of whom come from the Deobandi tradition.[3] 'Bury' itself had produced 260 *'ulama*, 250 Qur'an reciters and 290 Qur'an memorizers by 1995 (Sikand, 2002: 246). As such, uniquely in Britain, as compared with the rest of Europe, there is already a surplus of seminary graduates who have to look for employment opportunities outside of the traditional mosque *imamate* and supplementary schools. Instead, they turn to the burgeoning Muslim private schools sector (118 in January 2005), higher education, professional roles within the Muslim voluntary sector, and in state-sector chaplaincies.

The curriculum of the Deobandi seminaries is based upon the *dars-i nizami*, a traditional syllabus developed in India in the eighteenth century to serve both the *'ulama* and the Muslim elite (Robinson, 2001). In response to the bifurcation of education in British India, in which secular subjects were taught in the new English schools, the Deobandi *'ulama* took to preserving the core Islamic sciences, the Qur'an and *hadith*, learned commentary, law, Arabic and Urdu. Other elements gradually reduced or discarded include philosophy, logic, mathematics and Persian language and literature, although other groups of reformist *'ulama*, notably the Barelwis, retained these (Lewis, 1994; Birt and Lewis, forthcoming; Robinson, 2001).

In Britain, the *dars-i nizami* syllabus, to take the example of 'Bury', has been furthered attenuated – the Prophet's life, Qur'an commentary and formal theology receive limited attention. However, the emphasis upon direct study and commentary of the *hadith* literature, inherited from the reformer Shah Wali Allah (d. 1762), has been retained. Nearly all the seminaries, although formally registered as independent schools, have to provide statutory education up to the age of 16. In the early 1990s, there was little attempt to provide a cohesive curriculum at 'Bury' between Urdu or Arabic-based religious studies in the mornings and English secular studies in the afternoons (Lewis, 1994). However, over the last decade, the seminary has sent its graduates to higher studies in the Muslim world in jurisprudence, *hadith* and Arabic, and to doctorates in Islamic studies at British universities. A *mufti*-training course in Islamic jurisprudence was established at 'Bury' in 1995 and in 1998 links were developed with the Westhill College of Higher Education in Birmingham (applied theological studies and religious education), as well as the University of Central Lancashire (for various undergraduate degrees) in 2000. It has also developed its science and computing facilities and its post-16 secular education. Although previously there had been little outreach, subsequent to 9/11, the seminary has made some local effort to explain its work (Birt and Lewis, forthcoming).

The Emergence of New Social Roles for the *'Ulama*

The expectations that the pioneer generation of British Muslims had of a mosque *imam* consisted of leading the congregational prayer, teaching in the mosque supplementary school, giving the Friday address in Arabic and the sermon in Urdu, overseeing the rites of passage, and providing juristic advice and remedies to a host of personal and spiritual problems within the range of his training. However, with 52 per cent of British Muslims under the age of 25,[4] there is growing need for *imams* who can teach and lecture in English, address pertinent social issues and take up wider roles in society outside the mosque, especially pastoral youth work.

In the 1990s some of the younger Deobandi *'ulama* began to address this new set of expectations and to challenge the perspectives of the older generation. The first and most influential development has been the emergence of independent academies, which are firmly in control of the younger *'ulama*, for example those run by Riyadhul Haq in Birmingham, and Mufti Saiful Islam and Mawlana Ahmad

Ali in Bradford. These academies aim to get away from the negative associations that mosques carry with Muslim youth, and from the stultifying control of conservative mosque committees. They run a range of activities designed to keep students' interest in religion during adolescence, including homework clubs to boost academic performance at school, day trips and soccer leagues. They have more the informality of social centres, avoiding the strictures of correct comportment (*adab*) expected in the mosque. At the same time, direct sermonizing in English on core issues and concerns facing young Muslims is undertaken. For example, one of Ahmad Ali's most popular recordings is *Drugs: The Mother of All Evils*, and trips are undertaken to the Annual Youth Tarbiya Conference. With these new institutions, younger *'ulama* have sided with a youthful constituency in framing contextualized Islamic discourses in English.

The second development has been the encapsulation of many of the most able young Deobandi *'ulama* into various institutional chaplaincies, whereby the movement's quickness to create the first seminaries in the 1970s and 1980s has allowed them to provide the most able candidates in this new sector. One of the first prison chaplains, Khalil Ahmad Kazi in Batley, appointed in 1996, has taken the professional skills he has acquired to transform notions of what community and pastoral work by the *'ulama* might involve. In 2000, he set up the Institute of Islamic Scholars which has created new roles in prison and hospital chaplaincy, work with local schools and colleges, publishing, community liaison with the police, MPs and policy makers, public lecturing on Islam, interfaith and a support group for drug and alcohol abuse. He has also undertaken to reform the supplementary school curriculum in order to make it relevant to a younger generation (Institute of Muslim Scholars, 2002). Thus a new professionalism gained from experiences in chaplaincy has begun to inform the work of some independent academies.

The process of integrating Muslim chaplains into state-funded pastoral roles began with the Prison Service during the late 1990s in response to rising numbers of Muslim inmates. The appointment of a Muslim Advisor to the Prison Service in 1999 meant that serious deficiencies in the pastoral care of Muslim prisoners could be addressed such as the provision of Friday prayers and *halal* meals, as well as access to *imams*. One study found that Muslim chaplains were routinely excluded from chaplaincy team decision-making, and experienced direct and indirect discrimination along with inmates: 'there is a pervasive mistrust of Islamic culture. *Imams* are often treated with suspicion, verging on hostility'.[5] The Advisor instituted a centralized vetting procedure for chaplains, including Counter Terrorism Clearance, which allowed for the creation of paid positions. However, this procedure had still not been completely implemented following the events of 9/11, as there has been one case of an *imam* suspended for radicalism who had not been centrally approved (*Muslim News*, 25 January 2002). In 2003, out of a total of some 130 Muslim chaplains (as of 2001) across the country's 138 prisons, there were six part-time and 25 full-time paid positions (with wages of £25,000 a year, far outstripping mosque pay).[6] Most of these positions were taken by young Deobandi *imams*.

The National Health Service (NHS) has been slower to follow the example of the Prison Service. Historically, limited central funding has been available only to the Free Churches Council and the Jewish Visitation Committee, despite increasing religious diversity. In 2000, the Department of Health announced it was minded to take on paid minority faith chaplains with suitable qualifications, and provide some funds to train them. A survey of 72 NHS chaplaincy units in 2004 found that out of 105 full-time chaplains, seven were Muslim; of the 152 part-time chaplains, 13 per cent were non-Christian (*Muslim News*, 24 September 2004). Notably, the first Muslim 'faith manager' of a NHS Trust, Yunas Dudhiwala, appointed in 2003, was a graduate of 'Bury'.

Another sector in which a role for Muslim chaplains has emerged is the armed forces. For example, in December 2004, the Ministry of Defence announced that it would recruit civilian chaplains from the Buddhist, Hindu, Muslim and Sikh faiths in view of the fact that 740 service personnel, including 300 Muslims, came from these minority faith groups. While the armed forces and other sectors considered here have a statutory commitment to provide pastoral care, historically the Church of England, other denominations and the minority faiths have provided voluntary chaplaincies in the universities and colleges. Whether paid or voluntary, in 2005 the Association of Muslim Chaplains was launched in an attempt to network all chaplains across all sectors and represent their interests.

Arising out of its experience with under-qualified first recruits to the Prison Service, the Home Office encouraged a number of the seminaries, including 'Bury', to provide professional Muslim chaplaincy training, but was unwilling to fund such programmes despite requests from these institutions. In the end, two of the Islamic colleges were able to provide training at their own initiative: the Muslim College in London had already incorporated such elements into its core *imam*-training curriculum and, in 2003, the Markfield Institute of Higher Education (MIHE), in co-operation with the Anglican Diocese of Leicester, launched its first course. This has allowed a formalization of new state-funded chaplaincy positions, which now require a recognized qualification in Islamic Studies/Chaplaincy from MIHE or the Muslim College (see advertisement in *Muslim News*, 17 December 2004). Additionally, the Learning and Skills Council funded a pilot scheme in 2004 to train Muslim leaders, including *imams*, in management skills. Interestingly, this project was delivered by a multi-faith consultancy, Faith Regen UK, itself inspired by a moderate Islamist leadership.

For the most part, these initiatives have been undertaken with the logic of extending precedents in the church-state relationship to minority faith groups, although not without persistent lobbying, as these accommodations still have to be argued for. In Britain, the Anglican Church has retained an official status in many avenues of life, and has worked historically to incorporate dissenting Christian sects and more recently ethnic minority faiths into public life, the emergence of the 'Muslim chaplain' representing a paradigmatic example of such efforts (Fetzer and Soper, 2005). This precedent is important to Britain's political class in assessing the reasonableness of demands for minority faith accommodation, as well as providing the environment in which opportunities for accommodation present themselves. The creation of a credible Muslim umbrella body in 1997, the Muslim

Council of Britain (MCB), did allow for serious negotiations to promote opportunities for Muslim chaplains, and it is likely that security concerns post-9/11 have given the process of incorporation additional impetus.

Overall, it is important, however, to understand that at present the numbers of professional Muslim chaplains is small, and mainly confined to the prisons and the NHS. Indeed, it is expectations of traditional religious leadership roles, like the mosque *imamate*, that are likely to remain more salient in the foreseeable future, a fact that the government recognizes. Of long term significance to improving the pay and status of *imams* has been the harmonization of British and EU employment law, which meant that in December 2003 all ministers of religion received full employment rights in terms of pay, conditions and legal redress.

Muslim Religious Leaders and the Government After 9/11

It would be a grave mistake to assume that after 9/11 'everything changed'. The evidence in the British case is that while the government has pursued a robust anti-terrorist policy, it has remained cautious in formulating counter-terrorist policies in comparison with other European Union countries (see also Cesari, Chapter 3, this volume).

Anti-Terrorist Measures

Before 9/11, the government had already sought to change its policies to reflect the Northern Ireland 'ceasefire dividend' and developments in 'international terrorism'. The major piece of legislation, the Anti-Terrorism Act 2000 (TACT) allowed the Home Secretary to outlaw foreign terrorist groups operating within the UK by a process of 'proscription'. Since the Act came into force in 2001, 25 groups have been proscribed; in total, 16 are self-described as mainly Islamic in inspiration. Eleven are Salafi and nearly all Arab in origin, while three are subcontinental – Harakat al-Mujahidin, Jaysh-i Muhammad and Lashkar-i Tayba – growing out of subsections of the Deobandis and Ahl-i Hadith that were influenced by the global *jihad* movement of the 1990s. The police have been given extended powers of investigation, stop and search, and detention in relation to terrorism, and new criminal offences have been created such as incitement to terrorism, and seeking or providing terrorist training. After 9/11, the Anti-Terrorism Crime and Security Act 2001 (ACTSA) gave the Home Secretary additional powers to imprison, without arrest or trial, any foreign nationals suspected of international terrorism who could not be deported to their countries of origin without infringing fundamental human rights. ACTSA was overturned by the UK's highest judicial body in 2004 and replaced by the Prevention of Terrorism Act 2005 (PTA). This established a system of judicially-authorized 'control orders' for uncharged terror suspects, including British as well as foreign nationals, with the legislation to be reviewed on an annual basis.

The powers have all been used, but their efficacy and fairness have been vigorously contested by British Muslims, human rights activists, legal experts and opposition politicians. Post 9/11 up to the end of 2004, under TACT and other relevant legislation, there have been 701 arrests, 254 charges and 17 convictions, only three of which involved Muslims. Stop and search powers have been widely used under TACT, but even more extensively under the Criminal Justice and Public Order Act 1994: the combined figures for England and Wales rose from 29,100 in 2001/2 to 82,920 in 2002/3 (Statewatch, 2004). The government has admitted that these powers will 'inevitably' be felt 'disproportionately ... by the Muslim community' (Home Affairs Committee, 2005). While ACTSA was in force 2001-5, 17 foreign nationals have been held: 16 were identifiable as Arab nationals, 10 of whom were Algerian, and all were accused of links with officially-designated al-Qaeda affiliates such as the Tunisian Fighting Group or the Algerian Armed Islamic Group and the Front Islamique Salut. Six were released, and 10 were under PTA control orders in March 2005.

With regard to intelligence, a special MI5 unit, Britain's home secret service, was set up in 1998 to monitor known British radicals, to recruit informants and to disrupt their activities by making them aware of the surveillance (Hollingsworth and Fielding, 2003: 12, 176). Radicalized mosques and campuses, in particular, were targeted. After 9/11, combating radical Islamist terrorists became the top priority for national security and intelligence services as well as anti-terrorist policing, underpinned by the largest growth in funding since the Cold War and a centralization of intelligence assessment in 2003. According to press reports, five significant terrorist attacks have been thwarted since 9/11, and while it was initially believed that the main threat came from foreign nationals, as early as 2002, British Muslims were seen to constitute an equivalent security risk (*Observer*, 27 February 2005). One plot, stopped in preparation in March 2004, had at its heart eight British Muslims of Pakistani heritage; in February 2005, there was the first successful conviction of a British Muslim, Saajid Badat, in a UK court, for conspiring to commit a terrorist act.

After 9/11 there have been many incidents in which religious leaders or their followers have been questioned about alleged connections with terrorist groups, or attempts to recruit them as informants. Some have been charged or convicted under terrorist or other legislation. Those hardest hit have been the *jihadi* Salafi preachers, who came to prominence in Britain during the 1990s. Abu Hamza al-Masri, Abdullah al-Faysal and, the most significant figure, Abu Qatada, described at his appeal in January 2004 as 'at the centre in the United Kingdom of terrorist activities associated with al-Qaeda',[7] have all been detained or convicted since 9/11 (Birt, 2005). Salafis loyal to Saudi interests have worked hard after 9/11 to dissociate themselves from theological fellow travellers by offering full support for anti-terrorist measures. At the same time, some former Salafi radicals have moved away from the global *jihadi* rhetoric of the 1990s towards integrationist modalities like interfaith and political engagement. Beards have been trimmed and suits or street-wear have replaced *jalabiyya*.

The Deoband movement has also come under suspicion if to a lesser extent because of its perceived links with the Taliban government of Afghanistan, which gave shelter to Bin Laden. In the wake of the Richard Reid case (a British al-Qaeda operative caught trying to blow up a plane in December 2001), MI5 and Special Branch, the anti-terrorist police, instigated a mapping exercise interviewing British

Muslim individuals, mosques and organizations about radicalism. In particular, following intelligence leads from Afghanistan, subcontinental and particularly Indian Muslim communities from within the Deoband tradition, including some *imams*, were closely questioned as to their affiliations. After five months of 'cold calling', protests led to an apology from the Home Secretary in August 2002 (*Muslim News*, 30 August 2002).

During this period, there was some focus on the movement's seminaries. Zaki Badawi, Rector of the Muslim College, called for the closure of Taliban-style centres of radical indoctrination (*The Times*, 27 December 2001). Saajid Badat, later to be convicted for involvement in the Richard Reid case, was found to have enrolled at the Jami'atul 'Ilm wa'l Huda in Blackburn. However, as this was after his 'radicalization' and his eventual decision to abort his mission, the seminary was perhaps able to allay fears successfully as to its 'multiculturalist' bona fides and vetting procedures. However, the most significant event was the detention of Yusuf Motala in November 2003 at Heathrow airport, where he was questioned by MI5, Special Branch and Customs officers about the curricula of his seminaries, his views on aspects of Islam and alleged connections with *jihadi* groups. This had an immediate political impact: the MCB wrote to the Home Secretary expressing its outrage, privately reading this as a signal from the very top to stigmatize British Muslims as the 'new Irish', while a *Muslim News* editorial thundered that 'unless the Government stops ... harassment and intimidation ... confidence and trust in our security services will continue to slide ...' (*Muslim News*, 28 November 2003) As a result, outreach work commenced by the Deobandi seminaries after 9/11 has been halted, although given the need to strengthen employment skills, they will most likely continue to strengthen ties with educational institutions, both secular and religious.

Counter-Terrorist Measures

The key to the British government's counter-terrorism policies is long-term prevention, or stopping 'the next generation of people getting involved' (Home Affairs Committee, 2005). In early 2005, these were still in the early stages of development. The chief areas of concern regarding radicalization were the schools, the universities and mosque *imams*, with most work having been conducted on the latter.

The key perceived problem has been the role of foreign *imams* deemed unable to connect with the concerns of young British Muslims. As the argument has run since 9/11, this leaves them open to 'isolationist' or 'radical' tendencies. In the 1970s, when mosque-building began in earnest, while in theory foreign *imams* enjoyed permit-free employment,[8] the government felt that the absence of a religious hierarchy in Islam made vetting procedures more complex and lengthy.[9] In 1980, entry clearance was made compulsory so that these checks could be made abroad instead of risking rejection at the port of entry. Given the frequency of appeals during the 1980s, temporary visitors were often allowed to switch their status to 'working ministers of religion'. However, in September 2004 this 'switching privilege' was withdrawn (although 'switching' still applies to categories of managed migration). In December 2001, foreign ministers of religion trained in the UK were given leave to take up employment without having to return to their countries of origin. After a lengthy consultation, a pre-entry English language standard was made compulsory for foreign ministers of religion in September 2004. After two years this would be raised to the same level as that required by foreign students studying at postgraduate level, an effective ban on a technicality, given that seminary graduates would be even less likely to reach this standard. Further proposals have been announced that after a year, '*imams* and priests ... should be able to show knowledge of, and engagement with, British civic life, including an understanding of other faiths; and a requirement for *imams* and priests to have professional qualifications'.[10] In other words, applicants should not be of a radical 'anti-West' bent. This progressive tightening up of the rules obviously reflects the new security environment, but also a confluence of interest with reformers who had long viewed foreign *imams* as retrogressive influences but had no way to persuade conservative mosque opinion. In the medium term, this is likely to cement the dominance of the Deobandi tradition, which alone of all the theological tendencies in Britain, provides sufficient numbers of home-trained *imams*.

Conclusions

The Deoband tradition – in the form of Bury's graduates – has broadened the appeal of its reform message, re-imagining it outside of its South Asian context and scripturalizing it further in response to Islamist and Salafi polemics. New institutions have been shaped and new media employed to appeal to a younger, cross-ethnic constituency. Bury graduates have worked to bridge the professional and educational gap between the seminary and the university and between the mosque *imamate* and the new educational and pastoral careers available in the public sector. It remains a matter of speculation as to what extent those *'ulama* exposed to a new professionalism in terms of new social skills, a public service ethos and distinct intellectual formation in Western institutions – whether university, teacher training college, or chaplaincy training centres – will at some point seek to reintegrate this training back into the curricula of the seminaries.

Post-9/11, the British *imam*, long ignored in policy terms, has become a central figure in tackling extremism in the government's view, potentially displacing the community's current political leadership, the professional Islamic activists, a development that has been observed in France (Peter, 2003). He is now to embody civic virtues, interfaith tolerance, professional managerial and pastoral skills, and to work as an agent of national integration, most importantly on behalf of his young flock. A British peculiarity in European terms has thus far been to subcontract this training to moderate Islamist organizations. By contrast, the foreign *imam* has become the agent of divisive cultural and religious alterity to be deterred by multiplying bureaucratic hurdles, deported or imprisoned. At times, as counter-terrorist and anti-terrorist policies are conducted by different institutions, this may lead to formal incoherence. Yusuf Motala, for example, was simultaneously seen as the problem to which he is the solution (the subversive influence at one moment, the teacher of the new British *imam* the next). But beyond the oddities of governance, it will be the lived experiences of new generations of British *imams* that will do more to influence the multifarious ways they will seek to serve their community and wider society.

References

Birt, J. (2005), 'Wahhabism in the United Kingdom: Manifestations and Reactions', in al-Rasheed, M. (ed.), *Transnational Connections and the Arab Gulf*, London: Routledge.

Birt, J. and Lewis, P. (forthcoming), 'The Pattern of Islamic Reform in Britain: the Deobandis between intra-Muslim sectarianism and engagement with wider society', in Allievi, S. and van Bruinessen, M. (eds), *Producing Islamic Knowledge in Western Europe*, London: I.B. Tauris.

Fetzer, J.S. and Soper, J.C. (2005), *Muslims and the State in Britain, France and Germany*, Cambridge: Cambridge University Press.

Hollingsworth, M. and Fielding, N. (2003), *Defending the Realm: Inside MI5 and the War on Terrorism*, London: André Deutsch.

Home Affairs Committee (2005), 'Terrorism and Community Relations', Evidence heard in Public Questions 459-522, 1 March, [uncorrected transcript of oral evidence to be published as HC 165-v], at www.publications.parliament.uk, [accessed 1 March 2005].

Institute of Muslim Scholars (2002), *1st Bi-annual Report, 2000-2002*, Batley: Institute of Muslim Scholars.

Masud, M.K. (ed.) (2000), *Travellers in Faith: Studies of the Tablighi Jama'at Movement for Faith Renewal*, Leiden: Brill.

Metcalf, B.D. (1982), *Islamic Revival in British India: Deoband, 1860-1900*, Princeton: Princeton University Press.

Metcalf, B.D. (1999), 'Weber and Islam', in Huff, T.E. and Schluchter, W. (eds), *Max Weber and Islam*, New Jersey: Transaction Publishers.

Metcalf, B.D. (2002), '"Traditionalist" Islamic Activism: Deoband, Tablighis and Talibs', in Calhoun, C., Price, P. and Timmer, A. (eds), *Understanding September 11*, New York: Social Science Research Council.

Peter, F. (2003), 'Training Imams and the Future of Islam in France', *ISIM Newsletter*, 13, 20-21.

Robinson, F. (2001), *The 'ulama of Farangi Mahall and Islamic Culture in South Asia*, Delhi: Permanent Black.

Schiffauer, W. (1988), 'Migration and Religiousness', in Gerholm, T. and Lithman, Y.G. (eds), *The New Islamic Presence in Western Europe*, London: Mansell.

Sikand, Y. (2002), *The Origins and Development of Tablighi Jama'at (1920-2000): A Cross-Country Comparative Study*, New Delhi: Orient Longman.

Statewatch (2004), 'UK: Anti-terrorist state and searches target Muslim communities, but few arrests', *Statewatch Analysis No. 23*, February, at www.statewatch.org, [accessed 22 February 2005].

Taji-Farouki, S. (1996), *A Fundamental Quest: Hizb al-Tahrir and the Search for the Islamic Caliphate*, London: Grey Seal.

Tayob, A. (1999), *Islam in South Africa: Mosques, Imams and Sermons*, Gainsville: Florida University Press.

Zaman, M.Q. (2002), *The 'ulama in Contemporary Islam: Custodians of Change*, Princeton: Princeton University Press.

Notes

1 Figures for England and Wales (covering 97 per cent of British Muslims) derived from the National Census of 2001 (see www.statistics.gov.uk/census2001/). The largest non-Asian populations are Arab and Iranian (130,000) and Black African (96,000).
2 Islamists are simply those with a direct interest in applying Islam to modern political contexts (not necessarily implying a fixation on the modern state). The radicals aim to use persuasive or coercive means to overthrow the political system, while the moderates work to find a place within the system.
3 See Birt and Lewis (forthcoming). The original estimate of 25 omitted the Jaamiah Khatamun Nabiyeen established in Bradford in 1999. I would like to thank Mawlana Amjad Mohammed for the correction.
4 See www.statistics.gov.uk/census2001/.
5 *British Muslims Monthly Survey* (hereafter *BMMS*), September 2000, 8 (9), 2-3.
6 *BMMS*, January 2002, 10 (1), 6.
7 BBC News, 'Qatada's key UK al-Qaeda role', 23 March 2004, at www.bbc.co.uk, [accessed 17 February 2005].
8 Statement of Immigration Rules for Control on Entry, 25 January 1973, Para. 25(a).
9 Letter from Timothy Raison, Home Office, to Abduljalil Sajid, 1 June 1982.
10 Immigration and Nationality Directorate, 'New immigration rules on switching and ministers of religion', 22 July 2004, 252/2004.

Index